Sustainable Dual-Track Development

Every decade or so, the software development community reinvents itself to address the dominant problems of the day. Agile methods reacted against slow, bureaucratic, documentation driven development. The next big shift reacts against unsustainable development practices.

This book advances dual-track development as a unifying framework for the best way of designing great products (user-centered design), the best way of delivering software efficiently (agile methods), and strategies for balancing present and future needs (sustainable development).

This book does not just recommend practices. It explains how to implement practices and the surprising science behind the practices, in an approachable, sometimes cheeky style. You won't find a "Dual-track Master" telling you that you must do it exactly this way, otherwise you're a sellout. Rather, this book describes a set of sociotechnical tools and gives advice for adapting these tools to your unique context.

Welcome to the future of software engineering that you actually want: one that embraces clean code, hyper-productive programming, belongingness, empathy, environmental sustainability, economic feasibility, pro-social impact, and organizational justice.

Sustainable Dual-Track Development

The Future of Software Engineering for Co-located, Remote, and Hybrid Teams

Todd Sedano, Ph.D.
Paul Ralph, Ph.D.

CRC Press
Taylor & Francis Group
Boca Raton London New York

CRC Press is an imprint of the
Taylor & Francis Group, an **informa** business

Designed cover image: Alexander Minze Thümler
Vignette Sketches: Claire Sedano

First edition published 2025
by CRC Press
2385 NW Executive Center Drive, Suite 320, Boca Raton FL 33431

and by CRC Press
4 Park Square, Milton Park, Abingdon, Oxon, OX14 4RN

CRC Press is an imprint of Taylor & Francis Group, LLC

ISBN: 978-1-032-98409-4 (hbk)
ISBN: 978-1-032-98310-3 (pbk)
ISBN: 978-1-003-59803-9 (ebk)

DOI: 10.1201/9781003598039

Typeset in CMR10 Roman
by KnowledgeWorks Global Ltd.

To my wife, Karie, who grows more beautiful every day and reminds me of my heart's song; to my children, Claire and Colette, who taught me joy and wonder.

T.S.

For my mentor, Jeffrey Parsons, who put me on the right road, and my wife, Gianisa, who made the road worth taking.

P.R.

Contents

About the Authors

Todd Sedano, PhD (Carnegie Mellon University), enjoys creating inclusive engineering environments, empowering others to excel, and coaching others by listening and reframing from a growth mindset. He has more than 25 years of experience as a software engineer and engineering manager at leading organizations including NASA JPL, Pivotal Labs, VMware, Enjoy, Gusto, and ID.me. Dr. Sedano has published scholarly articles on software development waste, agile teams, product backlogs, and dual-track development. His academic research became the foundation for this book. His current hobbies include riding roller coasters, improvisational theater, and American Kenpo.

D. Paul Ralph, PhD (University of British Columbia), is an award-winning scientist, author, consultant, professor of software engineering, and director of the Dalhousie Software Engineering Lab. His cutting-edge research at the intersection of software engineering, human-computer interaction, and project management investigates how to improve the environmental, social, economic, and technical sustainability of software development. Dr. Ralph's previous research has been published in over 100 peer reviewed articles and used by leading technology companies including Adobe, Amazon, AT&T, Broadcom, Canon, IBM, Google, HP, Microsoft, Netflix, Oracle, PayPal, Samsung, Salesforce, Yahoo!, and Walmart.

Preface

Each of us is trapped in our moment of history and
can only engage in the dialectic of our time.
– Corey Mohler channeling Hegel

Turning the Dreaded News into a Non-Event

Bimpe was responsible for a team of six engineers, a product designer, and a product manager. In the back of her mind, she knew that the team relied heavily on one engineer, Dakota. Dakota knew how the system worked, mentored other engineers, and fixed complex issues quickly. Bimpe felt lucky to have Dakota but didn't think much more about it... until Dakota resigned.

Bimpe had mixed emotions: she was happy for Dakota because she'd found an amazing new position, but she was also concerned that Dakota's departure would significantly disrupt the team. She worried that a big chunk of the team's accumulated knowledge about the system was disappearing.

How long would it take for the team to relearn that knowledge? How would it affect the team's productivity and ability to ship the next release?

Sustainable Dual-Track Development is designed to make teams more resilient against disruptions caused by personnel departures. The practices recommended in this book help knowledge propagate rapidly throughout a team, such that no individual member is irreplaceable.

Teams using these practices no longer dread a team member's departure. Although a friend and colleague may be missed, the team will continue to deliver. Teams can wish their departing colleague well on their journey instead of fretting about the knowledge they'll lose.

Every decade or so, the software development community reinvents itself to address the dominant problems of the day. The Rational Unified Process (RUP) reacted against unpredictability and irresponsibility of prematurely diving into coding. Extreme Programming reacted against rigid planning, unnecessary documentation, and bureaucracy. Lean and Kanban reacted against waste. Scrum reacted against everything slowing down development, and DevOps reacted against everything slowing down deployment. Now we can see the beginning of the next big shift: reacting against unsustainable development practices.

Current approaches to software development are unsustainable. Between January 2020 and December 2021, Bitcoin mining "consumed 173.42 TWh of electricity," "emitted over 85.89 Mt of CO_2eq," consumed 1.65 km^3 of water and occupied 1870 km^2 of land [1]. This is obviously not environmentally sustainable, and sustainability is about more than just environmental impacts.

"Sustainable development ... meets the needs of the present without compromising the ability of future generations to meet their own needs" [2, p. 29]. We think about sustainable development in terms of four *pillars* [3]:

1. Development is *environmentally* sustainable when it meets present needs while enhancing or at least maintaining the natural environment.

2. Development is *socially* sustainable when it meets present needs while enhancing or at least maintaining individuals', families', communities', organizations', or societies' circumstances and capabilities.

3. Development is *economically* sustainable when the product is financially feasible, and the product and its development enhance or at least maintain the local, regional, national, or global economies.

4. Software is *technically* sustainable to the degree to which its codebase has long-term viability, and it enhances or at least maintains its surrounding technical infrastructure.

In other words, a sustainable project is not only profitable but also pro-social, environmentally friendly, and technically robust (maintainable).

Consequently, *sustainable software development* is a collection of practices for making projects more environmentally, economically, socially, and technically sustainable. A *sustainable software development process* creates economically profitable products that can be maintained and evolved for many years without damaging the environment, society or the well-being of its stakeholders, including the development team.

Focusing on developing features as fast as possible in the short term makes us all very slow in the long term. Many teams found that, when they first switched to Scrum, they progressed rapidly. Every sprint, Scrum helped them just crank out new features. Over time, though, it seemed increasingly difficult to turn the crank. Teams built features and whole products that no one used. Skilled professionals burned out and left. Projects were derailed by routine vacations and sick days. Rushed code became harder and harder to maintain. Knowledge was lost with every transfer and reorganization. Or worse, teams built enormously popular products that—*through their popularity*—irreparably harmed our environment or society. Only by refocusing on people and sustainability can we be fast *and safe* in the long term.

This trend will create winners and losers. Organizations that refocus on the human, social, psychological, and environmental aspects of software development will see their teams deliver fantastic products week after week, month after month, despite inevitable problems and disruptions, and without backlash from a concerned society finally waking up to the dangers of myopic innovation. Organizations that fail to appreciate their human capital will fall further and further behind. This book provides the practical recommendations and scientific concepts you need to stay on the winning side.

This book is unique in several ways:

1. It is the first book to advance dual-track development as a unifying framework for the best way of designing great products (user-centered design) and the best way of delivering software efficiently (agile methods).

2. It approaches software development from multiple perspectives—not only economic success but also environmental and social sustainability.

3. It was co-written by an expert programmer / engineering manager and a prolific scholar specializing in the psychology of software development and software project management, who synthesize first-hand experience with recommendations backed by scientific research including a three-year research study at Pivotal Software (now part of Broadcom) [4].

4. It respects the fact that software professionals have diverse educational and cultural backgrounds, and it provides recommendations for embracing our differences and excelling in multidisciplinary collaboration.

The software engineering industry is currently driven by opinions and "thought leaders." Most software engineers trust the opinions and anecdotes of peers and managers more than the results of rigorous scientific research [5]. Preference for opinion over facts leads professionals not only to misunderstand how the social process of software development works, but also to adopt ineffective practices and argue endlessly over trivialities.

Many of the models and ideas that the industry takes for granted (e.g., the Iron Triangle [6], [7]) are made up and not based on any data. Laurent Bossavit's book, *The Leprechauns of Software Engineering*, explores the origins of many of these myths including the exponential cost of change curve, the cone of uncertainty, the waterfall model, and $10x$ developers [8]. The Rational Unified Process hump diagram, showing the level of effort associated with each discipline during each phase of development, looks like a graph generated from data but is actually just a drawing of someone's intuitions.

We don't ask you to take everything on faith. We focus on practices that have been empirically validated by scientists, used extensively with good results at the companies we've studied, or implement the principles of well-established theories. For many, we'll discuss the evidence directly. We encourage you to think critically about all of our recommendations and, the next time you're faced with some 'guru' (or their writings), to demand evidence for their claims and keep an eye out for how they make their money.

We've worked hard to make this information approachable. We've done usability testing with this content. We're grateful to our many friends and colleagues that have reviewed this material, providing feedback to make this book more useful to you.

However, embracing the ideas in this book is easier said than done. Not everyone appreciates intense interpersonal collaboration. Some of the practices (e.g., Test-Driven Development) take years to master. Shifting from "go as fast as possible" to "focus on long-term sustainability" can be a major culture shift. Convincing some people that prioritizing environmental and social sustainability doesn't mean abandoning economic sustainability will be challenging.

Meanwhile, as we wrote this book, the COVID-19 pandemic pushed the imaginary software engineering pendulum away from tightly-integrated, co-located teams towards teams distributed across space and time zones.

This book therefore focuses on sustainable software development processes for *teams*: two or more individuals who work *together* regularly, are effective, and share compatible goals. Working together doesn't mean the team physically sits together in the same room, but it does mean team members collaborate synchronously, often completing tasks together (e.g., pair programming) rather than divvying up tasks to complete separately.

Then, while we were still writing, generative artificial intelligence (AI) and large language models (LLMs) in particular roared onto the scene. While large language models are undoubtedly useful in some situations, early predictions that they would revolutionize software development are likely exaggerated. LLMs do not address any of the core challenges we tackle in this book: the apparent disconnect between agile methods with human-centered design, the general lack of concern for sustainability, or the intrinsic challenges of organizing remote and hybrid remote / co-located teams. We haven't written much about LLMs because they just aren't relevant to the challenges we aim to address, and we haven't used LLMs in the writing of this book. This text is 100% written by us, for you, over seven years.

If you're reading this book, you must be one of the professionals who cares deeply about building quality software that delights its users without harming other stakeholders, the environment, or society. By the end of this book, you'll see the techniques, understand why they work, and know how to transition a team to use them.

Chapter 1

Overview

It's harder than you might think to squander millions of dollars, but a flawed software development process is a tool well suited to the job.

– Alan Cooper

 Key Takeaways

- Sustainable software development refers to practices that optimize the environmental, economic, social, and technical impacts of software.

- "Dual-track" development divides work into two *simultaneous, ongoing, parallel* activity tracks:

  - Track One involves making sense of the project context, imagining product features, and filling the backlog with good stories that represent those features.

  - Track Two involves writing code and tests based on user stories, integrating this code, and deploying the product.

- The most important artifact is the product itself. The second most important artifact is the backlog (a semi-prioritized to-do list of user stories, bugs, and chores), which sits between the two tracks.

- The product manager directs development by prioritizing the backlog. Product designers imagine product features and validate them with users. Engineers build, test, deploy and maintain the product.

A Day with Sustainable Dual-Track Development

Each day, the team coordinates with a daily sync. They share important decisions and knowledge they learned yesterday and any blockers to finishing today's work.

When working on production code, the engineers decide *pairing*. Yesterday, Isaac paired with Melissa, and they still have work-in-progress. They decide that Melissa will finish the work-in-progress with her new partner, Arthur. Isaac can pair with anyone except his partner from yesterday. He pairs with Jennifer, who has no work-in-progress. Yesterday, Li paired with Habib, but today, Habib has taken a personal day so that Li will finish their work-in-progress solo. The team might schedule an ensemble pairing session later in the week to work on something extra tricky.

When Melissa and Arthur need clarification, they talk to Taylor, the product designer. The team favors interruptions to keep work streams moving. If two people can't figure something out, it's OK to interrupt other people on the team.

The team prioritizes synchronous, person-to-person interactions when working during core hours. Distributed teams leverage differences in time zones for the team's benefit and leverage asynchronous communication technologies for knowledge sharing, coordination, and getting help.

Jennifer and Isaac write tests before designing or writing code. A failing test provides a short-term goal. The rhythm is to start a story, refactor if necessary, write a small failing test, write just enough code to get the test to pass and repeat until the story is done. Jennifer and Isaac take turns controlling the keyboard. Maybe Jennifer writes a test, Isaac writes the code, and then Isaac writes a test, and Jennifer writes the code. When they finish the story, they start a new story from the top of the backlog. Anyone can attempt any story.

Meanwhile, Taylor, the product designer, has two user interviews scheduled to validate potential features. Gill, the product manager, starts her morning prioritizing stories—identifying high-value work to start soon and delaying low-value work—and reorganizing the backlog. Later, Taylor and Gill get together with the team to draw mock-ups and write user stories for the features Taylor validated. Each story represents a small piece of interaction between the user and the system. The mock-ups will help the developers visualize how the system should look when the corresponding stories are complete.

If this were a Monday, the team might have a story showcase meeting: Gill and Taylor would go through upcoming stories, building shared understanding by providing context and detail while the engineers explain the complexity and risks associated with each story. If it were a Friday, they would have a retrospective meeting to examine what is working well for the team and what needs improvement. Regardless, the engineers aim to limit the frequency and length of meetings.

Two Challenges of Developing Software Today

The rise of agile development largely stamped out the idea that software projects comprise four or more separate processes (e.g., analysis, design, coding, and testing). Agile development refers to a family of software development methods that aim to improve software projects by making teams more adaptable and responsive to change. Each agile method (e.g., Extreme Programming, Scrum, Lean, Kanban) is different, but they all share similar principles: the development team is more important than the processes and tools it uses; the software product is more important than the documentation thereof; collaborating with customers and users is more important than negotiating contracts; adaptability and responsiveness are more important than planning and following plans [9]. Each agile method operationalizes these principles as a collection of practices for software teams to follow. While agile methods have made significant breakthroughs in the efficient delivery of working software, two interconnected problems appear ubiquitous in agile teams.

Ignoring Sustainability

The first problem is that the tech industry disregards sustainability. Many commercial products are built despite having no plausible route to profitability. Some companies build economically unsustainable software because they don't know any better; for others it's part of a deliberate strategy of first building a customer base with good quality and low prices, then intentionally degrading service to increase revenues—what Cory Doctorow dubbed "enshittification" [10].

Meanwhile software organizations disregard the environmental and social impacts of their products. They neither assess environmental impact nor prioritize optimizing it. They fail to consider how their products affect all relevant stakeholder groups or to mitigate social harms. Then they argue that addressing the harms they've caused is economically unfeasible.

Many software teams also struggle with *unsustainable ways of working*. Despite agile methods interdicting overtime, many teams suffer from crunch time, stressful work environments, antisocial colleagues, and toxic organizational cultures. In many projects, knowledge is so fragmented that losing a single team member can derail the whole endeavor.

All of these problems are exacerbated by both the software industry and the software engineering research community embracing the unfortunate view that success is about optimizing scope, cost, and schedule regardless of a product's impacts on human beings.

Sustainable Dual-Track Development addresses the sustainability problem using a collection of practices that: (1) make both the team and the product more resilient in the face of serious disruptions; and (2) incorporate environmental, economic, and social sustainability concerns into the design process.

Marginalizing Design

The second problem is that agile methods don't really explain how to design good software. Agile methods are all about building a product based on a backlog. They say, "There's a backlog of stories (i.e., feature descriptions), someone prioritizes them, and then the team implements the stories." But where do the ideas for these stories come from? How do we write good stories? How do we actually prioritize them? Some people say "the client writes the stories" or "the product manager writes the stories," but that doesn't explain how to design good software; it just blames the client or product manager for the bad design.

Major technical innovations including generative AI, low-code platforms, microservices, containerization, and edge computing address *neither* unsustainability nor design efficacy.

Sustainable Dual-Track Development addresses the design problem by reconciling agile methods with *user-centered design*. User-centered design (UCD) is a method for designing software by studying current or prospective users' characteristics, goals, environments, and actions [11]. User-centered design has made great strides in designing products that are more effective in improving their users' lives. But it usually assumes big-design-up-front, which is incompatible with agile methods. By splitting the development process into two parallel tracks of work, we can merge the best aspects of user-centered design with the best aspects of agile methods. While these twin aims seem very different, many practices contribute to both.

Dual-Track Development

Dual-track development is a way of organizing software development.[1] Development activities are organized into two tracks: *Track One* and *Track Two* (Figure 1–1). In between the two tracks is the product backlog (and some other stuff we'll discuss in Chapter 4: Boundary Spanning). Track One is about figuring out what to build and loading the backlog with these ideas. Track Two is about unloading items from the backlog and building, testing, and deploying product features based on them.

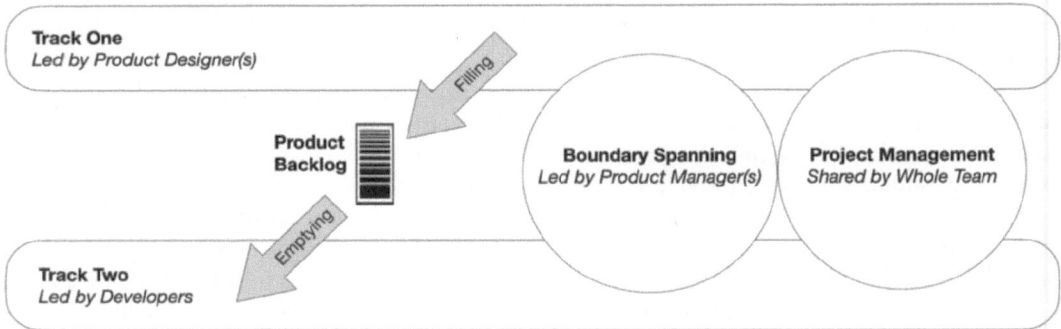

Figure 1–1: Overview of Dual-Track Development

Dual-track development has *tracks*. Tracks are not phases or stages. It doesn't have different groups of people or different blocks of time dedicated to different kinds of work.

---

[1]The term "dual-track" probably comes from a description of Alias Software's development process [14]. Alias was acquired by Autodesk in 2005.

The Science of Software Development Methods

Software development methods and project management frameworks are systems of prescriptions for building software and managing software projects. Examples include Scrum, Lean, Kanban, Extreme Programming, PRINCE2, the Rational Unified Process, Rapid Application Development, and the Spiral Model.

Teams don't really *use* methods to build software the way a plumber uses a wrench to fix a faucet. It's more like teams have a way of working that may be informed by one or more methods. Every project is unique, and software professionals often have good reasons for adapting or ignoring methods.

Some successful teams' ways of working are pretty chaotic; others are disciplined. Some apply the same sophisticated, homegrown method to every project. Others enact a unique process for each unique context. Some try to implement a specific method, like Scrum, but very few teams use a method exactly as its proponents intend. Some professionals claim to follow a method that they actually ignore [12].

The truth is that questions like, "Will using method X help my project succeed?" are extremely difficult to study scientifically. No compelling scientific evidence exists that any method outperforms any other method on any specific dimension (e.g., project success) in any particular context. There is very little evidence that any specific adaptation of any specific method in any particular context is helpful or harmful.

Yet, proponents of specific methods tend to claim that their method is the best and deride adaptations. The Scrum community, for example, bemoans *ScrumBut*; for example: "We use Scrum, but we don't have stand-up meetings" or "We use Scrum, but we have a project manager who assigns tasks" [13]. Unfortunately, many popular methods are promoted by people with a vested interest in selling consulting services or professional certifications.

This book proposes a software development method but does not claim that this method is always best or promote abandoning your current way of working without regard for your unique context. We trust you to adapt the ideas in this book to your situation and improve (not replace) your current way of working.

Throughout this book, you will find sidebars, like this one, that discuss the science of things. Although research has not produced compelling evidence for *methods*, it has produced compelling evidence for many *practices* (e.g., pair programming) and valuable insights about many relevant topics (e.g., teamwork).

It doesn't have iterations or sprints, yet it is nothing like a waterfall process. Dual-track is genuinely different and can be challenging to grasp.

In dual-track development, a project belongs to a *balanced team*: a cross-functional team with a 'balance' of engineering, design, and business expertise. The whole team is involved in both tracks and in bridging between them. The team carries the project from inception to dissolution. There is no transferring of the project from, say, the business analysis team to the development team to the operations team. There are no other teams, only *the* team.

In dual-track development, there are two main kinds of work: the work of loading the backlog and the work of unloading the backlog. The team does both kinds of work simultaneously and indefinitely. There is no cycling between the two kinds of work: no iterations, no sprints, no phases. (The team might have a release schedule, but releasing every x weeks does not imply x-week iterations.) The two tracks simply proceed together indefinitely. The only exception is that, in a brand new, greenfield project, Track One might need a little head start on Track Two.

The two tracks involve different skills, languages, norms and kinds of work, which create a disconnect between them. We call the work of overcoming this disconnect *boundary spanning*. Projects also include some coordination and optimization tasks that don't really fit in either track, which we'll group under *project management*.

To summarize, adopting dual-track development just means that a team organizes most of its work into two ongoing, interwoven tracks. Of course, doing dual-track *well* involves a fair bit more, as we'll see throughout this book. *Sustainable* Dual-Track Development involves augmenting dual-track with practices that encourage sustainability (below).

The Product and the Backlog

The most important artifact is the product itself. Everything else the team creates—tests, diagrams, user stories, etc.— exists only to deliver a better product.

The most important non-code artifact is the backlog. The *product backlog* is a collection of work items (e.g., user stories, bugs, chores). It can be implemented as a physical stack of cards or, more commonly, using project management software. In principle, the backlog is an ordered list, but in practice, only upcoming stories tend to be prioritized accurately. We'll return to the product backlog in Chapter 3: The Product Backlog.

Product managers direct the project by determining and prioritizing backlog items. Engineers work from the backlog. As they implement stories, they use the backlog to communicate status. The backlog is not a list of requirements or a design specification. Rather, backlog items remind engineers of conversations (e.g., with the product designers and product manager) and point toward aspects of the team's shared product vision.

Track One

Track One is about loading items into the backlog. *Product designers* typically collaborate with their product manager, prospective users, and other stakeholders to make sense of the project environment, situation, or context. They try to understand who is involved and their goals, values, and preferences. Building the product *changes* prospective users' goals, values, and preferences, so designers have to keep making sense of the evolving context throughout the project.

As product designers learn about the project environment, they imagine what the product might be. They begin with a superficial understanding of the context and a fledgling product concept. As they learn more about the context, new ideas for the product emerge. These new product details trigger new insights into the context. The product designer's understanding of the context and ideas for the product *co-evolve*.

Product designers interview stakeholders (especially prospective users) to learn about the project context and validate their ideas. They draw mock-ups and help the product manager write stories to flesh out potential product features. They perform usability testing to understand how users interact with the product and where things go awry.

The primary goal of Track One is to imagine a delightful, usable product that benefits its stakeholders. The team focuses on product fit by routinely studying stakeholders (especially users), deploying patches, testing assumptions and soliciting feedback.

Track Two

Track Two is about unloading items from the backlog by building features. *Engineers* code, test, deploy, and maintain the software product or system. Track Two includes determining the system's architecture, determining the low-level implementation details of stories, coding, all forms of technical testing, setting up technical infrastructure (e.g., a continuous deployment pipeline), receiving telemetry data, and sometimes operating a service (e.g., for cloud-based applications).

The primary goal of Track Two is to realize the product vision in terms of high-quality, thoroughly tested, and smoothly running code.

Project Management and Boundary Spanning

Agile teams are supposed to self-manage; there's no "project manager" who assigns tasks, sets schedules, and assesses performance. However, most projects still entail project management work (and associated artifacts and practices). Some of this work is suited to engineers (e.g., determining who should implement which story, running a retrospective meeting), and some is not (e.g., negotiating priorities with business stakeholders). Below, we therefore suggest that Sustainable Dual-Track Development teams have a *product manager* who does project management work that isn't well-suited to engineers, but who has no more or less authority than any other team member.

Meanwhile, organizing software development into two parallel tracks creates a boundary or gap between the tracks that inhibits communication and understanding. Sustainable Dual-Track Development therefore requires work and various practices and artifacts to improve communication by bridging the gap between the tracks. The product manager also leads this *Boundary Spanning* effort, including refining and prioritizing the product backlog.

We can think of both boundary spanning and project management as bridges that connect the two tracks.

Sustainable Software Development

Sustainable software development is a collection of practices for making projects more environmentally, economically, socially, and technically sustainable. In other words, a sustainable project is not only profitable but also pro-social, environmentally friendly, and technically robust (maintainable).

Furthermore, the people who most benefit from the product should also bear most of the costs. For example, suppose a social media platform harms students, educators, and school boards by facilitating distribution of child pornography, creating student-teacher conflict, encouraging cyber-bullying, and harming psychosocial well-being. Meanwhile the platform primarily benefits its shareholders and the corporations using it to market their products and service. This mismatch between those who suffer the harms and those who reap the benefits isn't sustainable.

An often overlooked aspect of sustainability is making software teams more resilient and steadily productive despite disruption and change. Maximizing the long-term health and effectiveness of the team is an essential part of sustainability. For example, in sustainable development, programmers work in pairs, and pairs change daily to improve team cohesion and knowledge transfer. Indeed, Sustainable Dual-Track Development is full of practices that promote resilience against disruption and contribute to *long-term* team effectiveness and project success.

Dual-track development is distinct from sustainable development. Dual-track development just means a cross-functional team organizing development into two parallel tracks that load and unload a backlog. Sustainable development means ensuring that our present product and development process don't compromise the ability of our team, organization, community, nation, or world to meet its future needs.

Sustainable Dual-Track Development

We combine dual-track development and sustainable software development into *Sustainable Dual-Track Development* because our twin goals of improving sustainability and reconciling user-centered design with agile development are synergistic. Having Track One dedicated to understanding stakeholders, validating features, and usability testing helps teams build economically sustainable products—products people want to use and *will pay for*. Meanwhile, only by studying stakeholders and project contexts can we appreciate our software's impacts on society and its unintended negative consequences. While considering the product's carbon footprint is part of Track Two, imagine the resource implications of building entire products that *no one wants*. Sustainable Development isn't just about incremental efficiency improvements; it's about questioning whether to create a product at all.

Sustainable Dual-Track Development helps each engineer understand the entire system, work on any story, share their expertise, learn from their peers, and consider the social and environmental implications of their work. Simultaneously, Sustainable Dual-Track Development elevates product design. For too long, software engineering has viewed the user interface as a thin layer of decoration for the "real" (i.e., back-end) system. And people wonder why so much software is bewildering. Sustainable Dual-Track Development allows each product designer to shape a product according to the user's needs—user experience drives features and architecture, not the other way around.

Meanwhile, the business benefits from *stability through agility*. Despite constant change, disruption, and the occasional cataclysm, the team continues to deliver software week after week, month after month. Things do not fall apart when the superstar developer leaves because nothing is critically tied to a particular individual. Vital work can be parallelized since

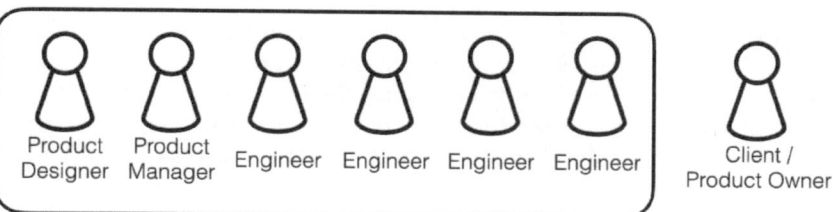

Figure 1–2: Team Roles

anyone can work on any feature. The team does not foment public relations catastrophes by creating systems with malignant unintended consequences.

Roles

Teams are organized into roles or jobs, as shown in Figure 1–2. Each role entails different responsibilities and requires different skill sets. Sustainable Development includes the following roles:

1. *Engineers* (i.e., programmers) build, test, deploy, and maintain the product. Most team members are typically engineers. Engineers are responsible for determining how to implement each story, including both system architecture and low-level design. Deciding how best to test new functionality is a large part of the engineer role. Engineers are responsible for assessing and managing technical sustainability.

2. *Product designers* research the project context, imagine product features, and validate features with users. For systems with graphical user interfaces, product designers draw mock-ups. Product designers come from diverse backgrounds, including human-computer interaction, industrial design, and fine art. Most teams have one or two product designers. Product designers are responsible for assessing and managing social sustainability.

3. *Product managers* set the overall direction for their products. A team typically has one product manager. Product managers research the business landscape (while product designers are more focused on users) and ensure that the project is economically sustainable. The product manager writes most of the stories and directs development by prioritizing the product backlog. In other words, they decide which features to build next. (In some companies, the engineering manager fills this role. They write the stories and prioritize the backlog.) The product manager typically collaborates with the product designer(s) to determine the product's features by balancing user preferences with business objectives. They also represent the team to upper management and the client or product owner. In small projects, one person may fill both the product designer and product manager roles.

4. The final role is the person or organization to whom the product is delivered—often called the *client* in outsourcing arrangements or the *product owner* for internal projects and commercial-off-the-shelf software. The client or product owner is typically concerned with meeting business objectives such as increasing sales, cutting costs, and return on investment. The client or product owner is not part of the team.

In Sustainable Dual-Track Development, there is no "project manager" in the traditional sense of a boss who gives orders, uses budgets and schedules to control the project, and assesses employees. The team manages itself. The product manager does not tell anyone what to do. The product manager directs the trajectory of the *product*, not the *team*. The team is the agent of change.

Furthermore, each person belongs to one and only one team. The team needs the product designer's design thinking skills, the product manager's business acumen, and the engineers' programming skills. While individuals can assume multiple roles, teams are most effective when each person has only one role. Roles exist to help diverse team members work together by clarifying responsibilities, not to create a hierarchy or figure out who to blame when something goes wrong.

Many important activities are shared among or supported by all the roles. Anyone on the team, for example, can take on important leadership work such as helping to onboard a new team member (Chapter 12), leading a retrospective meeting (Chapter 5), or proposing changes to the team's definition of done (Chapter 5). Other activities, including assessing and improving environmental sustainability, typically require collaboration among all team roles.

Artifacts

For our purposes, any object made by people is an *artifact*. Artifacts can be virtual, like code libraries and unit tests, or tangible, like whiteboards and sticky notes. Artifacts can be formal, like circuit diagrams, semi-formal, like Unified Modeling Language diagrams, or informal, like checklists.

Historically, software engineering suffered from too many non-code artifacts. Drawing diagrams and writing notes can help us remember, communicate, and make sense of complicated situations. However, using too many artifacts or artifacts that are too large is counterproductive. A 3000-page specification rarely helps reasoning, communication, or memory. Such documents tend to be ignored and quickly go out-of-date. It is crucial to find a good, minimal set of artifacts to help us think, communicate, and remember.

Sustainable Dual-Track Development includes the following artifacts. Each of these will be discussed more thoroughly (with examples) later in the book.

Track One Artifacts

- A *stakeholder map* is a visualization of individuals or organizations that have an interest in or are affected by the product.

Figure 1–3: Affinity Map

- A *persona* is a fictional stakeholder—similar to a novelist's character sketch—based on observations or interviews of real users, prospective users, or other stakeholders.

- An *interview guide* is a list of questions or map of topics to discuss with a user or other project stakeholder.

- An *affinity map* is a collection of notes organized into groups (Figure 1–3).

- A *mock-up* is a low-fidelity sketch illustrating the layout of a user interface.

- A *product roadmap* is a table that shows desired current (more specific), near-term, and long-term (more general) outcomes.

Boundary Spanning and Project Management Artifacts

- A *product backlog* is an informal model of work to be done including stories, epics, bugs, and chores.

- A *user story* is a brief, informal description of a small unit of functionality, typically expressed as a user action.

- An *epic story* is a brief, informal description of a large unit of functionality, typically expressed as a user action.

- A *chore* is a technical task that provides value without changing product features, such as reducing the test suite execution time, upgrading libraries, improving the development environment, removing dead code, or refactoring.

- A *bug* is a deviation from the intended behavior of a previously completed or delivered story.

- A *kanban board* is a visualization of the team's recently-delivered, in-progress, and soon-to-begin work.

Track Two Artifacts

- *Source code* refers to computer instructions written in a programming language.

- An *automated test* is a set of computer instructions for verifying that the source code functions as intended.

- A *test suite* refers to a collection of automated tests.

- A *version control system* manages files and changes to them.

- A *build system* pulls code from a repository, compiles it, runs test suites, and (optionally) pushes code to a staging environment or production. Build systems are crucial for continuous integration and delivery.

- A *build monitor* displays the results of running the latest tests against the latest source code: green for a successful build and red for a failed build.

Artifacts not used directly by the development team (e.g., financial plans, accounting ledgers, personnel records, marketing materials, and operational logs) are outside the scope of Sustainable Dual-Track Development.

Practices

A practice is a specific pattern of behavior adopted and used intentionally. Sustainable Dual-Track Development includes the following practices, each of which is discussed more thoroughly in subsequent chapters. Figure 1–4 illustrates how we conceptually organized these practices.

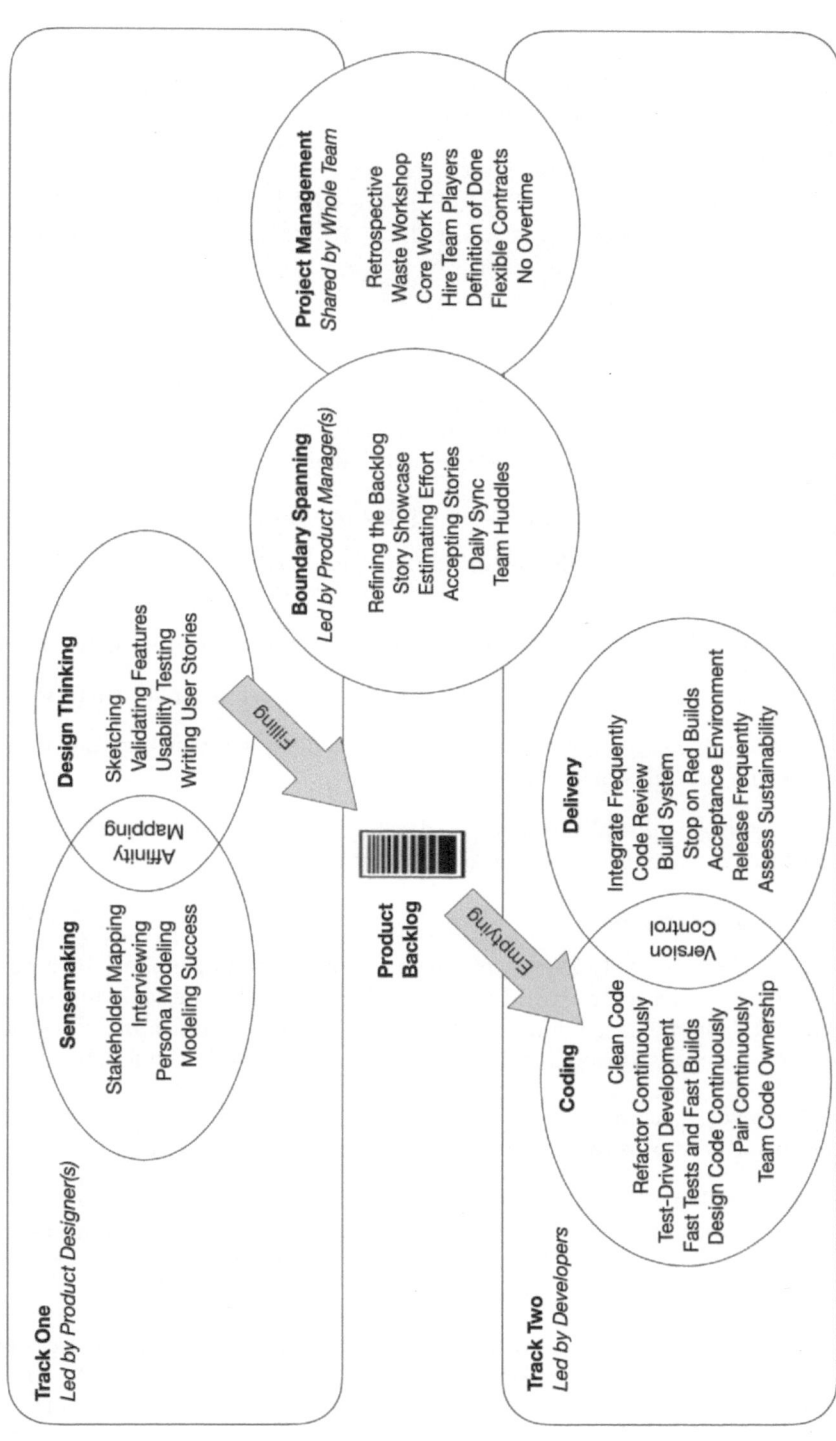

Figure 1–4: Detailed Overview of Sustainable Dual-Track Development

Track One Practices

Track One aims to understand stakeholders, especially users, and generate design concepts—that is, ideas for the product—based on this understanding. The product designer typically leads Track One, including:

- *Stakeholder mapping*: (1) identifying individuals and groups who have an interest in the success of the project or are affected by it; and (2) drawing a diagram that organizes these "stakeholders" in some way (e.g., according to their relationships to one another or their influence over the project).

- *Interviewing*: semi-structured, typically one-on-one conversations between a team member and a stakeholder.

- *Persona modeling*: creating descriptions of fictional stakeholders, similar to character sketches, to reason about who will use product features.

- *Modeling success*: visualizing the product's impacts on its stakeholders over time.

- *Affinity mapping*: generating design insights by categorizing data (e.g., notes) from user interviews or ideation sessions.

- *Sketching*: drawing informal models (e.g., mock-ups) of graphical user interfaces.

- *Validating features*: checking whether ideas for the product resonate with users.

- *Usability testing*: investigating the product's usability by reviewing the product, a simulation of the product, or mock-ups with users.

- *Writing user stories*: literally writing and refining stories that represent potential product features (sometimes based on epic stories).

Boundary Spanning Practices

Boundary Spanning practices help the team synchronize its mental models such that the product manager, product designer(s), and engineers share basically the same understanding of the product and its context (see Chapter 4: Boundary Spanning for more). The product manager leads these practices. Boundary Spanning practices include the following.

- *Refining the backlog*: the product manager routinely re-sequences the backlog, keeping the highest priority stories on top and ready for engineers to start.

- *Story showcase*: a 60-minute weekly meeting to discuss stories that the team will begin shortly. The product manager describes upcoming stories, and the engineers provide feedback on the expected difficulty of each story. The story showcase helps improve the team's shared understanding of the product.

- *Estimating effort*: only if necessary, the team forecasts the time and resources needed to implement a story using a mathematical model, or by comparing stories to a small set of reference classes (groups of previously-completed stories that took similar effort).

- *Accepting stories*: after the team delivers a story, the product manager verifies that the delivered work meets expectations. The product manager tries to break the feature with unexpected input.

- *Daily sync*: a daily 5–15 minute meeting where team members discuss changes that affect the team from the previous day's work and impediments to the current day's work. If physically possible, people stand to encourage a short check-in.

- *Team huddle*: an ad-hoc team meeting to solve a specific problem.

Track Two Practices

The primary purpose of Track Two is to deliver the product vision to stakeholders as high-quality software. The engineers lead Track Two including the following practices.

- *Clean code* means writing code that is easily understood, easily changed, and complies with any coding standards the team has adopted.

- *Refactor continuously* means systematically improving code quality concurrently with new feature development. It means both optimizing software architecture and addressing technical debt as we go.

- *Test-driven development* means incrementally building the software by iterating between refactoring, writing a failing test, then writing just enough code to get that test to pass.

- *Fast tests and fast builds* means that tests and builds execute reasonably quickly to provide speedy feedback when something breaks and encourage integrating frequently.

- *Design code continuously* means engineers continue reformulating and reorganizing code to satisfy readability, performance, or other quality attributes for the entire time the product is actively being developed.

- *Pair continuously* refers to two engineers synchronously co-creating source code and tests. Pairs rotate daily.

- *Team code ownership* means that all code belongs to a team and any engineer on a team can change any of the team's code.

- *Version control* means having a system for storing and managing code, including change history, work-in-progress, and labels showing what code shipped in each release.

- *Integrate frequently* means that developers integrate as often as practical—typically several times a day. Any code branches are short-lived.

- *Code review* refers to examining a change request before merging it into the product's main branch (or development branch, depending on the pipeline) in version control.

- *Build systems* automate compiling code, running tests, and (sometimes) pushing changes to the staging, acceptance, or production environment.

- *Stop on red builds* means that when a build fails (the build monitor turns red), one pair immediately stops what they are doing and fixes the issue; engineers only merge code into version control on builds for which all of the tests pass.

- An *acceptance (AKA staging) environment* is a simplified version of the production environment that supports manual testing.

- *Release frequently* means shipping or deploying as often as is practical, which could be anywhere from several times per day to biennially depending on the project.

- *Assess sustainability* refers to quantitatively or qualitatively evaluating the environmental, economic, social, or technical sustainability of the product or its development process.

Project Management Practices

The primary goal of project management is maximizing the *long-term* health and effectiveness of the team. The whole team owns these practices since it has no project manager.

- *Retrospective* (or *retro*): a meeting in which the team reflects on recent events, celebrates successes, and identifies ways to improve in a safe environment for constructive discussion and feedback.

- *Waste workshop*: a meeting in which the team systematically identifies and eliminates things that consume resources without providing any value to project stakeholders.

- *Core work hours*: the team prioritizes working together in the same office during the same hours. Flexibility with the schedule helps with outside-of-work constraints, provided that the team has enough time in common.

- *Hire team players*: valuing job candidates' ability to work well with others and get along with current team members as much or more than technical skill.

- *Definition of done*: the conditions under which a backlog item can be marked as completed.

- *Flexible contracts*: establishing an ongoing relationship between a development organization and a client organization without stating a fixed scope, schedule, budget, or other unnecessary details.

- *No overtime*: no one is allowed to work overtime except in genuinely exceptional circumstances.

How Is Sustainable Dual-Track Development Different?

Dual-track development just means that a product is built by a balanced team, which organizes work into two continuous, parallel tracks dedicated to loading and unloading a backlog. *Sustainable software development* means building software that is economically feasible and can be maintained and evolved for many years without damaging society, the environment, or the well-being of its stakeholders. When you put them together, you get *Sustainable Dual-Track Development* (Figure 1–4).

Sustainable Dual-Track Development builds on previous software development methods and project management frameworks including Extreme Programming, Lean Software Development, and Scrum. Like other agile methods, it rejects managerialism, bureaucracy, excess documentation, litigiousness, and over-planning. However, it differs from previous guidelines in several ways:

1. Sustainable Dual-Track Development incorporates user-centered design techniques to ensure software products are appropriate for stakeholders. Most software projects go awry because of misunderstanding the project context and writing the wrong stories. Yet, most of the advice in the professional literature is about estimating, implementing, and deploying stories after they're written. Sustainable Dual-Track Development focuses on getting the right things into the backlog as much as effectively realizing the backlog as working software.

2. Sustainable Dual-Track Development overcomes disruption using numerous practices that help team members share knowledge.

3. Sustainable Dual-Track Development incorporates many techniques for improving team cohesion, resiliency, health, and well-being. Software development is a group process—team cohesion and collective intelligence eclipse individual talent and intelligence. Team members' health and well-being outweigh capricious short-term deadlines.

4. Sustainable Dual-Track Development focuses on continuity. A balanced team replaces multiple specialist teams, handing the project back and forth. Parallel tracks of work replace phases, iterations, or sprints. Frequently integrating and releasing replace arbitrary deadlines that only served to sow division and discord.

5. Sustainable Dual-Track Development encourages a sustainability-first mentality. It includes numerous practices for prioritizing the long-term health of the development team, long-term performance and profitability of the product, and long-term benefits for the natural environment and human society.

Part I

Spanning Track One and Track Two

for everyone

We need a set of practices to help the team build the system incrementally yet smoothly. Track One is about identifying what to build, and Track Two is about implementing features.

Chapter 2: Balanced Teams explains how individuals become work groups, and those work groups mature into high-performing teams. It discusses considerations for team composition, team size, group decision-making, working across time zones, building large projects with small teams and forging resilient teams with clear boundaries, effective communication, and a focus on sharing knowledge.

Chapter 3: The Product Backlog clarifies that the product backlog is a model of work to be done, describes common misconceptions about product backlogs, and explains how to manage a backlog.

Chapter 4: Boundary Spanning illustrates how the team spans different social worlds: development, use, and business. Product managers span the boundary between business and development; product designers span the boundary between developers and users. It explains how to span these boundaries more effectively, using evidence-based practices.

Chapter 5: Project Management describes the mechanics of running a project, including how to organize development without iterations, eliminate software development waste, establish sustainable core work hours, and minimize overtime.

Chapter 2

Balanced Teams

If you could get all the people in an organization rowing in the same direction, you could dominate any industry, in any market, against any competition, at any time.
– Patrick Lencioni

 Key Takeaways

- Forging effective, mature, and cohesive teams is vital for software project success.

- Team members interact regularly, pursue shared goals, and collaborate effectively. Just calling people a "team" does not make them a team.

- Welcome new team members and capitalize on their fresh perspectives.

- Software teams need a balance of design, development, and business / management knowledge.

- 200-person teams don't exist. Large systems are built by a bunch of small teams.

- Remote and hybrid teams can struggle to mature when they don't get enough intense collaboration.

- The secret to effective knowledge management is continual interpersonal collaboration (e.g. pair programming), not formal documentation.

- The drawbacks of knowledge silos usually outweigh the benefits of specialization.

Joining an Unwelcoming Team

When I (Todd) am not developing software, I like doing improv (improvisational theater) and riding roller coasters. To me, software development projects feel like improvising while riding a roller coaster. The developers are always adapting to changing contexts (like in improv), while projects give the illusion of hurtling toward the dangerous unknown (like roller coasters).

Years ago, I was excited to join a high-profile project developing a connected car application for a major automotive company. It was my first iOS development experience and my first automotive project. I knew and respected some of the people already involved and was looking forward to joining them.

My first day, however, was pretty disappointing. After the daily sync, the developers moved to their work area, paired up and began working. There were an odd number of engineers, so everyone had a pair except me, and I had no idea what I was supposed to do. I felt like I was standing against the wall at a junior high school dance: excluded, unwanted, and unnecessary. I should have asked for help, but I just couldn't.

Todd

Later, I discovered that the team lead had intended to brief me that afternoon but was stressed by the aggressive project schedule and distracted by the project's complexities. But because no one mentioned it, the implicit message I received was *you are on your own*.

This first impression set the tone for the remainder of the project. When my teammates tried to integrate me later, I struggled to get past the feeling of being unsupported.

Is Your "Team" Really a Team?

Arguably, the most powerful determinant of success in software development is the extent to which individuals coalesce into a team. Simply assigning people to work together does not create a team.

A *team* is a group that has matured enough to be effective [15]. A *group* is three or more people who (1) share goals and (2) interact to perform tasks [16].

If your "team" is ineffective—always fighting, distrustful, don't feel like they're in it together—they aren't a team at all. If some people don't interact with each other regularly or have different goals, perhaps with a hidden agenda, they aren't even a group.

Group members do not have to be in the same physical location. Your workgroup can all be working from home. What matters is that you all interact regularly to pursue approximately the same goals.

Most teams have 4–8 members. If your workgroup has more than about fifteen members, it's probably multiple groups. Fifty-person teams do not exist. Pretending that 50 people are all on the same team is misleading and dangerous. To be effective, you must transform your collection-of-individuals-who-are-supposed-to-work-together into one or more teams. That is not possible if you are pretending that the 50 people on your floor and the 25 in the satellite office are all one big team.

There are four basic steps to develop your group into a high-performing team [15]:

1. Make a list of who is in your group. Basically, it's the people you interact with regularly to get things done. It's the people you work *with*, not work *near*.

2. Make sure members have a sense of inclusion. (For suggestions, see the next section, *A Welcoming Team*, and the *Team Cohesion* sidebar on page 25.)

3. Ask everyone in the group about their goals. Resolve differences in perceived goals through conversation. Take turns talking and listening (don't talk over each other). Perfect agreement is not necessary. You just need to agree enough so everyone is pulling together in the same direction. If agreement is elusive, look into conflict resolution techniques.

4. Resolve mistrust among team members by: (A) building trust by acting in a trustworthy manner; and (B) overcoming distrust by apologizing for past mistakes. Getting everyone to share information freely without playing power games is crucial. Clarify that politicking is not welcome.

When all the group members work together, feel like they belong in the group, share broad goals, and trust each other, then the group is a team.

In addition to working toward their goals, groups must manage their internal dynamics. If we ignore group dynamics, we will waste time dealing with conflict instead of pursuing our shared goals. If we develop the group into a team, the percentage of time needed to keep the team together will decrease substantially, and the team will be more productive.

Welcoming and Onboarding New Team Members

First impressions matter. A developer joining a team is a critical transition point for the individual and the team. Adding a new team member fundamentally changes the team's dynamic.

Welcoming and integrating (i.e., *onboarding*) a new team member is essential because we are more productive when we feel like we belong. Belonging is a core psychological need, and feelings of belonging are essential for motivation and morale [17]. When the team welcomes new members, they are more likely to pay it forward and welcome the next team member joining the team.

The opening vignette illustrates how a bad onboarding process can disempower a new team member and undermine team effectiveness. Contrast this experience with joining a welcoming team.

Joining a Welcoming Team

Some time after the iOS automotive project described in the opening vignette, I (Todd) joined a new, much different team. "We are glad to have you on the team," said Maryam when I first met them. "Welcome friend!" chimed in Kalen.

"We see you joining the project as a unique opportunity for you to provide us feedback," explained Eyram, the most experienced engineer on the team. "We've been working on this project for a while. We've grown accustomed to the assumptions we've made. We're blind to problems that we take for granted. We want your help with removing waste, improving our dev flow, and making the code easier to discover and understand."

Later, during a meeting, the team rehashed a thorny problem. They asked for my opinion first because they thought I could offer a fresh perspective. Being new, I didn't have all the context, but offered what I could. Some of my half-baked ideas helped, and my naïve questions framed the problem in a useful way that the team had not considered.

At the end of the first day, Eyram asked how my day went. His tone conveyed that he really meant it. He wanted to hear about any issues that made my day less than ideal. He asked if there was anything I needed to be productive or if I had any questions about the project or the way the team worked.

At the end of his first week, the product manager asked me, "What do you think we should be doing differently?"

I got the message loud and clear: "you are welcome, and we value your opinion." This first impression set the tone for the rest of the project, during which I consistently felt supported, included, motivated, and capable of doing a great job.

Every New Team Member Is an Opportunity

Teams grow accustomed to how they work. Whenever a new person joins a team, there's a unique chance to benefit from their perspective and make them feel valued. Asking new team members for feedback can:

- bolster morale;

- improve employee retention;

- empower both new and existing team members to remove issues they discover;

- identify assumptions, waste, hard to discover or understand code, or better practices or tools; and

- create a culture where "it's OK to ask questions" instead of spending time relearning what the team already knows.

Teams that say, "We've always done it this way" or "It's pointless trying to change the bureaucracy" miss these valuable opportunities to improve. The fresh-eyes perspective only lasts for a few weeks before the new team member acclimatizes to the team's ways of working. Welcoming a new member is not expensive; it just takes some forethought and consideration.

Team Cohesion

Group conflict negatively affects team performance [18] and project success. These negative effects cannot be erased through effective processes [19]. We asked Dr. Lucas Gren, an expert in group dynamics, how software teams can improve their cohesion. He had the following recommendations:

1. Continuously reflect on how you collaborate and the social processes within your team. Write a dynamic "team agreement" where the team defines the team norms; that is, how do we treat each other and conduct our work? Is it OK to be ten minutes late? Is it OK to not listen and interrupt? What do we expect from our team's output? What do we expect from our team members? How do we know if we fulfill our goals?

Dr. Lucas Gren

2. Discuss where the team is in Tuckman's forming, storming, norming, and performing stages of group development. For example, if some members do not share their opinions, the group might still be forming. Ask yourself, why are some members still concerned with their dependency and inclusion in the team? What can we do about that?

3. Discuss why the team exists at all. What is our purpose? What competencies do we have and need? Do we have too few or too many team members to fulfill our purpose?

4. Accept that conflicts are an essential part of team building and find good conflict resolution techniques.

5. A vocal member (often a person in a leadership role) can drive a newly formed team and provide safety through structure. However, as the team matures, move to participatory decision-making methods such that all members help drive the team forward.

Cross-functional and Balanced Teams

A *cross-functional team* combines individuals with complementary skill sets into one collaborating team. In software development, these knowledge areas are usually design thinking, management / business, and software development. The team needs development knowledge to build software, design knowledge to build software that *users will want*, and management / business knowledge to build software that *someone will pay for*.

A *balanced team* is a cross-functional team in which power is distributed across relevant knowledge areas. (*Balanced team* can also refer to the movement that promotes

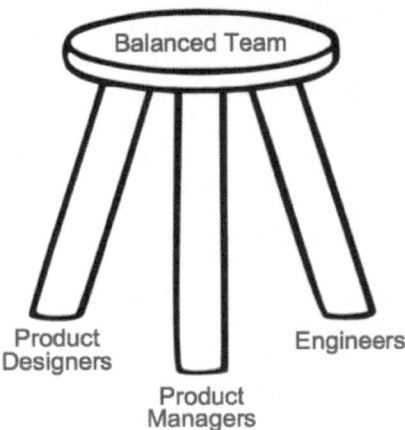

Figure 2–1: Balanced Team

cross-functional teams.[1]) A balanced team is like a stool with three legs (Figure 2–1). Take away a leg and the stool falls over. For example, if no team member understands the business environment, the team may create an unsellable product. Make one leg longer than the others, and the stool falls over. For example, if the product manager makes all the decisions, ignoring the engineers, the code may accumulate so much technical debt that it becomes unmodifiable. A balanced team has no boss. Team members combine their complementary knowledge and skills to determine together what to do and how to do it.

Design, management, and development are skills, not people. Individual people can be skilled in multiple areas. However, gaining proficiency in these areas requires significant training and experience. Few people have excellent programming, design, *and* product management skills, so balanced teams typically combine different people with complementary skills. In fact, having a designer who is not a programmer can help because their design work can't be displaced by programming work. So even though these are skills, not people, it's usually best for each person to stay focused on one role.

A balanced team has the following advantages.

- **Faster and easier collaboration.** On a balanced team, there are no organizational barriers between the different roles. A product designer can easily ask engineers about a design concept's feasibility; engineers can easily ask a product designer to clarify user needs.

- **Respect for the other disciplines.** Continuously working together helps team members better understand and appreciate each other's work.

- **Alignment of vision.** The team works towards a common goal. There is no competition between groups. The team succeeds together.

---

[1]https://balancedteam.org/

- **Self-direction.** A self-managed team can react more easily to change and feel greater ownership of the product. Feelings of ownership help with motivation and quality.

- **Reduced politics.** Balanced teams feel like "we're all in this together" rather than "it's us versus them." By contrast, groups of specialists operating in a functional silo inevitably have more conflict and politicking as each faction pursues their own agenda.

Balanced teams shift the manager role from an external boss to an internal teammate. The product manager's goal is to say "yes" to the next piece of work to be done and "no" to everything else. If upper management is not yet aligned with agile software development, the product manager shields the team from arbitrary external forces and communicates expectations outwards.

Team Size

Teams should be large enough to progress towards a goal while small enough to avoid communication and coordination problems. For most projects, the ideal team has one product designer, one product manager, and between four and six developers. Teams with close to 15 members may benefit from a second product designer. Having two designers enables pair design, which may increase creativity and design quality. However, good product designers are in short supply, so the designer and manager can pair up for some activities.

While approximately seven-person teams work well in many contexts, the optimal team size depends on how many developers can work on the product simultaneously without getting in each other's way. Assigning 20 people to a two-person job will not make it go faster. That is why adding more team members can make a late project later [20].

As teams grow, there's a trade-off between the business goals of efficiency and throughput. Small teams are more efficient because they have less communication and coordination overhead. They keep all the context of their decisions and quickly learn each other's strengths. However, such small teams are fragile due to a low truck number (described later in this chapter) and can't build anything large. Larger teams can ship more features and tolerate more disruption. Larger codebases need more help dealing with defects and upkeep. But the larger team is less efficient because it needs additional communication, coordination, and sharing of knowledge. Teams of 12 engineers feel large, as it is hard to keep track of all the changes happening in the codebase. Even with continuous pair programming and overlapping pair rotation (see Chapter 10: Clean Code and Tests), information propagates slowly.

For large projects with dozens or hundreds of contributors, people must be organized into multiple teams. Many organizations divide up the workers by skill group, creating a business analysis team, design team, architecture team, front-end team, back-end team, maintenance team, etc. This tends to create communication and knowledge transfer problems as one team hands off work to another. It is usually better to divide a large product into multiple components and have a balanced team work on each component.

Large Projects

Large projects are not built by large teams. Large projects are built by a bunch of small teams. Groups larger than approximately 6–8 people become increasingly difficult to hold together. It's not that larger groups necessarily fight more, it's that the more people there are trying to work together, the more difficult it is for everyone to:

- interact regularly;

- maintain homogeneous goals;

- maintain a feeling of belonging together (cohesion); and

- maintain consistent, shared mental models.

Despite what proponents of Scaled Agile Framework and Large Scale Scrum would have you believe, *no one knows how to build a monolithic software project effectively.* However, we do know a lot about how to organize large groups of people for effectiveness. So, let's focus on what we know and see how far it gets us.

First, as we just said, large projects necessarily have many work groups. Success depends on how those groups are organized. In one project we observed, all 145 people were treated like they were on a single team. They had a single, shared codebase without clear boundaries or team responsibilities. Small changes in one part of the system would break supposedly unrelated features. The team-that-wasn't-really-a-team couldn't maintain a shared mental model, so everyone kept stepping on each other's toes.

Meanwhile, this mega not-a-team couldn't communicate effectively. A 15-minute daily sync with 145 people is either impossible or useless. Story showcases didn't work because there were too many stories; retrospective meetings were ineffective because 145 people can't really have a group discussion. It's just not possible for that many people to synchronize shared mental models, and the codebase quickly became too large for any one person to comprehend.

Faced with this situation, many organizations backslide into pre-agile ways of thinking and working: requirements specifications, planning meetings, hierarchy, command-and-control, etc. They start thinking about development in terms of "phases" or propose separate development, operations, and testing teams. These pre-agile structures undermine productivity and effectiveness in large projects just as they do in small projects.

Instead, we must keep workgroups small enough to maintain shared mental models, embrace a shared identity, and mature into teams. To build a large product with multiple work groups, we need two things: (1) good ways of dividing work among the groups and (2) good structures to help the groups collaborate. To divide work effectively, we have to exploit Conway's Law... backward.

Inverting Conway's Law

Conway's law states that organizations create systems that reflect their communication structures (see the sidebar on page 29). A small product's architecture should emerge from continuous refactoring. Part of being agile is avoiding premature commitment to a particular architecture. However, as soon as enough people are involved that we need

> ### Conway's Law
>
> Way back in 1964, Christopher Alexander (the famous architect who proposed the concept of design patterns) explained that systems should be organized to maximize stability by splitting them into components that have lots of internal connections (similar to cohesion) and few connections to other components (similar to coupling) [21]. The problem, as he saw it, was that people tend to organize systems into components for which we have convenient names instead of optimizing cohesion and coupling.
>
> In 1968, Mel Conway observed that "organizations who design systems are constrained to produce designs which are copies of the communication structures of these organizations" [22]. Fred Brooks called this *Conway's Law* [20].
>
> In other words, developers *should* organize systems to optimize their stability, understandability, security, etc., but they actually organize systems based on the way the developers themselves are organized and the concepts for which they have names. For example, instead of weaving safety and security throughout every system component, the "security" team might try to build a "security system" and somehow attach it to an otherwise insecure product. If you have a security team, an engine team, and a command-line-interface team, the code tends to have a security component, an engine component, and a command-line-interface component *regardless of whether that architecture makes any sense.*
>
> We can work with Conway's Law (and Alexander's observations) backwards. Organize developers into corresponding teams to get software with certain components and boundaries. Give them names that reflect what the components actually do and boundaries that reflect the desired boundaries between components. For example, if we have a simple base system augmented through a plug-in architecture, we make a "base system" team for the generic framework and then one team for each plug-in.
>
> To summarize, organize people into teams corresponding to the components you want the system to have—an "inverse Conway maneuver" [23]. If you want two components to have a clear interface, have separate teams own them and set a clear boundary between them.

multiple work groups, we must start making architectural decisions. If we have n groups, we must divide the system into *at least* n quasi-independent subsystems so that each group can work simultaneously without breaking each other's contributions.

Therefore, the larger the project, the more difficult it is to delay at least a tentative architecture. Over time, we can revise the architecture (and reorganize teams), but as soon as we have more people than can form a single team, we need to make some tentative architectural decisions.

Sometimes, the project begins with more than 20 people. Before they can get down to any real coding, they should ask, "how should we organize the system into subsystems?" and "how should we divide the developers into teams?" The point here is that these are really *the same question*—if the initial architecture doesn't reflect the division of labor, the developers will trip all over each other.

Other times, the project begins small, with a single workgroup building a product. The group and the product grow until there are too many people for a single work group, and they implicitly or explicitly split into multiple groups. Implicit deterioration into multiple work groups invites conflict and working at cross-purposes. It is better to recognize that the workgroup is getting too large and have an intelligent group discussion about how best to divide the system into subsystems and the developers into corresponding groups.

For some projects, the components are obvious. For example, if you have some large, database-driven product with an Android app, iOS app, web app, and a back-end that runs all of them, these are your four teams. For other projects, it's less clear. For example, in an enterprise system that handles inventory, purchasing, scheduling, marketing campaigns, forecasting, etc., those sound like they're going to be the components because that's what we have names for, but these activities may be tightly coupled from a technical perspective, and a totally different division may be needed. There are no generalizable rules for this—you need domain knowledge to figure it out case by case.

The main symptoms of misalignment between work groups and system architecture are:

1. Multiple groups frequently needing to collaborate on a single change (or worse, one group modifies another's files).

2. Teams frequently blaming each other for technical problems.

3. Individuals frequently struggling to determine who is responsible for fixing a particular defect.

Furthermore, several organizational anti-patterns are rarely a good idea:

- Combining "technical leads", "senior engineers", "engineering directors", and "domain experts" into an "architecture" team. Having any kind of separate architecture team is a pre-agile anti-pattern that reinforces hierarchy and interferes with bottom-up architecture and team code ownership.

- Separating the "back-end team" from the "front-end team." This means every time we want to add a feature, we must coordinate with both teams, and the subsystems can't maintain loose coupling. We realize this is a contentious recommendation, as many organizations separate the back-end from the front-end since they often involve different programming languages, but we stand by it.

- Separate analysis, design, coding, testing, and operations teams. Testing involves analysis, design, and coding; coding involves analysis, design, and testing; and analysis and design are the same cognitive processes. Having teams named after pre-agile lifecycle phases is simply out of whack with reality.

In small- to medium-sized projects with a single, cohesive team, that team gets to make all the decisions. When there's more than one team on a project, we have a new problem to solve: team boundaries and inter-team coordination.

In summary, the first step to scaling up Sustainable Dual-Track Development for large projects is *divide and conquer.* Every large project is really a bunch of interconnected small projects. Every large workgroup is really a bunch of small workgroups (or a set of individuals). Ideally, any large subsystem is divided into n loosely coupled subsystems, one for each of n work groups. We wish this were easy, but in practice, companies periodically shift their team structures based on a better understanding of good team boundaries.

A Real-life Inverse Conway Maneuver

For an enterprise database, one team built a "Command Center" while another built a "Workload Manager" using pre-agile techniques. Since two separate teams built the two products, each had its own code repository, just as Conway's Law suggests.

The Command Center team began adding "metrics" to the Command Center. Eventually, however, user research revealed that "metrics" and "workloads" were equivalent from the customer's perspective. Both teams had independently implemented the same features because the system's structure was based on the organization's structure instead of its feature structure. Engineering management leveraged Conway's Law by merging the teams and their backlogs. Eventually, the two products become one product.

Merging the teams was complicated by the fact that they were located in different parts of the world. One team hired new team members while context was shared both during overlapping hours and by flying team members to each site for continuous pair programming. When it became clear that the combined team was too big, several team members were rotated onto other projects, but only after the teams were fully integrated and there had been sufficient knowledge sharing.

Coordinating between Multiple Teams

A single team working on a product can be fully self-managed, but when a project needs multiple teams, the organization needs a way to coordinate between teams and manage the product's technical direction. Meanwhile, teams need authority, autonomy, and control over their environment (see the Psychological Ownership sidebar on page 173).

Management Support

Each company has different expectations for their managers, whether they code, whether they manage people, whether they manage zero, one, or several teams. Usually, there's a progression from engineering manager to director to VP of Engineering, but who is doing what changes from company to company and group to group. Whatever they call it at your company, here we'll use the term *engineering manager* to denote the person who coordinates multiple teams working on the same project.

While each team generally makes its own decisions, the engineering manager helps teams identify and collaborate on decisions that affect multiple teams. For example, if one team is considering introducing a new library that impacts another team with different needs, the engineering manager can identify the conflict and help the teams find a mutually-acceptable solution. The engineering manager considers cross-cutting concerns such as security, logging, and coding conventions. The engineering manager helps avoid duplication of effort. Very large projects may need a team of engineering managers.

Engineering managers can be configured in two main ways: 1-to-1 and 1-to-many. With 1-to-1, as shown in Figure 2–2a, one engineering manager works closely with one team and coordinates with other engineering managers. With 1-to-many, as shown in Figure 2–2b, one engineering manager coordinates multiple teams.

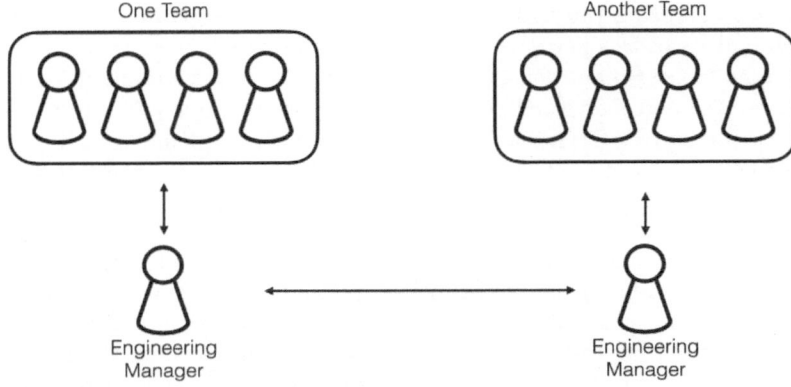

(a) One Manager Coordinating One Team

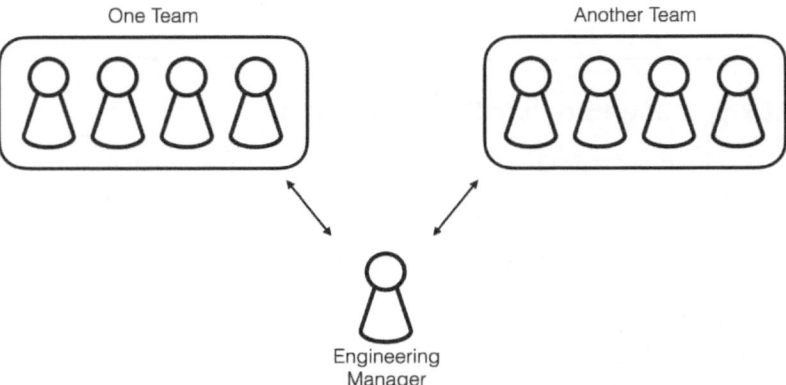

(b) One Manager Coordinating Several Teams

Figure 2–2: One-to-one (a) vs. one-to-many (b) manager configurations

There are three common coordination styles: led by product managers, led by an engineering manager, or led by someone outside the team. If the teams are organized well, most day-to-day tasks should not require coordination among teams. When coordination is required, it is usually best for the product managers of the affected teams to coordinate with each other. However, the more deep technical understanding of the product is needed, the more valuable it is to have an engineering manager lead the coordination effort. When an outsider leads an initiative, they coordinate with the product managers and engineering manager(s). For example, when multiple teams struggled with upgrading versions of their Kubernetes clusters, an external Kubernetes expert was brought in to review the issue and then coordinate with many teams to make improvements.

Multiple teams solving the same problem differently is wasteful and confusing, and often creates systems that are difficult to understand. On one large enterprise database project we observed, each team developed its own way of provisioning a cluster, leading to 16 different mechanisms—not 16 configurations; 16 different provisioning mechanisms. Solving the exact same problem 16 times over is just waste.

Large projects may need additional coordination rituals; for example, a *product sync*—a project-wide meeting to introduce new people, seek help, share interests, and remind people about upcoming events—immediately following individual teams' daily syncs. Some organizations may have a regular meeting for engineering managers and technical leaders to discuss cross-cutting concerns.

Decision-Making

As explained above, when a product has only one team, they get to make all the decisions. As a product grows, having clear expectations about who makes each type of decision becomes helpful. Some companies create guidelines regarding who is responsible for different kinds of decisions (see Table 2–1 for an example). Without clear guidelines, role expectations might

Table 2–1: Example: Who Makes Which Decisions?

Decision	Decision-Maker
Programming language selection	Engineering leadership
Team assignments (and rotations)	Engineering leadership consulting PM's and team leads
Prioritizing stories	Product manager
Prioritizing bugs	Product manager
Prioritizing escalations	Product manager
Prioritizing chores	Team lead or engineering manager
Paths of work	Product manager with input from engineering leadership
Which team owns which code	Engineering leadership with product managers
When to rewrite a class	The team
When to rewrite a product	Engineering leadership with input from the team
When to wake up engineers for a customer escalation	Engineering leadership
When to end support	Product owner

not align with reality. Agile organizations prefer to decentralize decision-making so decisions are made by the people with the most relevant information and first-hand experience.

In one multi-team project that we observed, one engineering team was making solid engineering decisions that were ideal for their team, but they didn't have the perspective of the entire product. The team slowly realized that they needed to involve engineering leadership and other teams in certain types of decisions. On another, one product manager had an outward-facing emphasis and limited involvement with the engineers. This caused issues when engineering leadership assumed the product managers were coordinating product features, and this particular product manager thought coordination was an engineering problem.

Working Across Time Zones

Sam lives in the United Kingdom and has worked on distributed teams for many years. He enjoys traveling the world, seeing new places, meeting new people, and learning about their different experiences. He likes hearing about the different customs and cultures where his teammates live.

For a while, he worked for an education software company in Silicon Valley. Since all his teammates were many hours away, he did not pair program. His teammates often checked on him in a way that made him feel like they didn't trust him. He often struggled to get the information he needed. When he had a problem, he'd have to wait for someone else to wake up. He could be blocked for 12 hours waiting for an answer. It reminded him of the novel *The Martian*; because of the huge communication delay, he felt like he was on Mars waiting for answers from Earth.

Sam thought a lot about how to hand off work between people in different time zones and how to maintain a sense of belonging in a team with little face-to-face interaction, but his team wasn't interested. Luckily, he joined a new company that was receptive to his ideas. His new team is more spread out; their day spans 15 business hours. High-priority work "follows the sun": as team members start their day, they join an engineer already working on the problem.

Sam

Sam begins his day by reading his teammates' *stand down notes*, describing progress while he slept. As he works, he takes notes about his goals and progress. When a developer in Chicago starts her day, Sam pair-programs with her. Once California comes online, he joins the team's daily sync and shares his progress. Since Sam values pair programming, he shifted his working hours to have more overlap with his teammates. Sam appreciates that the team schedules key meetings when he is available. Once his day is over, the team continues working on the feature. At the end of the global work day, the remaining team members will write more stand-down notes, documenting the current status and suggestions on what to try next, for Sam and others to read the next morning. Although following the sun requires more coordination, the work can be completed faster. Not cheaper, but faster.

Working this way helped Sam's team trust each other and feel more connected. While distributed work remains challenging, Sam wastes less time waiting for information or trying to determine the status of work-in-progress.

Distributed and Hybrid Teams

Many companies that begin in a co-located office eventually struggle to attract enough good developers in their local community, so they open offices in other locations or go remote-first to facilitate growth. If you need specific expertise (e.g., a Postgres or Kubernetes core contributor), you might find no one with those skills is willing to move to where you are. However, going distributed or remote-first has many drawbacks including coordination, communication, and trust problems. The success of distributed and remote-first teams depends on three key issues: communication approach, time zones, and team configuration. How you handle these three dimensions affects the tools and practices you'll need to support your teams.

Communication Approach

Real-time Conversations

Some teams prefer real-time conversations where everyone can join a virtual meeting or enter a conference room. Meetings with real-time conversations have many benefits: better communication, achieving alignment, accelerated team maturation, and more trust.

A 30-minute meeting often achieves desired outcomes faster than waiting for every team member to respond asynchronously. Synchronous communication gets quick responses to clarifying questions and picks up on non-verbal cues (e.g. that participants don't understand a topic or oppose a decision).

A *well-run* meeting helps participants align on a shared understanding of a problem, a shared solution with actions, or a shared vision of the future. Attendees might not necessarily agree with the course of action, but in a well-run meeting, they may feel more buy-in from their participation. Many meetings are not well-run (see the Run Inclusive Meetings section in Chapter 12).

Of course, we've all had meetings that should have been emails, and we are not advocating endless meetings. Rather, we are saying that groups need synchronous conversations to mature into teams. They needn't be scheduled meetings. A co-located team can call an impromptu huddle for five minutes to make an emergent key decision and then return to work. A distributed team might have an impromptu video call to decide how to handle a critical bug. The more time zones the team is distributed across, the more difficult these conversations become (see Time Zones below).

Asynchronous Conversations

Some teams prefer asynchronous conversations via a wiki, email, documentation, instant messaging, or chat rooms (e.g., Slack, Discord). The main benefit of asynchronous communication is time shifting. Each person can decide when they respond. This means a parent picking up a child from school in the afternoon can still participate in the conversation. You also have more time to think through what you want to say before responding.[2]

Some teams argue that asynchronous communication is better because others can read the conversation later and see how decisions were made. This is a great argument for recording meetings or taking minutes, not for asynchronous communication.

Throughout this book, we advocate for real-time conversations for co-located and distributed teams. Yes, open source communities have invented many practices that allow disconnected individuals to work simultaneously on the same project without breaking each other's stuff, but it's better to just work as a team and build trust, belonging, and alignment.

Time Zones

Same Time Zone

Even when all team members live in the same time zone, some may prefer different work hours or have responsibilities that interfere with their work schedule. However, having everyone in the same time zone usually maximizes core work hours (see the Core Work Hours section in Chapter 5). The team's daily sync meeting can demarcate the beginning of the team's shared schedule.

For teams that pair, engineers that arrive early might work on chores, catch up on emails, and take care of HR tasks prior to core work hours. Likewise, engineers who work after core work hours take care of these tasks at the end of the day.

A fully distributed team in the same time zone can leverage impromptu meetings during core work hours. Some teams all hop onto a virtual meeting and mute their lines until the team needs to discuss a topic. Engineers pairing might be in breakout rooms; when the team needs an impromptu meeting, everyone joins the main room. We want to minimize friction in making team decisions.

Overlapping Time Zones

Some teams hire across time zones. With a three-hour time difference (e.g., California and New York), there are roughly four hours of shared time for pairing or meetings. Scheduling around lunches reduces overlap. The more time zones a team is distributed across, the more scheduling friction they experience and the more they rely on written, asynchronous communication. Teams with less shared time may need to spend more of that time pairing or in meetings to make up for less impromptu synchronous communication.

Disjoint Time Zones

Some companies will create teams in disjoint time zones (e.g., California-India, or Bejing-Montreal). This structure is often motivated by a desire to reduce labor costs, which rarely

---

[2]Or cool down if someone just set fire to your *last nerve*. You hear me, John? MY LAST NERVE.

works out as well as companies expect [24]. In this case, there is no overlap of normal working hours, no one can schedule a coordination meeting, there's no impromptu synchronous conversations, and so the "team" usually devolves into separate teams, one at each office. Thus, it is better to treat the different offices as separate teams, create well-defined team boundaries, and have managers who routinely meet between time zones to coordinate, mitigate communication issues, and align their mental models.

Team Configuration

Team configuration broadly refers to times and locations of work. There are three high-level configurations, as follows.

1. A *co-located* team predominately works together in the same physical space. Members may occasionally work from home or collaborate across offices.[3]

2. A *remote-first* team predominantly meets virtually or asynchronously. Most or all team members work from home or an office environment separate from any other team member.

3. A *hybrid* team combines elements of remote and co-located teams. Hybrid teams may be configured in *many* ways and new configurations are still being developed. Some have members who always work remotely and others who are always co-located. Others have everyone work co-located on certain days and remotely other days. Some let each individual choose when and where to work.

Adding one or a few remote team members to an otherwise co-located team is highly problematic because virtual meetings are inferior for co-located members and hybrid meetings are very challenging for remote participants.

Some organizations upgrade conference rooms for better remote experience: microphones at every desk, high-quality speakers in the ceiling, and video cameras that can identify and zoom in on the person speaking. Carnegie Mellon upgraded several classrooms in this way so that students at its Silicon Valley, Pittsburgh, and Rwanda campuses could participate in courses together [25]. Even with these upgrades, hybrid meetings and courses remain challenging. Remote participants often struggle to hear what is happening in the room, contribute to the conversation, or see diagrams drawn on a whiteboard. Today's best remote collaboration tools still cannot fully recreate the co-located experience.

Remote participants will want, and benefit from, a remote-first experience. That does not mean every organization should go remote. It means that teams considering adding remote members should carefully weigh the possible contributions of these remote members against the costs of switching to a remote-first team configuration.

Meanwhile, no one really knows the best way to configure a hybrid team, or the conditions under which any particular hybrid configuration is better or worse. Preliminary research in Paul's lab suggests that realizing the benefits and mitigating the challenges of hybrid teams depends on having sufficient co-located core work hours.

---

[3]Co-located, spelled with a hyphen, means in the same place. Collocated, spelled with two l's, refers to seemingly unconnected words that often appear together like 'artificial' and 'intelligence.'

Onboarding Remote Team Members

Sam was onboarding a team in India remotely from his office in the United Kingdom. Their afternoon overlapped with Sam's morning. The Indian engineers would start their day with learning activities, attempting to fix an issue, exploring the codebase, or ensemble programming. They would record questions to ask Sam. In their afternoon, Sam would come online and do a training session for 2 hours. Then, the Indian team would form breakout groups working on different stories, rejoining Sam as needed. The team found this successful as there were sufficient cross-over periods of working together.

Practices for Distributed Teams

Spin-down Meetings

Spin-down (or *stand-down*) *meetings* are brief events that occur at the end of a workday to facilitate knowledge handoff to team members (or a separate but dependent team) in a different time zone. A spin-down differs from a daily sync in that it includes writing stand-down notes to communicate asynchronously (e.g., using email or Slack).

Gaining a remote engineer in a distant time zone can necessitate changing coordination practices. On one project we observed, a UK engineer was working with a US team. During the UK day, he would finish a task and show it to the US team during the daily sync, at the end of his work day. He found this frustrating experience:

> *Someone will then say, 'Oh, we fixed it last night while you were sleeping.' That's a duplication of work. You don't know what they did. I then feel forgotten. Tell me what you did, it's not that hard. USA is not doing stand-down notes. They aren't communicating freely enough. Duplication of work still happens.*

So, when writing stand-down notes, remember to:

- Overshare information. Don't assume that someone understands something. Add a little more detail. Anticipate their questions.

- Be flexible with the work schedule. Be prepared to work outside of regular hours. Someone needs to accommodate differences in time zones and lunch breaks.

- Ask questions when you have them. Have a policy of disabling notifications outside of work hours so that team members can ask questions anytime without worrying about disrupting teammates' home lives. Someone may answer a question during their evening if it's convenient for them, but don't expect people to be always online.

Sharing and Retaining Knowledge

Many software teams have high levels of disruption, for instance, existing members leaving and new members arriving. People change jobs, change teams, receive promotions, and eventually retire. Even stable teams have a steady flow of members taking vacations, leaves of absence, sick days, personal days, etc. A crucial and underappreciated aspect of team effectiveness is resiliency in the face of this kind of disruption. Resilient teams continue to deliver value week after week, month after month, even when experiencing significant disruptions. Resilient teams survive disruptions by: (1) actively sharing knowledge and removing knowledge silos; (2) cross-training team members; and (3) caretaking the code and tests (described in Chapter 10: Clean Code and Tests).

A quick and dirty way to think about a team's sensitivity to disruption is *truck number*: "The size of the smallest set of people in a project such that, if all of them got hit by a truck, the project would be in trouble" [26]. For example, if productivity dramatically declines every time a certain person is away, the team's truck number is one. *Many* teams, especially in start-ups and small organizations, have a Truck Number of one because so much relies on a single founder or leader. Having a truck number of one or two means that disruption risk is very high.

Many factors undermine resilience and keep the truck number low, for example:

- dividing engineers into "the front-end developer," "the back-end developer," "the database developer," and so on;

- individual engineers hoarding knowledge to increase their job security (in fact, information hoarding lowers team performance, which usually lowers job security) or bolster their egos;

- disorganized, impenetrable code that can only be understood by the person who wrote it;

- a culture of distrust and individualism.

Team disruption combined with a low truck number results in significant organizational knowledge loss. Teams lose knowledge whenever a team member becomes unavailable. This knowledge loss can lead to bad decisions, rework, unfixable bugs, wasting months trying to relearn lost knowledge, and, in extreme cases, total project failure. Indicators that knowledge silos are forming include:

- putting tasks on hold until someone returns from vacation;

- developers skipping over stories in the backlog (because they don't feel confident working on some high-priority stories); and

- requiring specific developers for certain stories.

When knowledge silos form, team members can share what they learned through a demo, code walk-through, team huddle, or pair programming. Team members should rotate people through the code such that each member is exposed to more areas of the codebase. Pair rotation (see Chapter 10: Clean Code and Tests) is an excellent mechanism for improving code base exposure.

Surviving Disruption on Project Relevance

Mladen was looking forward to joining Project Relevance, as it had good upper management visibility and was vital for the client. He hoped performing well on this project would turbocharge his career.

The client company was well-established in their marketplace but concerned that their competitors had added innovative features to their product lines. Project Relevance would fix all that in 23 weeks when the team would deliver a new product to the Apple store.

The team was concerned about the aggressive schedule. By routinely delivering working functionality, the team demonstrated progress and enabled the product owner to ship whenever necessary. Unfortunately, the client demanded everything done. By refusing to prioritize any of the features, the client added unhelpful psychological distress to the team.

Over the first 10 weeks of the project, the team ramped up to eight engineers and progressed steadily until Zornitza was promoted to management, Felix went on a multi-month medical leave, Shelby transferred to another office, Joëlle was needed on another project, and Dany took a multi-month unpaid leave to travel. They were all replaced, one after another, by good engineers, but there was so much churn that it was difficult to keep track of who was even on the team.

Yet, with all of this disruption, the team continued to make steady progress toward their goal. They successfully completed the product and released the application through Apple's capricious approval process. Given the project's success, the client extended the engagement for a second iOS release on week 43.

The client was delighted, even claiming that the team delivered a multi-year project in five months by delivering the first release. The team's secret to coping with such severe disruption? Aggressively sharing knowledge and caretaking the code (see Chapter 10: Clean Code and Tests).

There are three basic mechanisms for preserving knowledge against disruption:

1. externalize knowledge through documentation;

2. acquire knowledge as a person leaves the team; and

3. share knowledge through routine interpersonal interaction (e.g., pair programming, code reviews, daily syncs).

The only trouble is the first two don't work.

Externalizing Knowledge into Documentation Doesn't Work

In the 1980s and '90s, software teams had much more documentation. They wrote binders full of architecture diagrams, user manuals, use case descriptions, test cases, and requirements and design specifications. The logic was, 'Write it down so we don't lose it.'

Figure 2–3: No One Reads Instructions (Source: `https://www.schlockmercenary.com/2017-12-26`; **by Howard Tayler, used with permission)**

However, such documentation quickly becomes unwieldy. A single expert knows too much to write down. For example, a product designer attempting to document everything they know about a product's current and prospective users might compose more than a thousand pages. A mid-sized project could have many such documents, which are collectively so voluminous that no one can find needed information without the documents' writers showing them where to look, which defeats the whole purpose of documentation. And even if all the documentation is expertly organized and indexed so that needed information can be found, everything changes so fast that the information quickly goes out of date.[4]

Furthermore, experts can't anticipate every unexpected situation. Suppose a new product enters the marketplace, and we need to integrate our code with it, or a new standard comes along, and we need to know if our system will support it. A human expert might be able to manage these situations easily, but wouldn't think to document them. Without the expert, the documentation alone cannot rise to the challenge.

With the shift to agile methods, most of the software industry realized that the limited value of prodigious documentation does not justify the cost of creating and maintaining it. Some highly regulated industries still require lots of documentation even though there's no evidence that documentation-centric knowledge management is effective. The rest of us make do with fewer, simpler, non-code artifacts such as those listed in Chapter 1 (e.g. interview guides, informal notes, user stories.)

(Please do not misinterpret our documentation skepticism as a license to stop commenting your code. While many programmers believe code shouldn't need comments, and many programmers are bad at commenting their code, ostensibly self-documenting code can only go so far. We'll return to the art of commenting in Chapter 10.)

---

[4] At the start of my (Todd's) career, I interviewed at an aerospace company making air traffic control software. The interviewer proudly pointed to a shelf of books containing the requirements. I naïvely asked when he'd last opened one of those. He replied that it had been a few months. I didn't get the job.

When you do come across a detail that seems to demand some kind of documentation, ask yourself these questions:

1. **Is this important?** If it's not important, it doesn't need to be documented.

2. **Would this be obvious to a newcomer?** If it will be obvious even to someone unfamiliar with the system, it doesn't need to be documented. The trouble with this is that most people are wildly optimistic about what is or is not obvious about their code. If you have a new team member, you can ask them, "what does this do?" If they can't answer or answer wrong, it's not obvious, even if it seems obvious to you.

3. **How will we keep it all current?** Documentation quickly becomes out of date and unreliable [27], and incorrect documentation may be worse than no documentation. Will this information realistically be kept current, when, how, and by whom? If there's no mechanism to keep the documentation reliable, you're better off without it.

4. **Where would a future team member look for this information?** If you don't think people would look for this in documentation, documenting it won't help. Where would you look for it? In the code? The tests? The readme? The wiki? How do we index it or otherwise make it discoverable? If no one will be able to find something, there's no point writing it.

In summary, information should only be documented if it's important, non-obvious, going to be kept current, and likely to be discovered when needed.

When a Team Member Leaves, It's Too Late

Many good organizations interview outgoing employees. *Exit interviews* are highly effective for revealing organizational problems but are hopeless for knowledge retention. Furthermore, people who leave on short notice or on bad terms may not cooperate with knowledge extraction. Though morbid to consider, if a team member unexpectedly dies, there won't be an opportunity for a transfer-of-knowledge interview.

Furthermore, as explained in the previous section, individuals simply have too much knowledge to codify quickly. Implicit knowledge, in particular, typically can be shared over time but not explicated and codified. If you find yourself recording interviews with exiting employees about system aspects or rushing to document some crucial thing before so-and-so leaves, your team isn't sharing knowledge effectively.

Share Knowledge through Continuous Interpersonal Interaction

Proactively sharing and replicating knowledge around a team makes it more resilient to disruption. The agile manifesto favored "working software over comprehensive documentation" [9]. Extreme Programming sees unnecessary documentation as waste and prefers "open, honest communication." Following this sentiment, Sustainable Dual-Track Development emphasizes knowledge sharing through continuous interpersonal interaction rather than externalizing knowledge into documents. We want knowledge to spread from one developer to the next and eventually reach the entire team.

> ### Knowledge Management
>
> "Knowledge management and organizational learning" has been an active area of research for at least three decades. The basic idea is that the combined knowledge of an organization is a significant source of competitive advantage. However, that advantage can only be realized by effectively managing all the knowledge and can only be maintained as long as the knowledge isn't lost. Knowledge management is crucial for knowledge-based organizations, like software companies, because their success depends much more on their employees than on access to natural resources or expensive machinery [28].
>
> The "knowledge" in knowledge management is used broadly to include real knowledge (justified, true belief), explicit knowledge (facts), implicit knowledge (the ability to do something) and the combination of beliefs, conjectures, assumptions, and mental models that constitute an organization.
>
> Some people incorrectly believe that you have to make knowledge explicit to share it. Consequently, many organizations overemphasize formal, written approaches to knowledge management (documentation). Much early knowledge management research implicitly supported the focus on codified knowledge by investigating databases, data warehouses, decision-support tools, and "groupware" [29].
>
> The truth is that knowledge can be shared one-on-one or one-to-many through writing, speaking, or collaborating, formally or informally, horizontally or vertically. Indeed, underutilized informal, collaborative approaches like pair programming are usually better for distributing knowledge throughout a team. Because "interactions involving people transfer more readily within than between firms ... by embedding knowledge in interactions involving people, organizations can both effect knowledge transfer internally and impede knowledge transfer externally. Thus, knowledge embedded in the interactions of people, tools, and tasks provides a basis for competitive advantage in firms" [30, p. 150].

Pair programming is exceptionally effective for all sorts of knowledge sharing [31]. It provides just-in-time help, such that developers don't waste hours solving a problem that a teammate can fix in five minutes. Pair programming is especially good not only for onboarding but also for routine development. Each day that an engineer works solo, they are creating knowledge silos. During pair programming, engineers co-create shared knowledge. Those two people know the code they wrote and the rationale for their design. Frequently rotating pairs (as described in Chapter 10) amplifies knowledge sharing.

Another practice that helps with knowledge transfer is peer code review. During code review, one engineer inspects another engineer's code, looking for defects, potential improvements, and compliance with team agreements like coding standards (see Chapter 11 for more about code review). Code review helps spread knowledge because developers read different parts of the codebase, see other developers' ways of doing things, and reconstruct why changes have been made. In open-source communities, code review is also the main mechanism for determining which changes are accepted into the project.

Some teams meet occasionally to discuss or demonstrate new work. Presentations and discussions are good for raising awareness of important, time-sensitive changes. If we can't wait for knowledge to percolate across the team naturally, an explicit discussion, presentation, or demonstration is a good choice.

However, reading code and watching presentations are less effective for knowledge transfer than pair programming with pair rotation. During pair programming, team members actively cross-train on programming languages, frameworks, tools, refactoring techniques, and processes. They experience code at a deeper level than a reviewer or demo-watcher. For programming, learning by doing is simply more effective than learning by listening or reviewing. Therefore, peer code review and occasional demos cannot fully replace pair programming and pair rotation. Rotational pairing is *the* knowledge transfer practice in Sustainable Dual-Track Development.

Indeed, becoming an expert requires a combination of first-hand experience (e.g., pair programming), second-order observation (e.g., peer code review), and mastery of applicable theory (e.g., reading and reflecting on this book). Just as some implicit knowledge can only be gained through practice, some explicit knowledge is extremely difficult to grasp without a formal education or extensive reading. Most developers don't get enough second-order observation and theory integration to master their craft.

Specialization vs. Knowledge Management

Some people complain that two engineers working independently are faster than a pair and that specialization increases efficiency. And that's true ... *in the short term*. However, *in the long term*, the knowledge loss, inflexibility, and sensitivity to disruption caused by specialization and solo programming outweigh short-term productivity gains.

The move-as-fast-as-possible-and-to-hell-with-the-consequences culture endemic to Silicon Valley is not sustainable. The proponents of this mindset are walking, talking manifestations of survivorship bias. Prioritizing short-term feature delivery over long-term sustainability is intrinsically perilous; it entails risks like burnout and low morale that intelligence and hard work cannot mitigate. For every company that gambled on an unsustainable development process and won, a hundred more lost. But you only hear from the winners.

Summary

In summary, *groups* share goals and collaborate on tasks, while *teams* are mature, effective groups. Most groups need intense, synchronous interaction to share knowledge and mature into teams. Large groups quickly fracture into smaller groups, so big products must be modularized and built by multiple small groups. Onboarding is important because new teammates temporarily reduce maturity and effectiveness. This is often challenging for remote-first and hybrid groups, and more research is needed to determine how to address it. As we will see in subsequent chapters, Sustainable Dual-Track Development includes many practices that help improve team cohesion, maturity, and effectiveness.

Chapter 3

The Product Backlog

Stories aren't a different way to write requirements, they're a different way to work.
–Jeff Patton

 Key Takeaways

- A backlog is a model of work to be done.

- A backlog is **not** a requirements specification or a design specification.

- A backlog usually includes user stories, epic stories, bugs, and chores.

- A backlog can be visualized using a list, product roadmap, or Kanban board.

- A backlog can be organized into quasi-independent paths of work.

Navigating through Chaos

Joëlle—a product manager—was excited to join a new project developing management and control software for offshore wind energy. She knew that offshore wind had enormous potential and couldn't wait to be part of solving some of the critical technical challenges. But it wasn't long before the project floundered.

The team was anxious. There were many unknowns and technical risks. The engineers felt overwhelmed and unsure of how to proceed.

Joëlle focused on what was known. She divided the preliminary work into small steps. She presented to the team the simplest thing possible as the first user story, clearly defining its acceptance criteria. The engineers knew how to build that. She then presented the next story; the engineers knew how to build that as well. The engineers responded to the clarity Joëlle imposed on the initially unclear situation. By focusing on what was known and what could be done, the engineers could compartmentalize the long-term uncertainty surrounding the project and start building.

Joëlle

After a few weeks, the team was surprised to see that they had built a minimal viable product (MVP). The engineers appreciated how Joëlle guided them through their uncertainty and apprehension. She understood that engineers are most effective when focused on individual, clear tasks. A good product manager simplifies and clarifies initially uncertain situations, helping prioritize the stories that comprise the backlog.

What Is a Product Backlog?

To understand contemporary software development, we start neither at the beginning nor at the end but in the middle. In the middle of most software projects is *the backlog*, one of the most widely misunderstood parts of agile development.

A *product backlog* is a collection of work items to be done. A *work item* could be many things: a Kanban card, use case, scenario—some backlogs are basically just 1980s-style requirements statements. However, the most popular backlog items are as follows.

1. **User story:** a brief, informal description of a feature in terms of a user taking some action, where the *user* can be a human being or another system.

2. **Epic story** (or simply **epic**): a large, vague user story.

3. **Bug:** an error or fault that causes undesirable system behavior (not to be confused with a missing feature).

4. **Chore:** an action that provides value directly to the team but only indirectly to external stakeholders (e.g., reducing technical debt, configuring the build system).

In a new product, user stories are the most numerous backlog items. In a mature product that is being maintained rather than actively developed and extended, bugs and chores might outnumber stories.

The product manager is typically responsible for the backlog and uses it to control the direction of the product. The product manager decides which stories are sufficient to deliver a feature and which features to build first. A subset of the total backlog is typically sufficient to create a minimal viable product, deliver most of the possible business value, release a new feature set, or receive additional user feedback. Many stories are simply never delivered, and that's a good thing.

Purpose of the Backlog

Before agile, many teams tried to document everything. This didn't work because a team's understanding of the world is too complicated and evolves too quickly to document effectively. Now, successful teams develop a shared understanding of their products and contexts by conversing and working together. A backlog simply collects reminders of these conversations.

This sounds simple but can be challenging to digest, especially if you have a formal education in software engineering or have worked in pre-agile organizations. You may be tempted to conceptualize the backlog as the agile equivalent of a requirements specification or design specification. But it's not. Specifications are meant to stand alone. Backlog items are not. Backlog items remind team members of things they already know and conversations they've already had.

The backlog is a model of work to be done (by the developers—product designers and product managers typically have separate lists). It's a glorified to-do list. The backlog's job is to keep the team from forgetting important actions and to give the product manager a way to prioritize work. The backlog is also a great example of a *Boundary Object* (see sidebar on page 48).

In a new product or a product under active development, most backlog items should be user stories (rather than use cases, requirements statements, etc.) because user stories are most consistent with the backlog's purpose: modeling work to be done. Over-complicating or over-formalizing the backlog items reinforces the misconception that the backlog is a specification.

Visualizing the Product Backlog

Stories can be written on physical index cards or sticky notes and arranged on tables or walls or organized into envelopes or small boxes. However, most teams now store their backlogs in integrated project management tools, which typically provide a list-like view of the backlog, sometimes organized into different categories. The team can create additional visualizations, including product roadmaps and Kanban boards. Different visualizations have different purposes.

Boundary Objects

In 1989, Star and Griesemer [32] proposed the concept of *Boundary Objects*—things that sit at the boundary between two social worlds [33]. The two social worlds could be management and development, developers and users, or a software company and its client.

The boundary object is supposed to be flexible enough for people from different social worlds to use it for different purposes. Sometimes, someone modifies the object to make it more generally useful; other times, someone modifies it to make it more useful for their specific work. Without consensus, the boundary object is constantly in flux.

A product backlog is a boundary object. It inhabits the boundary between two social worlds—the world of figuring out what to build (Track One) and the world of building it (Track Two). Even though product designers and software engineers work together, deep down, they come from different social worlds.

Realizing that the product backlog is a boundary object helps us understand what the backlog does and how it works:

- it facilitates communication within the team;

- it allows designers and developers to cooperate despite different perspectives;

- it helps team members remember;

- it allows team members to externalize their thinking about things too complicated to hold in working memory;

- it evolves; and

- it simultaneously includes details that are specific to each track and important for both tracks.

Remote and distributed teams need virtual visualizations to facilitate coordination. In a co-located team, physical cards make it easier to see the whole backlog simultaneously. Hybrid teams can benefit from both, depending on their configuration.

Product Roadmaps

Some people see epic stories as mistakes: stories too large to implement. In contrast, we view writing epic stories as a natural part of designing a product and determining which features to prioritize. The mistake is asking engineers to implement an epic. Instead, the product manager, the designer, or the whole team should use epics to organize feature development and inform more atomic user stories (see Chapter 8).

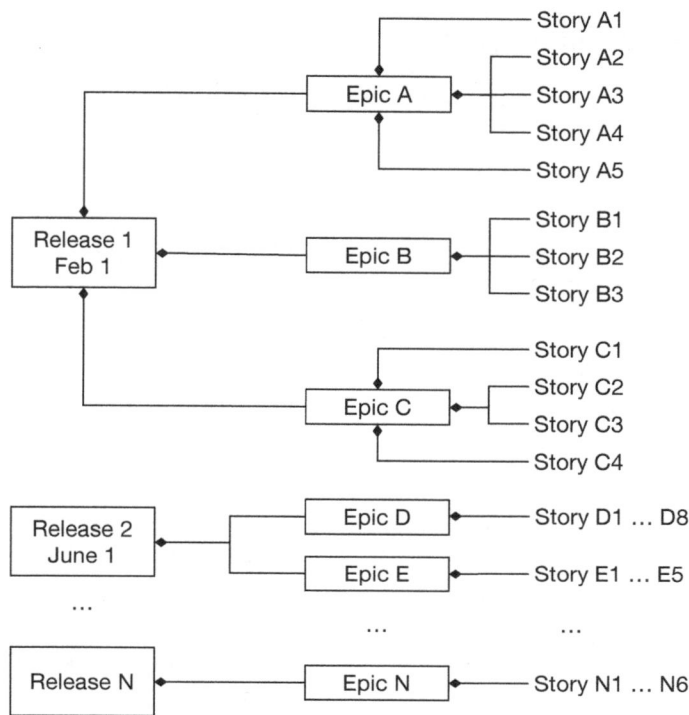

Figure 3–1: Simple Product Roadmap Template

The product manager might organize all of the epics into a *product roadmap* (e.g., Figure 3–1) that depicts the long-term product vision. The roadmap helps the product manager communicate their vision of the product, prioritize features, schedule releases, and determine which features can be built in parallel (see Paths of Work on page 51 for more detail).

Used judiciously, a product roadmap can help synchronize and maintain the team's mental model of the project. However, product roadmaps can also encourage over-planning like filling the roadmap with *stories* rather than *epics* or specifying six months of work in advance. In principle, each release contains one or more epics, and each epic is implemented as many stories. In practice, only upcoming releases would be mapped out down to the story level; more distance releases should be shown in decreasing detail to reflect increasing uncertainty. Furthermore, roadmaps must be updated frequently to avoid departing from the team's evolving mental model of the product.

Kanban Boards

The backlog can be divided into several sections (see Figure 3–2). Most stories in commercial backlogs are not ready to implement. In principle, a "ready" story becomes "work-in-progress" when a developer starts implementing it and "delivered" when the developers

Figure 3–2: Product Backlog

think the story is complete. A story is "finished" when someone—usually the product manager—approves it. However, pipelines vary greatly across organizations.

Kanban boards have several advantages:

1. They show what everyone is doing. This was critical in the early days of agile when teams needed to broadcast their productivity to their organizations.

2. They clearly show which work should be started next.

3. Management can see when important stories are finished.

4. The Kanban board makes it obvious when work-in-progress starts piling up. Limiting work-in-progress is important for efficiency (see Chapter 5).

5. With physical boards, moving story cards from "work-in-progress" to "delivered" is cathartic. Tearing up a card for a particularly troublesome story feels even better.[1]

---

[1] For maximum catharsis, take turns burning old story cards in a fire pit at your next team retreat.

History of Kanban Boards

The Toyota Production System [34], [35] (the way Toyota builds its cars) transformed manufacturing from batch-and-queue to just-in-time. The similarities between batch-and-queue and waterfall software development, as well as just-in-time and iterative software development, inspired several software development methods, including Lean Software Development [36] and Kanban [37]. Taiichi Ohno enjoyed removing waste from the manufacturing process, which included producing material only when needed (resulting in less inventory), slowing machines to the same cadence, and rearranging equipment to improve the flow of the car through the system.

Toyota engineers were curious about how American supermarkets worked. They noticed that when an item is sold from the shelf, a request would be generated to restock it from a distribution center. The distribution center then might, in turn, place an order from the producer of the product. There's a direct link between the sale of a product and its creation. The system knew how to restock each sold item. Toyota applied this idea of "pulling" inventory or "just-in-time" inventory to car manufacturing.

Toyota would attach a card called a kanban to each manufactured part that would describe how it was made and how to make another one when that part was used. When a customer ordered a car with the enhanced speaker package, a request for another car with an enhanced speaker package was created. When the package is pulled off the shelf for that car, its kanban will cause a replacement to be ordered.

Early agile methods adapted manufacturing kanban cards as story cards. Engineers would place story cards on a kanban board that illustrated the work to be done, the work-in-progress, and the work done. Unlike manufacturing, each software kanban card uniquely describes a new feature to be added to the system. Instead of planning for a quarter, the team could determine what to build at any moment in time. In 2010, Anderson created a set of software practices called Kanban [37]. Software developers sometimes refer to the kanban *board* as a kanban.

Paths of Work

Ideally, any developer should be able to work on any story in the backlog. However, teams must coordinate so different developers can simultaneously work on different files, components, or parts of the system without constant merge conflicts.

A *merge conflict* occurs when two separate developers modify the same piece of code in different ways. The conflict is detected when the second developer attempts to commit their code to the version control system. Merge conflicts can be very annoying; it's better to organize work to minimize merge conflicts.

Just as some technical processes lend themselves to multi-threading, some development tasks can be broken into quasi-independent *paths of work*. (Some companies call them "tracks of work," but we we'll stick with *paths* to avoid confusion.)

The team can, at least tentatively, use the backlog to figure out paths of work. Different features (represented in the backlog by epic stories) often align with quasi-independent tasks. For an e-commerce website, for instance, paths of work might be "showcasing products," "onboarding a new user," and "the checkout process." Paths of work, therefore, can be created by grouping related epics. The product manager can label each story with its path of work or the epic story it partially implements.

Organizing the backlog into paths of work can help the team in several ways:

- it helps engineers minimize merge conflicts if they are working in different parts of a codebase;

- it helps the product manager plan capacity for bugs, customer escalations, and chores; and

- it helps management determine the optimal team size.

In other words, software projects have a kind of innate decomposability, which is what Brooks was trying to say in the *Mythical Man Month* [20]. Most people only remember the one quote: "adding manpower to a late software project makes it later." But what Brooks was really trying to explain was that, if you can divide available programming work into n mostly-independent segments, you want n programmers. If you have $n + 1$ programmers, there's nothing for one of them to do that won't impede someone else. Conversely, if you have fewer programmers than paths of work, adding more developers should help.

It is possible to have more developers than paths of work. Pair programming increases optimal team size because you can have $2n$ programmers work in pairs on your n paths. Pairs will complete tasks faster than solo programmers, accelerating the project.

You can add even more people if you can handle the extra explicit coordination. On one observed project, a product manager was willing to take on additional communication and coordination overhead of having more pairs than paths of work because they were more concerned about time-to-market than overall cost. In this case, it worked, but only because the product manager was very good at coordinating. It doesn't usually work very well because the coordination effort increases quadratically (maybe exponentially) with each additional developer.

Occasionally, the entire team may need to focus on finishing one path of work. On another project we observed, the team struggled to complete an epic. One pair figured out what was needed to get the work done. On a whiteboard, they created a diagram showing all the tasks that needed to happen. The team huddled to discuss the plan and made sure that everyone on the team knew what needed to happen. Pairs took on different parts of the work. Since everyone knew the entire plan, possible merge conflicts could be avoided, and six engineers quickly finished the work in two days.

Meanwhile, teams with a released product might have a path of work for "bugs, customer escalations, and chores." This is a way of reserving capacity to deal with important interruptions without affecting the team's ability to deliver new features. If the work in this path of work is temporarily low, the developer or pair might pick up another feature story.

Summary

In summary, the backlog is a model of work to be done by the developers in Track Two. Most backlog items are user stories; other items include bugs or chores. The backlog is used to facilitate communication and prioritization. The product manager is in charge of the backlog.

A backlog of user stories is not a requirements specification, a design specification, or product documentation. The backlog is a mechanism for sequencing work, and the stories are pointers to aspects of the team's shared mental model. In other words, the backlog does not encapsulate knowledge as much as it refers to team members' knowledge.

The backlog can be visualized in many ways, including using product roadmaps and kanban boards. Organizing the backlog into quasi-independent paths of work helps developers work in parallel, and management determines the optimal team size.

We can think of the backlog as sitting between Track One and Track Two within a broader activity of *boundary spanning*. As we'll see in Chapter 4, the backlog can change rapidly, so managing it can be a major challenge.

Chapter 4

Boundary Spanning

Bridging the Gulf between the Two Tracks

What is a scrum team's velocity formula? A bloody mistake, that's what it is. If I invented velocity, I'm sorry. I know I supported it, and I'm sorry for that too.
— Ron Jeffries

 Key Takeaways

- *Boundary spanning* is work that helps team members understand and communicate across different social worlds; *boundary spanners* are people who do boundary-spanning work.

- Product managers span the boundary between business and development.

- Product designers span the boundary between developers and users.

- Product managers constantly refine the backlog by updating, elaborating, and reprioritizing stories.

- The team regularly discusses upcoming stories in a meeting called a story showcase.

- If formally estimating stories is necessary, teams should consider model-based forecasting or reference-class planning poker.

- Daily syncs, team huddles, and retros help teams communicate and resolve conflict.

A Balanced Team Bridges Track One and Track Two

Aaron, a product designer, enjoys surfing and embodies a quiet patience and flexible attitude. He believes in "strong opinions loosely held," which helps his design research. He enjoys identifying, questioning, and validating assumptions. He reassesses previous decisions as new information arises. He loves delighting users with elegant, innovative designs.

Aaron's team makes book publishing software. Authors upload the contents of their book, and the system prints a physical book and sends it to them. Authors can be anyone, including people with limited computer skills, so Aaron aims to design an easy-to-understand system.

Aaron

While the engineers implement ready stories, Aaron and Melissa, the product manager, elaborate the next feature set. With the team, Aaron interviews prospective users to understand their needs for the next feature set (Track One activities), while Melissa continues competitive analysis (Track One activities). Aaron creates low-fidelity prototypes, while Melissa writes stories that would incrementally accomplish the next feature. Once the stories and mock-ups are ready, the team holds a story showcase meeting. Aaron walks the team through the user flow, and Melissa reviews the stories. With a shared understanding of what to build next, the developers implement the stories at the top of the backlog (Track Two activities).

Later in the week, as developers Chris and Shelby manually tested the website, they realized that the way the user selects a color for the book spine is unintuitive. They interrupt Aaron for clarification and suggest a different interaction. To Aaron, the proposal makes sense since it fits with his understanding of the Author personas. Aaron asks the developers to implement it. When they reconvene to see how the new experience works, they decide to ship the feature.

Melissa

Aaron reflects on the benefits of fast feedback loops. At a previous company, he would have handed over the design to the engineering team to build. The feature would be built and shipped to a customer. Issues with the user interfaces might be reported to the company's support organization, and if he was lucky, the feedback might reach him some day. Here, feedback is much faster. The original interface made sense to Aaron and seemed reasonable during the story showcase. Only during implementation did the team realize that the design needed reworking. The engineers closed the feedback loop since they were all on the same team.

Aaron looks forward to usability-testing the new design to validate that users, without the biases of the development team, will find the revised user interface intuitive. But he is more confident in the new design than the previous one.

Between the Tracks

In Chapter 3: The Product Backlog, we explained how the product backlog sits between Track One and Track Two in Sustainable Dual-Track Development. But the backlog is not the only thing between the two tracks. The backlog is part of a broader process of *boundary spanning*.

To succeed, teams need a shared understanding of their project environment and the product they are building. Barring telepathy, however, this sharing is incomplete. Each team member has their own individual understanding of the context and product—their own *schemas*—and these schemas can get out of sync.

If all team members had identical schemas, the product manager could just write user stories and hand them to developers without further communication. The developers would understand and interpret the user stories in precisely the same way as the product manager and designers.

In reality, however, team members' differing skills and experiences drive their schemas apart as the project proceeds, undermining their shared understanding. This desynchronization is most pronounced between the two tracks because, although the whole team participates in both tracks, Track One and Track Two are driven by different goals, skills, and knowledge.

Therefore, the team must regularly sync up, that is, share their diverging viewpoints and rebuild common ground. This process is called *boundary spanning* (see the sidebar on page 58). Boundary spanning includes artifacts (especially the backlog), meetings (especially the story showcase), and practices (especially refining the backlog).

Practices

Refining the Backlog

Refining the backlog involves assessing, improving, prioritizing, blocking, accepting, and rejecting stories. Product managers assess stories against the criteria described in Properties of a Good User Story in Chapter 8. For example, they check whether stories provide value to identifiable stakeholders. They rewrite stories to improve clarity and update stories for better consistency with the product vision. They delete outdated stories, combine duplicate stories, and generate smaller stories from larger ones. As the project environment changes, and the team comes to understand it better, the product manager continually updates the backlog to reflect the team's evolving product vision. Part of this process is deciding the order in which to deliver the stories—prioritizing.

Prioritizing

Product managers periodically examine the backlog to verify that upcoming stories are developer-ready and prioritized to deliver the most value to the user quickly. The prod-

Boundary Spanners

In the Boundary Objects sidebar on page 48, we explained how a boundary object occupies a space between social worlds, is flexible enough to be used in both worlds, and helps people from the two worlds collaborate without perfect consensus.

Boundary spanners are like boundary objects, but they are people instead of artifacts. Boundary spanners simultaneously inhabit two social worlds [38]. Boundary spanning is a kind of work (e.g., activities, practices, rituals) that helps people from different social worlds communicate and understand each other.

Product managers and designers are both boundary spanners. Product managers span the social worlds of business and development. Product managers need to know enough about both the client's business and the process of software development to prioritize stories and advise the developers. Similarly, product designers span the worlds of users and developers. Designers need to know enough about both the users and the development process to lead Track One, imagine appropriate features, generate good low-fidelity prototypes, and promote usability.

We call the space between the two tracks *boundary spanning* because Track One and Track Two represent different social worlds, and bridging those worlds requires specific boundary-spanning work. The artifacts and practices encompassed by boundary spanning bridge the gap between the two tracks. When product managers lead these efforts, they *are* boundary spanners, and they *use* boundary objects (including the backlog).

Seeing the product manager as a boundary spanner helps us differentiate product managers from pre-agile *project* managers. A product manager is responsible for delivering the product but is not the project boss in a traditional management sense, because balanced teams are self-managed and self-organizing (see Chapter 2: Balanced Teams). The product manager does not give orders, assign tasks, or appraise the developers' performance. Rather, the product manager uses knowledge of the business environment to imagine and prioritize features and helps the developers understand enough about the business to build an appropriate product.

When we understand the product manager as a boundary spanner, we understand that the product manager's job is to help people share knowledge, not tell people what to do.

uct manager represents the business, and business considerations typically determine story priorities.

Many prioritization approaches exist [39]. Ideally, the team has both: (1) access to sophisticated financial modeling from which the team can estimate the net present value, rate of return, and payback period associated with each new feature; and (2) enough experience, history, and stability for accurate estimates of feature costs. Then the product manager can simply prioritize features based on the ratio of their economic value and difficulty. However, few teams have access to such information.

Most teams, therefore, adopt more qualitative techniques. For example, in the MoSCoW method, stories are divided into the following four categories.

1. Must have: high-priority stories that must be included in the next release.

2. Should have: medium-priority stories that should be in the next release.

3. Could have: stories that would add value to the next release but aren't necessary.

4. Won't have: stories that wouldn't add value at all (and should be deleted).

MoSCoW helps teams classify features according to risk and value. However—and this is the counterintuitive part—teams implement high-risk / high-value stories *first*. If the product is doomed, we want it to fail now before we waste lots of time and money on it. We could spend a year doing all the low-risk stories, only to discover that a critical high-risk story was impossible and scuttle the whole project. Contrastingly, the more high-risk stories we complete, the more confident we are that the product will be delivered. So, we do the highest-risk critical features first, followed by lower-risk critical features, and then a mixture of less critical features.

Some product managers prioritize stories themselves. Others lead the team through a prioritization workshop, with each team member voting on what to do next. If knowledge of the business and project environment is distributed throughout the team, the whole team should help with prioritizing. In contrast, if the business knowledge is concentrated in the product manager, they should handle prioritization.

In either case, prioritizing the *entire* backlog every week is not necessary. The backlog is often described as a 'prioritized' list of stories, but we've never seen a *completely* prioritized backlog. Real backlogs are messy and evolve rapidly. Most contain stories that are half-baked, outdated, or unimportant. Some stories conflict with each other. In a changing environment, routinely reprioritizing the entire backlog wastes time. Product managers usually just keep the highest-priority stories at the top of the backlog.

In a semi-prioritized backlog, an imaginary line separates the stories that are ready to start from the rest. The product manager should ensure that there are always enough ready stories for the developers to work on. We also recommend making that imaginary line visible so the developers don't inadvertently start a non-ready story, and the product manager can clearly see how much work is ready.

Another question to consider is how to prioritize bugs. Some teams automatically give each bug the highest priority; that is, all known bugs must be corrected before new features are implemented. This strategy minimizes technical debt and greatly reduces the chance of having to abandon a codebase and start over. However, some bug fixes entail so much work that it's not practical to suspend feature development for them, and external pressure on the team can prevent the bugs-first strategy. Moreover, *misfits* are often more damaging than bugs (see the sidebar on page 60), and the bugs-first strategy marginalizes misfits.

Misfits Are More Important than Bugs

A *bug* is when the product doesn't behave the way the development team expects. A *misfit* is when the product doesn't behave the way a user expects [21].

For example, suppose the developers make a rule that passwords must contain at least one special character. If a user can create a password with no special characters, that's a bug because the system violates the developers' intentions. In contrast, if a user is prompted to create a new password and thinks, "why is this asking me to create a new password when I'm already signed on?" (because the user's organization uses single sign-on), that's a misfit.

Users don't distinguish between bugs and misfits. Users just see the product not behaving right and want it fixed. From a user-centric perspective, there is no difference between bugs and misfits because the user is the final arbiter of correct behavior. From a *legal* perspective, however, software development agencies may be allowed to charge for "new features" (fixing misfits) but not for bug fixes. This incentivizes software companies to argue that everything is a "new feature request," which frustrates users and clients. Clients don't want the extra bill, and users feel like the product should have been designed better in the first place.

Sustainable Dual-Track Development minimizes misfits by validating features and user interfaces *before* implementing them. Minimizing misfits is crucial because most major software project failures are due to misfits, not bugs.

Blocking and Re-sequencing

When a story cannot be implemented yet, we say that it is *blocked*. Refining the backlog includes marking blocked stories or moving them later in the backlog so developers do not start them. Stories can be blocked for many reasons, including the following.

- The story needs clarification from an unavailable stakeholder or agreement between stakeholders.

- The story is waiting for content from marketing or legal.

- The story is awaiting approval, possibly from legal, upper management, or a government agency.

- The story depends on an unfixed bug or other unfinished story.

Bugs and chores can also be blocked. For example, on a client-server system project that we observed, the team had identified a resilient bug where data was being assigned to the wrong user. However, the cause of the bug was difficult to identify because of poor client-side logging. The bug backlog item was therefore blocked until the client-side logging story was implemented.

Sometimes, developers ask product managers to resequence work to make the implementation easier; for example, creating user profiles before implementing a login screen. On another project we observed, the engineers were concerned about unknown risks. The product manager sequenced stories in such a way that engineers could see the next immediate step in front of them and navigated the team through the uncertainty without the team realizing it.

Story Showcase

A *story showcase* is a meeting where the team discusses stories they will be working on in the immediate future (e.g., in the next week or two). The team discusses stories one at a time. The product manager typically reads the story and the acceptance criteria out loud to the team. If there are user interface mock-ups, the product designer walks the team through the desired user interactions. The engineers discuss the story, ask questions, and provide feedback on its difficulty. If the team identifies additional work, the product manager takes notes and creates corresponding stories later. If the team struggles to understand a story, the product manager will stop the discussion and rework the story outside of the meeting.

Our memories degrade rapidly over time, so it is better to have frequent short story showcases: 60-minutes each week is better than a half-day each month. Weekly story showcases should not take more than 60 minutes unless the team is unusually large, the stories are unusually complicated, the team is showcasing more than a week's worth of stories, or the stories are poorly written.

The point of the story showcase is for the product manager, the designers, and the developers to co-construct a shared understanding of the work to be done. Part of this is the product manager explaining the upcoming stories, but it's a discussion, not a presentation. The stories and the product manager's vision of them are tentative. The whole team works together to create a more nuanced, shared understanding of the stories. This may involve discussing the difficulty of a story or, more formally, estimating effort (next). The team might briefly discuss implementation details when it serves to understand the story better. However, these activities must serve the purpose of the story showcase: to share, synchronize, and co-construct meaning.

When introducing a new epic, the product manager or product designer might provide a high-level overview of the entire feature and then walk the team through the stories achieving the feature, one by one.

The story showcase meeting is easy to misunderstand. Many teams have "estimation meetings" or "sprint planning meetings" in which 'the product owner selects stories, the developers estimate the stories, and someone decides who will implement each one.' A story showcase is different. A story showcase is about updating and synchronizing the team's mental models of the product and context. It's not *planning*—it does not assume work is organized into sprints, and formal effort estimation is optional.

A story showcase should be a synchronous meeting. In hybrid teams, the story showcase should be scheduled when the maximum number of team members are co-located.

Estimating Effort

Formally estimating the amount of time, effort, or resources that each story will require is not necessary to build great products. Estimating stories is a lot of work and does not provide value directly to users. In many projects, it may be better not to estimate at all or only very roughly.

If you must estimate every story, there are two broad approaches for doing so: model-based forecasting and expert-based forecasting.

Model-based forecasting means you have a mathematical model for estimating the time and resources required based on the story's parameters. It is typically more precise than expert-based forecasting, and any bias in the estimates can be systematically identified and corrected over time. The problem with model-based forecasting is that very few software teams have enough information to do it. If your team uses model-based forecasting, your software process is probably very different from the one described in this book.

Expert-based forecasting is when "experts" make educated guesses about a story's time and resource requirements. Expert-based forecasting is relatively straightforward and does requires little information or math; however, it is typically biased and imprecise. *How* you should do expert-based forecasting depends on *why* you're estimating in the first place. Estimation serves at least four purposes:

1. **Providing feedback to the product manager.** Some developers estimate stories simply to help the product manager refine and prioritize the backlog. For example, team members tell the product manager if they think a story is an epic, in which case the product manager should refine it into several more specific stories. Similarly, differentiating between high- and low-effort stories helps the product manager prioritize the "low-hanging fruit:" high-value, low-effort stories. Expert-based forecasting works well here because rough estimates are sufficient.

2. **Making sense of stories.** Group estimation techniques like planning poker (below) can help teams make sense of stories. Different team members producing different estimates for the same story triggers a conversation about why. One team member may show the others that a story is more or less challenging than it seems. Such discussions are one of the main benefits of estimation rituals.

3. **Measuring productivity.** Estimating stories to measure your own productivity is misguided (see the sidebar on page 63). Some teams will assign each story a number of points and then measure *velocity*: the number of story points completed per time period. Velocity is made-up nonsense. If velocity increases, is it because the team was more efficient, worked more hours, or estimated more pessimistically? No one knows!

4. **Providing estimates to clients.** Having to provide formal estimates to clients for approval contradicts the fundamental agile principle of preferring collaboration over contract negotiation. Teams should strive to overcome the mistrust that drives demands for formal estimates. If you must provide estimates to clients, you should use model-based forecasting. If you don't have enough data for model-based forecasting and must provide estimates to clients anyway, use reference class planning poker.

Measuring Productivity and Performance

Most organizations want to maximize employee performance and productivity. Many organizations and managers are obsessed with *metrics* (ways of measuring something) and *key performance indicators* [40] in a doomed attempt to replace subjective human judgment (about who's doing a good job) with objective facts and math.

This industry-wide metrics fixation has many negative consequences. Performance measurement entails workplace surveillance, which harms "employee well-being, work culture, productivity, creativity, and motivation" [41]. Moreover, software professionals do a lot of different things besides coding: they review code, watch user interviews, have meetings, research APIs, help each other, find bugs, fix bugs, research testing strategies, onboard new developers, talk to clients, prioritize backlogs, and so on. Constructing metrics that encompass all of the activities that contribute to organizational goals is impossible [42]. "Measuring performance" by counting lines of code written, function points implemented, features shipped, or stories completed does not accurately reflect an employee's contributions.

Meanwhile, human beings can *react* to the measurement of their activities. If management pays bonuses for lines of code written, programmers will generate verbose, repetitious code. Incentivize bug fixing, and programmers will begin bug-farming to have more bugs to fix later. Promote developers who add novel new features and suddenly no one will maintain existing code.

A dramatic example of such unintended negative consequences was the "stack ranking" system used by Microsoft in the early 2000s. Under stack ranking, "every unit was forced to declare a certain percentage of employees as top performers, then good performers, then average, then below average, then poor" [43]. This led to an entirely predictable mess. Employees actively sabotaged each other's work to get a better ranking, avoided working with high performers, and played politics instead of advancing Microsoft's goals. The journalist Kurt Eichenwald said, "Every current and former Microsoft employee I interviewed—everyone—cited stack ranking as the most destructive process inside of Microsoft; something that drove out untold numbers of employees" [43]. For more on fixing promotions, see Fix Your Promotions Process in Chapter 12.

Reference Class Planning Poker

If you must use expert-based forecasting, you should account for two cognitive biases that affect estimation: optimism and anchoring.

Lots of things can lead to optimistic estimates, but one pattern is so common it has a name: *the planning fallacy.* The planning fallacy works like this: suppose we ask you to estimate how long a task will take. You mentally break down the task into a bunch of subtasks, you estimate each one, and then add them together. This produces optimistic estimates in three ways: (1) subtask estimates are more often optimistic than pessimistic; (2)

most people are more likely to miss a subtask than to imagine an unnecessary subtask; (3) most people don't budget enough time for resolving unanticipated problems. Consequently, the divide-and-conquer approach to estimation typically produces optimistic estimates.

The cure for the planning fallacy—*reference-class forecasting*—has been well known to researchers for decades. Instead of estimating a task by breaking it into subtasks, we create a *reference class*: a group of previously completed tasks similar to the current task. If previous, similar tasks took, on average, about a week, the current task will probably take about a week.

Meanwhile, anchoring works like this: suppose there are two developers, Simon and Jennifer. In scenario A, Jennifer and Simon use an estimation technique called *planning poker*. They each hold some cards labeled "one hour", "two hours", "four hours", "one day", "two days", "four days", "one week", and "epic."[1] The project manager reads the story, and Simon and Jennifer each select a card without letting the other see. Simon chooses the two-hour card. Jennifer chooses the two-day card. They show their cards simultaneously and then discuss their different conceptions of the story. Jennifer explains that the story requires a large number of non-obvious changes that Simon hadn't considered. Simon agrees with Jennifer's estimate.

In Scenario B, there are no cards. We ask Simon to estimate the story, and he says "two hours." Then we ask Jennifer what she thinks. She thinks *two hours* is not enough. Still, she generates her estimate by *anchoring on* Simon's estimate and adjusting it upward to, say, four hours, drastically underestimating the true time. Anchoring is a very robust cognitive phenomenon—it crops up in all kinds of situations and biases estimates even when anchors are chosen randomly and people *know* they are random.

To mitigate both optimism and anchoring, combine reference class forecasting with planning poker. First, the team needs at least a few dozen completed stories and some data on how long they took or how difficult they were. If your team has a system that tracks time spent on each task down to the minute, you can use that, but more granular estimates are often sufficient. If your team doesn't have this data, you can collect it over a few months by recording the time or effort associated with each story *after* it's completed.

These effort numbers do not have to be precise. You could just label stories "easy", "medium", "hard", "epic", or on a scale from one to five, or using the non-linear scale described in the anchoring example above.

Next, the team categorizes all the stories (and acceptance criteria, if applicable) by effort as shown in Figure 4–1. You don't have to use 1-2-3-Epic; you can name the categories whatever works for your team. You can write the names of the categories on your planning poker cards. Or just use your fingers rock-paper-scissors style to ensure everyone shows their estimates simultaneously.

Generate estimates during the story showcase after the product manager reads the story (and acceptance criteria, if applicable), and the product designer presents mock-ups and walks the team through the intended user experience (if applicable). Then, each developer secretly selects a card corresponding to the reference class in which they think the story best fits. At first, the developers may have to consult and read the reference stories, but the reference classes will quickly become ingrained. The developers all show their cards at once, discuss any discrepancies, and reach consensus.

---

[1]We use times, but many teams prefer effort points to avoid false precision and schedule fixation.

Figure 4–1: Reference Class Wall for Planning Poker

If formal estimates must be provided to clients, the team can carry on recording how long each story actually takes, and the product manager can use the average completion time for each reference class to produce the estimates. The only real challenge with this approach is that developers like to estimate *effort* rather than *cost*. Effort and cost *should* be highly correlated, but the product manager will need to monitor the effort-cost relationship to continue producing reasonable estimates. Teams should periodically review and update their reference classes, especially as new people join the team.

However, to reiterate, you should only estimate effort if you absolutely have to. Most projects will not benefit from effort estimation at all. If you absolutely must estimate effort, use model-based forecasting. If you don't have enough data for model-based forecasting, try explaining to whoever wants the estimates that expert-based forecasting is usually unnecessary, inaccurate, and increases costs and risk. If all else fails, reference class planning poker is less bad than other approaches to expert-based forecasting.

Accepting (or Rejecting) Stories

Once developers deliver a story, the product manager verifies that the completed work meets expectations. The product manager is the first user of the feature and provides the first line of defense against quality issues. They consider what could go wrong or what could break the implementation. The product manager may try to break the feature with unexpected input. In larger teams, the product manager might have a quality assurance specialist to help with opaque-box testing.

Some teams write specific expectations for each story, called *acceptance criteria*, as explained in Chapter 8. If so, the product manager appraises the story implementation against its acceptance criteria, sometimes—especially when acceptance criteria are vague or the team's mental model is desynchronized—the delivered work fulfills the acceptance criteria but is not what the product manager intended. Then, the product manager has a choice: either accept the story and write a new story that will refine the system into the desired state, or reject the story and provide a new set of acceptance criteria. Adding more work to a delivered story can demoralize the team, so avoid capriciously moving the finish line. However, sometimes changing a story is inevitable.

The product manager rejects stories that have quality issues or fail to meet expectations. A rejected story should be placed at the very top of the backlog, where the next available developer or pair should pick it up. If the team has knowledge silos, the story may have to wait for the developer who originally implemented it. Indeed, if a different team member cannot easily pick up a rejected story implemented by a colleague, that's an indicator of unacceptable knowledge silos.

Changing a Story Once Started

We often discover new information while we are working on a story; for example, an application programming interface (API) doesn't work as expected, we realize the user interaction isn't intuitive, the code is more difficult to change than we expected, or we learn a key bit of information that changes everything.

Some teams embrace the imperfection of breaking down work and will say, "we discover the work to be done while doing the work." No matter how hard we try to break down the work into smaller pieces at the start of a new epic or feature set, we're going to learn new information. Some teams will quickly sketch the breakdown of the work, expecting it to change.

Some approaches to dealing with new information that requires us to change the work include the following.

1. Create a new story encompassing the new work.

2. Clarify the acceptance criteria that were revealed as vague or incomplete.

3. Block the story, because it can't be implemented without information and research, another team implementing a needed feature, or access to another system.

4. Delete or de-prioritize the story because delivering the expected user value is impossible, or the cost-benefit calculus has flipped.

Whatever we do, we should avoid increasing the scope of the story (see Commit Only to Work-in-Progress in Chapter 5). Changes are not so bad if they do not increase scope. Adding new work can be OK if just getting it done is less work than creating a new story and running it through a story showcase. However, avoid the anti-pattern of management adding "minimal" new work that doesn't seem minimal to the developers.

Daily Sync Meetings (with a Twist)

Daily sync meetings (also known as stand-ups) have become very popular in software projects. The primary purpose of daily sync meetings is to help the team reconnect and maintain their shared mental models.

Early agile methods used stand-ups to replace weekly status meetings and recommended discussing what was done yesterday, what will be worked on today, and any obstacles faced by the team. Reporting what was done yesterday has become less common because it turns the meeting into a status report. Discussing obstacles ("blockers") remains essential. Teams also use daily syncs to determine who is doing what and to share recent decisions or changes that may affect other team members. Physically standing for the daily sync (to remind everyone to be concise) is less popular these days because it doesn't make sense in remote or hybrid teams, and it may leave some professionals with physical disabilities feeling excluded.

To prevent the daily sync meeting from turning into a status meeting, some teams will post their previous day's status updates in a daily Slack thread before the meeting. This keeps the daily sync focused on knowledge sharing, short discussions, or brief walkthroughs of code changes that everyone should know about.

In co-located teams, daily syncs typically occur at the start of core work hours (see Core Work Hours in Chapter 5). Team members intuitively recognize that missing the sync is a problem, so the sync helps motivate people to arrive on time. In distributed teams with overlapping time zones, daily syncs are scheduled when everyone is present. In distributed teams with non-overlapping time zones, each office typically has their sync (or "spin down") at the end of the day to facilitate asynchronous knowledge handoff to the other office(s).

Tips for effective sync meetings include the following.

- Time-box the meeting to 15 minutes.

- Sometimes, participants need to be cut off a few times before they get used to being concise.

- Schedule follow-up meetings with clear agendas.

- In some organizations, only the developers speak at the stand-up; in others, all team members speak. Do what works for your team.

When the meeting is quick, some teams will stop when done, or have a deeper conversation about one topic that came up during the sync. Teams that use pair programming decide on pairing at the end of the daily sync (see Chapter 10).

Team Huddles

Team huddles are impromptu meetings called by a team member, typically for one of several reasons:

- Communicate a recent, critical decision that affects the rest of the team (e.g., "We just re-sequenced the build steps so that the build is faster; let us show you what we did").

- Inform the team of new, time-sensitive information (e.g., "The build is red" or "There's a high-priority customer escalation").

- Resolve a disagreement between two team members (e.g., "We can't decide between using A or B. Here are the pros and cons of A. Here are the pros and cons of B. What do you all think?").

- Ask for ideas (e.g., "We can't figure out how to reproduce this bug; any suggestions?").

- Seek expertise from another team member (e.g., "Does anyone have experience navigating Apple's certificate process?").

Many people hesitate to start a team huddle, so it's important to minimize the friction of doing so when appropriate. Co-located teams can move and talk to each other. The greater the movement, the greater the barrier to starting a team huddle. Teams that are distributed and always present on the same channel can quickly meet. A huddle might only last for a minute and allows the team to resolve an issue immediately instead of scheduling a meeting later in the week.

Summary

In summary, a boundary spanner is a person who inhabits multiple social worlds and bridges the gulf(s) between them. The product manager spans the boundary between Track One and Track Two. Even though the whole team is involved in both tracks, the tracks represent different social worlds with different norms, logic, and knowledge bases. Developers are typically more comfortable in Track Two; product designers are typically more comfortable in Track One. The product manager must, therefore, use artifacts (e.g., the backlog) and rituals (e.g., the story showcase) to overcome boundaries between the two tracks and create shared mental models. The product manager also spans the boundary between the team and the broader business (or social) environment of the software product. Similarly, the product designer spans the boundary between the social world of the product's users and the social world of the development team. Meetings including story showcases, daily syncs, and team huddles help with boundary spanning.

Chapter 5
Project Management

No mission plan can prepare you for the unexpected because that doesn't make any sense.
—The Ninja Handbook

 Key Takeaways

- x-week iterations are arbitrary and unnecessary.

- Iterationless, continuous development reduces waste, stress, and burnout.

- Each developer (or pair) should commit to one story at a time.

- The product manager should avoid altering a story once developers begin implementing it.

- The optimal external release schedule depends on many factors and need not align with the internal rhythm of work.

- Systematically removing waste is the key to efficiency.

- Hiring good team players is more important than searching for mythical $10x$ developers.

- Regular retrospective meetings help teams identify and mitigate problems.

- Teams benefit from core work hours, flexible contracts, no overtime, and a clear definition of done.

Stress-based Project Management

When Noreen joined Project Cumulus, it was a high-priority project for the company, with most of engineering working on it. It was also one of the company's most complex projects, relying on unfamiliar technology and requiring unprecedented coordination between teams.

To help motivate engineers into "action," engineering leadership introduced status meetings for the entire organization several times per week and assigned specific deadlines for numerous intermediate deliverables. And yet, they were not forthcoming about when the project needed to be delivered. Everything was Quadrant 1 work: important and urgent. New deadlines would emerge as the dates slipped. The engineers were not consulted about the complexity, risks, or effort involved. Although there was a list of stories, the list was incomplete, and new stories were routinely discovered while doing the work.

Instead of asking, "how can we help?" or "how can we remove blockers?", engineering leadership increased pressure on teams, reminded them that they were behind schedule, or created arbitrary story deadlines, all of which induced unnecessary and unhelpful stress. Suggestions for improving tooling, process, or communication were ignored.

Leadership maintained that there was no time to make course corrections; however, changes occurred daily.

As delays continued and pressure mounted, there was no slack, no time to coordinate, no time to communicate, just a rush to the finish line. Teams didn't coordinate dependencies on each other, which resulted in nasty surprises as one team's change broke another team's code. Teams independently solved the same problems, duplicating each other's effort. A whisper network emerged where people would informally share tips and tricks, but this information wasn't broadly communicated. Nothing that worked seemed to work for long.

Eventually, despite much stress and overtime, the product shipped late due to the ineffectiveness of the software process.

The preceding story highlights what goes wrong when management fixes an unrealistic scope and schedule without getting sufficient feedback on feasibility from engineering: the project falls behind, deadlines are missed, stress increases, important activities are neglected, and the pressure to ship makes it impossible to reflect on what's going wrong and how to address it. Reprimanding people for not meeting an unrealistic deadline instead of investigating why deadlines aren't being met is counterproductive. Consequently, this chapter recommends (1) flexible contracts, which decrease overall project risk; (2) retrospective meetings and waste workshops, which create space for reflection, feedback, and identifying and addressing ongoing problems; and (3) *iterationless development*, which enables teams to embrace change, manage scope, and deliver key features as early as possible.

Instead of having a project manager *role*, project management *work* should be shared dynamically among team members. As we see in the preceding vignette, centralizing management work in a single person or "leadership team" decreases team performance [44] and causes many problems due to conflicting priorities and poor information sharing.

Iterationless Development

The Problem with Iterations

One of the main ways Sustainable Dual-Track Development differs from development methods is its denial of *both* iterations and waterfall-like development "lifecycles."

In most agile methods, teams commit to delivering a set of stories within a specific period. Scrum originally recommended 30-day "sprints" [45, p. 117] while Extreme Programming recommended 1–3 week "iterations" [46]. Sprints begin with a planning meeting in which teams estimate upcoming work and agree to an amount that fits within their capacity, minus some slack for uncertainty. The product manager "freezes" (doesn't change) the sprint backlog, limiting scope creep and creating a valuable illusion of short-term stability. Short iterations energize teams toward near-term deadlines and facilitate frequent releases, thus accelerating feedback and decreasing risk.

The thing to remember is, in 1999, most software was released once—when it was done. Some large projects aimed to release a new version every year or two. Releasing weekly seemed ridiculous. The DevOps movement and the technologies underlying continuous deployment didn't exist. Back then, sprints were a way to speed up *release cycles*. Iterations were both a development rhythm and a release cycle.

But, the development rhythm doesn't have to align with the release cycle. Today, many projects with automated deployment pipelines can be released multiple times per day or push a release whenever it's ready. Once you realize that the development rhythm and the release cycle are mostly independent, the benefits of iterations no longer outweigh the problems:

- Sprints induce conflict. Managers (and marketing) fight with developers over expectations, often creating unrealistic schedules.

- Teams waste effort negotiating what an iteration can include instead of just getting on with the work.

- The short-term stability sprints introduce isn't real. Receiving a customer escalation, uncovering a high-priority bug, experiencing a critical shift in the project environment, or just a story that takes longer than expected can derail an iteration. Then testing gets marginalized, and teams waste more time replanning the sprint.

- Racing to finish a derailed iteration is stressful; stress wastes energy.

- In many countries were programmers have less autonomy, two-week iterations mean that employees are under constant pressure—unable to take a sick day or attend to family responsibilities.

All of this stress and conflict just interferes with achieving the team's goals and furthering the organization's mission.

The "two-week sprint" is arbitrary. Chunks of interconnected work should be done together. Some chunks take one day. Some take six weeks. Sometimes, you can't neatly break chunks of work into x-week segments. Sometimes, you can't accurately predict how long a chunk of work will take. Iterations were a necessary scaffolding to get off Waterfall processes, but now we have the technology and ideas necessary to move on to iteration*less* development.

Continuous, Iterationless Development

To move beyond the problems with iterations, we can adopt continuous, iterationless development. The two keys to iterationless development are committing to one story at a time and decoupling the release schedule from the rhythm of work.

Commit to One Story at a Time

Sustainable Dual-Track Development reduces the commitment window from an iteration to a single story. This means that the product manager can alter a story until a developer starts implementing it. Before a story is started, the product manager can quickly adjust course as new information emerges. Important bug fixes or emergent feedback from user research can be slated for the next free developer to work on.

By picking up a story, the developer (or pair) commits to completing it as efficiently as possible while keeping the codebase shippable and producing high-quality, refactored code. In return, the product manager commits to neither altering the story nor replacing the work-in-progress with new, unrelated work. There are reasonable exceptions as described in the following section.

In our observations, most developers are dedicated and diligent in finishing their stories. They strive to deliver high-quality work as soon as it is ready without over-engineering solutions. (See Chapter 10 on balancing code quality with timely delivery.)

Narrowing the commitment window to stories-in-progress allows the product manager to change course by changing or re-sequencing stories without antagonizing developers. It removes the waste of meeting to agree on the scope of work, tracking progress, resetting expectations mid-iteration when things do not go according to plan, and hurrying to get work done by the end of the iteration. When the product manager can alter the backlog at any point, there is no need for iteration planning.

One might argue that having a finish line helps energize the team. While being energized about work is a good thing, falling into cycles of rushing, crunch time, and burnout is stressful, wasteful, and inefficient. Emphasizing diligence and steady productivity instead of estimates and deadlines empowers the developers, improves morale, and typically increases productivity by interrupting crunch-burnout cycles. When a team moves to iterationless development, developers are no longer unduly stressed by arbitrary internal deadlines. However, management can still pressure developers to cut corners by taking on technical debt (see Avoid Technical Debt in Chapter 9 for advice on handling this issue).

Changing Work-in-Progress

The product manager must be allowed to stop work-in-progress stories to address unexpected, high-priority situations including customer escalations, time-sensitive bugs, the build breaking during continuous integration, or new Common Vulnerabilities and Exposures (CVEs). When the engineers *agree* that the situation warrants an interruption, it doesn't damage motivation or morale. A retrospective meeting is a good place to build consensus around what justifies interrupting the current work-in-progress.

Notwithstanding such interruptions, the product manager should only alter in-progress stories when asked to by the developers working on that story. Developers might request a change if:

- They discover that a story (or acceptance criterion) is ambiguous to the point that they no longer know "what done looks like." Effective story showcase meetings should reduce such discoveries.

- They discover a problematic user-system interaction. Product designers often see the developers as the first users of the system. If the people building the system can't figure it out, then the end user will probably also struggle. In this situation, the developers iterate with the product designer to find a good user interaction, layout, or flow.

- They discover new technical information that makes the story infeasible. Such stories are often temporarily abandoned or substantively modified.

If something is not working during implementation, developers will usually want to fix it now rather than have to deal with it again later. These changes are challenging to predict. What frustrates developers is agreeing to complete task X by time Y, only to have someone add seven new pieces to X while moving up Y. The developers feel like Charlie Brown when Lucy yanks the football away right before he kicks it. So product managers should add new work to *the backlog*, not to stories-in-progress. Regardless of who identifies the problem, changes *agreed* by the engineers and product manager do not damage morale and motivation compared to changes *imposed* by the product manager.

If developers estimate effort for every story, alterations should trigger reestimation, which can affect release planning. However, as explained in Chapter 4, formal estimation should be avoided.

Disentangle Release Cycles from Work Rhythms

Meanwhile, human beings' natural work rhythms revolve around days, weeks, and (sometimes) seasons. Our project cycles should match natural work rhythms. That's why so many teams have *daily* syncs, *weekly* meetings, and *quarterly* planning. Project cycles work better when they line up with natural rhythms. For example, in teams that use pair programming and rotate pairs each morning, we often observe pairs pressing to finish their task near the end of the day.

Once we realize that external release cycles do not have to match internal iterations, we can consider how often to release the software. Early agilists promoted releasing as often as possible, but what is possible has changed dramatically. An unregulated consumer web application with a fully automated deployment pipeline and excellent testing and recovery infrastructure, like *Netflix*, can be released multiple times per day. Meanwhile, firmware for forklifts that can only be updated by physically plugging a device into thousands of forklifts in multiple countries, might be released yearly or even less often. There's no definitive recipe for determining how often to release, but we can identify some factors to consider.

Release more frequently when:

- the delivery pipeline is highly automated;

- the test suite is comprehensive;

- pushing a bug into production will do limited physical, environmental, or financial damage (i.e., no one's going to get hurt);

- the product has serious bugs that need to be fixed immediately; and

- you can roll back or otherwise correct errors quickly.

Release less frequently when:

- each release creates lots of manual work for customers (e.g., updating thousands of devices one at a time);

- project stakeholders don't want frequent releases (e.g., because each release creates work);

- the team is working in a regulated environment where an auditor must approve each release;

- the cost of releasing is high (e.g., because an auditor has to approve the release); or

- frequent releases are somehow frustrating or destabilizing for users (e.g., frequently changing the syntax of a programming language).

Today, developers tend to underestimate the potential harms and risks of their releases. While we still recommend releasing frequently, more attention to the negative impacts of new releases is needed.

Practices

Much of conventional project management doesn't work for software development or self-managed teams. Agile software development teams don't have a boss who assigns tasks, controls a project through scheduling and budgeting, draws Gantt charts, derives model-based forecasts, sets key performance indicators, and (quantitatively) monitors performance. All that stuff comes from *managerialism*—the ideology that the same professional management techniques work for everything from from mining lithium to cutting hair to operating hedge funds to aerospace engineering. How such foolishness took hold is beyond us, but the whole reason we have agile methods is that managing software development like manufacturing didn't work.

So, what does project management mean for a self-managed team? Well, self-managed teams still do management work; they just don't centralize that work into an individual boss. The team still adopts a software development process like Sustainable Dual-Track

Development, which entails many other management decisions, like how to organize work (into two simultaneous, parallel tracks), development cycles (continuous, iterationless development), rituals (e.g., daily syncs, retros) and artifacts (e.g., user stories). The work of allocating tasks, scheduling, and resolving conflicts is still done; it's just done by team members instead of a separate boss.

A comprehensive account of all useful software project management practices would fill a large book, so we merely highlight the practices we think are most important and supported by scientific theory and evidence.

Retrospective Meetings (or "Retros")

 A *retrospective, retrospection meeting*, or *retro* for short, is a meeting in which a team celebrates successes and reflects on its development process, team dynamics, and any barriers, obstacles, or issues about which team members are concerned. Teams must reflect on their software process, product, and external forces to respond effectively to changing situations. During retros, teams identify specific action items to resolve problems and improve their performance and well-being. There is little point in having retros unless they lead to concrete actions.

Retros should be held at the end of each week (e.g., Friday afternoons). A short weekly retro is generally better for rapid process improvement than a longer monthly retro. Frequent retros help the team stay agile and avoid getting overwhelmed by difficulties.

The ideal retro is a safe environment where team members are comfortable discussing any work-related topic. Retros can become unhealthy in several ways, including: (1) members becoming dismissive or non-constructive; (2) one or a few team members dominating the discussion, marginalizing others; (3) not following up on action items; (4) having an overly negative tone. To avoid these anti-patterns, consider the following suggestions.

- Each retro should have a designated leader responsible for facilitating the discussion and ensuring everyone is respectful, constructive, and heard (i.e., no one dominates the discussion). Team members can take turns leading.

- Record *action items*, that is, concrete steps the team will take to resolve the issues. At least one team member should take responsibility for each action item.

- At the beginning of each retro, review action items from previous retros and discuss what has been done. While some action items will invariably be slow to resolve, hold each other accountable for agreed actions.

- Try varying retro formats (below) to see what works for your team and keep things interesting.

There are many ways to conduct a retro [47]. One good way is the emotion-based format where "happy," "neutral," and "sad" faces are written on the top of a whiteboard (e.g., Figure 5–1). Any team member can add any topic to any column. In the happy-face column, write items that work well and should be continued or expanded. In the neutral-face column, write items that the team needs to keep an eye on. In the sad-face column, write problems that the team should try to fix.

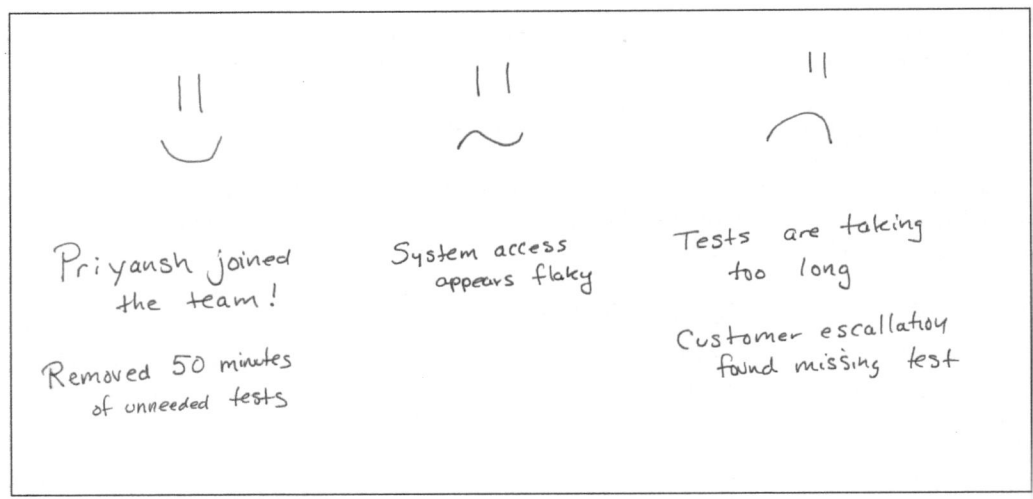

Figure 5–1: Example Retro Whiteboard

After a few minutes of writing, the team dot-votes on the topics to discuss [47]. Dot-voting is a simple prioritization technique in which each group member has the same number of "dots" (usually stickers) and distributes them across the topics they want to discuss. For example, if you have three dots and really want to discuss crunch time, you can put all three dots on the crunch time topic. Alternatively, if you want to discuss three different topics, you can put one dot on each.

After voting, the team discusses the topic with the most dots, followed by the topic with the second most dots, and so on, until time runs out. Sometimes, simply discussing an issue is sufficient to bring about change. Otherwise, the team creates action items, and someone volunteers to tackle each action item.

One limitation of dot voting is that an issue that is very important to just one or two people may never be discussed. Another approach is to follow a round-robin style and let each team member take turns picking the next topic.

Other retro formats include the following.

- **The Sailboat.** The team draws a sailboat on a whiteboard and discusses wind (things that are helping the team), anchors (things that are slowing down the team), icebergs (threats), and islands (opportunities).

- **The Futurespective.** The team members imagine that they will have a retro in the future (e.g., right after the next release ships). They discuss what went well and what went badly in this hypothetical future and then what they might do now to avoid the problems and exploit the opportunities.

- **Waste Workshop.** The team focuses on identifying and eliminating sources of waste (see next section).

- **Circles and Soup.** The team divides concerns into three circles: those they control, those they can influence, and those outside of their control (the "soup"). For issues the team controls, they brainstorm direct actions to resolve the issues. For issues the team can influence, they brainstorm what to recommend and how to persuade the relevant stakeholders to adopt their recommendations. For the soup, they brainstorm ways of mitigating or responding to any threats.

- **Timeline Retro.** The team uses a timeline to structure their discussion:

  A set of focus questions ... [and an Evidence-based project timeline (EBT)] are constructed by collecting evidence from various systems, e.g. scope and prioritisation systems, requirements databases, planning tools, defect management systems, etc. Project history is visualised by displaying this evidence along a timeline for each aspect... [The] goal and [timeline] are presented at the meeting. The moderator then leads a discussion based on the focus questions... The participants add clarifications, corrections and additional information to the [timeline]... The final part of the meeting consists of jointly summarising findings and lessons learned with a set of sum-up questions...: things that worked well; what was learnt; what needs improving; what is still puzzling; and what needs to be discussed further. [48]

Different formats work for different teams, and variety can improve creativity and motivation. Regardless of the format, weekly retros should be time-boxed to 60 minutes.

If the team is implementing Sustainable Dual-Track Development incrementally, retros are a great place to start. Retros create space to discuss challenges and consider practices for overcoming them. Additional practices can be added based on the team's concerns.

At the end of a project or major milestone, a team can schedule a longer, *project retro* to reflect on the experience. Some teams will kick off the conversation using a mood timeline: a visualization of how people felt throughout the project (milestone, etc.). Other teams will use one of the retro formats already described. If more than one team is involved, we recommend bringing in a facilitator to help run the meeting.

Retros are especially good for revealing different kinds of waste or friction in the software development process. Removing waste is discussed in more detail in the next section.

Waste Workshop

Anything that consumes resources without providing any value to project stakeholders is *waste*. Systematically identifying and eliminating waste is one of the best ways to improve any sociotechnical process, including software development.

One of the largest sources of waste in most organizations is unnecessary bureaucracy. Here, we use the term *bureaucracy* to refer to an organization's policies, procedures, rules, records, and hierarchical relationships. *Some* bureaucracy is reasonable; for example, asking job applicants for a CV describing their education, experience, and skills. But other kinds of bureaucracy are unnecessary; for example, asking job applicants for a CV, a portfolio of recent work, three letters of reference, a statement of interest, a cover letter, an essay on the ethics of technology, a presentation, a credit check, and two technical interviews followed by an informal dinner. Most of that work won't lead to better hiring decisions.

Sedano Waste Workshop™

During a *Waste Workshop*™, a team systematically examines its practices to identify the most pressing waste(s) to address. You can run your own workshop using our free facilitator's guide [49] and the following steps.

1. **Prepare.** Have each team member read through the waste identification worksheet (which asks questions about each of the wastes listed in Figure 5–3) and briefly reflect on possible sources of waste around them.

2. **Generate.** Have each team member write an identified waste or problem on a sticky note.

3. **Filter.** Ask each team member to choose the 3–5 wastes they are most concerned with *from their individual list.*

4. **Visualize.** Draw a 2x2 grid on a whiteboard. Label the X-axis "Effort to Remove" and the Y-axis "Impact" as shown in Figure 5–2.

5. **Plot.** Each person describes their top waste and places the corresponding sticky note on the grid. Focus on problems, not solutions. Do not debate or push back at this point, but clarifying questions are OK. Keep going around until everyone runs out of ideas, time permitting.

6. **Prioritize.** As a group, combine duplicates and organize waste notes into appropriate quadrants. The relative positioning need not be perfect; rather, focus on which items belong in the high-impact/easy-to-remove quadrant.

7. **Select.** Discuss the highest-impact, easiest-to-remove wastes. Select one or a few wastes to remediate first.

8. **(Optional) Plan.** If time permits, create an action plan to address the most pressing waste(s) and ask for volunteers to execute the plan.

9. **(Optional) Wrap Up.** If this is your first waste workshop, or you're an outsider introducing the workshop to a team, leave time at the end for reflection and feedback on the usefulness of the workshop itself.

Alternatively, you can run a one-person waste workshop on any pet project. Just list every waste you can think of, pick one that seems like the best combination of high-impact/easy-to-remove, and make a plan to mitigate it.

Unnecessary bureaucracy comes from the mistaken beliefs that (1) policies prevent problems, and (2) valueless work must be completed anyway because it is the "proper" way to do things. Policies often fail to prevent problems because they are rarely evidence-based and people don't follow them anyway. When things go wrong—and they will—instead of

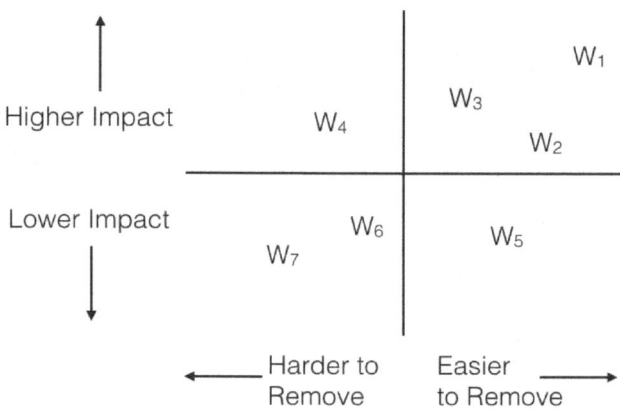

Figure 5–2: Waste Workshop Impact vs. Effort 2x2 Matrix

adding policies, find ways to prevent the mistake from happening. Did a commit get to the build system that could not possibly work? Add a developer command that runs all the quick tests before pushing a commit. Did the product manager release the product before it was ready? Let developers remove a release when they discover it's broken. Did someone pick the wrong option because the interface was confusing? Simplify the interface.

Bureaucracy is often tricky to remove since "we've always done it that way," and someone often insists that the waste is absolutely essential. When this happens, ask *why* they think it's essential. If they say, "it's policy," find out who has the authority to change the policy and ask them to do so. If they say it's a legal requirement, ask them where they got this information. Many bureaucrats are victims of bad legal advice.

Small experiments are an excellent way to reduce bureaucracy. For example, one team found that their daily syncs were mostly status updates. They experimented with reporting status asynchronously and then leveraged team time for more valuable conversations. If the experiment succeeds, advertise its success to other teams; otherwise, try something else.

That said, unnecessary bureaucracy is not the only kind of waste (see Figure 5–3) [50]. Other types of waste include the following.

1. **Building the wrong feature or product**: the cost of building a feature or product that does not address stakeholder needs.

2. **Mismanaging the backlog**: the cost of duplicating work, expediting lower value user features, or delaying necessary bug fixes.

3. **Rework**: the cost of fixing problems with delivered work *that could have been reasonably anticipated* at the time the work was completed.

4. **Unnecessarily complex solutions**: the cost of creating code, user interfaces, features, etc. that are more complicated than needed to satisfy stakeholders.

5. **Extraneous cognitive load**: unnecessary mental effort caused by poor presentation or organization of tasks.

Figure 5–3: Common Software Development Wastes

6. **Psychological distress**: negative impacts of stress on the team's well-being and performance.

7. **Knowledge loss**: the cost of reacquiring information that the team once knew.

8. **Ineffective communication**: the cost of incomplete, incorrect, misleading, inefficient, or absent communication among project stakeholders.

9. **Waiting / multitasking**: the cost of unnecessary task-switching or idling (often hidden by multitasking, which decreases cognitive performance [51]).

10. **Unnecessary bureaucracy**: the cost of doing / awaiting / following unnecessary or outdated paperwork, approvals, processes, regulations, permits, or reporting requirements.

11. **Electricity**: the energy consumed by the software, especially any power consumption above that which is necessary to deliver stakeholder value.

12. **Unknown**: while we have observed many types of wastes over many projects, as humans we are clever and creative in finding ways that waste energy and time.

Often, the hardest part is realizing that something is waste—some wastes aren't apparent unless you're specifically looking for them. We recommend occasionally holding a Waste Workshop (see the sidebar on page 78) to identify waste. But don't be overzealous—developers sometimes misperceive all non-coding work as waste, exacerbating the problem of building the wrong thing due to insufficient research, or neglecting important interpersonal work like onboarding new employees.

Once you've identified waste, there's no cookbook approach to eliminate it, but often the fix is obvious. If everyone's filling out a form that provides no value, stop filling out the form. If the release countdown clock stresses out the team, throw it in the bin. If the build takes an hour, look for ways to speed up the build while waiting on the build.

Core Work Hours

Sustainable Dual-Track Development emphasizes real-time collaboration and recommends that all production code be written in pairs to improve code quality and reduce knowledge silos. To work in pairs, developers have to work similar hours. However, employees appreciate flexibility in their work hours, which improves work-life balance. We need a middle ground between everyone working 9–5 and everyone setting their own hours.

Core work hours are a period during which all team members work. Daily syncs should occur at the beginning of core work hours unless prevented by time zone differences among team members. Important rituals, including story showcases and retrospectives, should occur during core work hours. Team members should take advantage of core work hours for pair programming.

People don't have to work in the same *place* to collaborate, share knowledge, and mature as a team, but they do have to work at the same *time*. If team members have slightly different schedules, they have to do some work solo. To avoid knowledge silos, solo developers should focus on chores, code reviews, and any non-coding tasks, then switch to pair programming for feature development when a partner becomes available. Shorter core work hours make it harder to fill solo time with non-coding tasks, reduce collaboration, and slow team maturation. If employees are so spread out that core work hours are short or nil, the employees will not be able to coalesce into a team. Asynchronous communication is too ineffective to foster team cohesion or prevent knowledge silos.

One team we observed had members on the east and west coasts of the United States (a three-hour time zone difference). The team agreed to have a daily sync from 9:30 am to 10:00 am Pacific / 12:30 pm to 1:00 pm Eastern and ensemble pairing time from 10:00 am to 12:00 pm Pacific / 1:00 pm to 3:00 pm Eastern. These were the team's core hours; the rest was flex time. Individual team members might adjust to accommodate a whole company meeting or ad-hoc meetings between teams. In this case, team members enabled others to skip meetings by repeating key takeaways or outcomes. If a meeting was particularly important, they'd encourage the team members to watch a recording later.

Hire Team Players

Early books on agile methods (e.g., [46]) often emphasized the importance of hiring the best possible people. It was believed that much of the unnecessary bureaucracy and documentation slowing down software was a kind of crutch for holding up mediocre developers—topnotch developers don't need that stuff. This coincided with the myth of the $10x$ developer: gifted engineers who could build a system ten times faster than average programmers. While individual skill varies among developers, the existence of $10x$ developers has been greatly exaggerated. Furthermore, coding speed is not the primary driver of team performance or project success.

In recent years, this preoccupation with getting the very best developers has returned to the argument that every software company has to hire remote workers to get "the best" people, whatever best means. Choosing between co-located, distributed, remote-first, and hybrid working arrangements is a complex, multifaceted issue. While some people dislike working from conventional shared office space, remote-first and hybrid groups experience additional challenges around team cohesion and maturity.

This raises a more general point about hiring the best people. *Team cohesion is more important for team performance than individual skill.* Hire people who work well with others and will get along with current team members. Hiring an engineer who ignores the backlog and only does work they think is important, refuses to pair program, demands individual code ownership, and derails the team's sense of self is counterproductive regardless of their technical skills.

Policies

Definition of Done

Teams need to clarify when they can mark a story as completed in their backlog.

Many conflicts between management and development stem from people having different definitions of "done." Consider a student who is just learning to program. The assignment is to make an array and fill it with ten random numbers. The student writes some code, and when it looks right, proclaims the assignment "done." But does it compile? It's not "done" until it compiles without errors.

Now, let's consider a developer working on a track-changes feature for a diagramming web application. The code compiles. Unit tests pass. They commit their code; integration tests pass. The engineer marks the story complete in the project management system. Later, the product manager asks why the story was marked complete before the code had shipped to production. The product manager and the developer had different definitions of "done." Clarifying the change request (or code submission) process avoids this kind of conflict.

Teams should clearly define what "done" means in their context. A retrospective meeting is a good time to define or revise a team's definition of done. Product managers and engineers must share the same definition of done to avoid conflict.

Some software professionals use *definition of done* as a synonym for *acceptance criteria* (see Chapter 8). We only use *definition of done* to refer to criteria that apply to all stories.

Flexible Contracts

Contracts with a fixed price, schedule, and scope are incompatible with Sustainable Dual-Track Development. Fixed contracts appear incompatible with software development in general. Fixed contracts work in manufacturing, where design and construction are separate activities. In software development, where design and construction are inextricably entangled, fixed contracts significantly increase risk to both parties and undermine economic sustainability.

Figure 5–4: (In)flexible Contracts (Comic used with permission)

Since Track One continually evolves the product concept, all business agreements need a flexible scope. Agreements with other business units or signed contracts for outsourcing companies focus on how the inter-business relationship will be managed or set a budget or schedule, but they do not fix scope or features. Explicitly acknowledging flexibility allows the team to change with emerging information. Ideally, the product manager keeps key stakeholders informed about not only implementation progress but also what the team is learning.

No Overtime

Overtime is not sustainable. Overtime undermines work-life balance, invites burnout [52], reduces efficiency [53], lowers customer satisfaction [54], and results in "poorer perceived general health, increased injury rates, more illnesses, [and] increased mortality" [55]. No-overtime policies, therefore, help business sustainability and reliability.

Management should not ask the team to work evenings or weekends. Since features are prioritized, it becomes a product decision whether to ship ready features (thus cutting scope) or wait until the necessary features are finished. When the team has a regular release cadence, teams prefer to ship on time and delay unfinished features for the next release instead of rushing to ship (which typically produces lower-quality code).

Occasionally, a customer escalation requires engineering support to resolve an issue outside of regular business hours. When overtime happens, give the affected engineers time off to recover from solving a stressful problem. Consider the rate of two hours off for each hour worked after hours, as this motivates management to minimize overtime.

Summary

In summary, x-week iterations are arbitrary and no longer necessary to reap the benefits of agile methods. Sustainable Dual-Track Development recommends iterationless, continuous development in which each developer (or pair) commits to one story at a time, and product managers commit to not altering work-in-progress. For teams that want to stick with x-week iterations, the optimal external release schedule depends on many factors and need not align with internal iterations.

Iterationless development isn't new. Many mature products, for which developers are mainly fixing bugs and making minor updates rather than building new features, use an iterationless process. The developers produce a steady stream of updates and fixes. Organizing these into a set schedule provides no demonstrable value. Dividing tasks into two-week increments, arguing about what is feasible in two weeks, over-promising, and then feeling like you've let down your stakeholders... it's a lot of work to accomplish what exactly? In contrast, we recommend a host of project management policies and practices including:

- removing all kinds of waste to speed up the development process;

- hiring team players;

- managing internship and mentoring programs (see Chapter 12);

- negotiating a shared definition of done to avoid management-developer conflicts;

- setting core work hours, during which all team members should be working and ideally co-located;

- insisting on flexible contracts; and

- having a no-overtime policy to maintain not only reliable productivity but also employee health and morale.

Part II

Track One: Loading the Backlog

*for product designers
and product managers*

Before we load the backlog with stories, we need to know what to build. In Track One we reduce the risk of building features that users don't want by exploring product market fit.

Chapter 6: Understanding Track One provides an overview of Track One: the roles, principles, and what a steady state could look like.

Chapter 7: Making Sense of the Project Environment examines research practices to verify we understand the project environment, including identifying who to interview, how to interview, and how to analyze interview notes.

Chapter 8: Design Thinking describes common practices to iterate towards something the team can build and inexpensively verify that the proposed solution delivers market value to the users. Our understanding of the problem evolves as we consider different solutions to the problem. The primary output is user stories.

Chapter 6

Introducing Track One

Design is not just what it looks like and feels like. Design is how it works.
– Steve Jobs

 Key Takeaways

- The purpose of Track One is to determine what to build and load the backlog with appropriate stories.

- The product designer is in charge of Track One, but all team members participate. The product manager writes most stories. The developers give technical feedback.

- Reject preconceived ideas while accepting ambiguity and disagreement.

- Track One is about understanding and modeling stakeholders' conflicting beliefs—not requirements—while resisting premature solutionizing.

- Greenfield projects typically have an initiation phase where Track One gets a head start on Track Two.

- Software teams need a product designer and product manager because most engineers do not have the information or skill set to envision or prioritize features effectively.

When the Engineers Are in Charge

In Eve's last company, the most convincing (i.e., the loudest) engineer, Bob, had the most impact on the direction of the product. Bob might say that the users will definitely need this feature to work this certain way, but no one ever talked to any users. The team wouldn't get feedback that the interface or feature wasn't working the way users needed until after the code was complete, sometimes a year after the decision. Sometimes the only feedback was users not renewing their license with no details as to why. Sales declined. Eve felt like she was building shelf-ware: software that users purchase only to avoid using.

Eve moved on to a new team who validated their ideas with current or prospective users. New products and features were grounded in a deep understanding of users and their contexts. Eve felt like her contributions mattered. The team delivered features that provided value. Eve's new team had a rhythm of continually identifying, validating and delivering practical, high-quality software.

Overview of Track One

Track One is concerned with the question, "How does a team know what to build?" The purpose of Track One is to understand the project environment, imagine the product (or product enhancement), and then create an appropriate backlog of user stories for Track Two. The project environment includes stakeholders (especially users), the business landscape, opportunities, and threats. Imagining the product means figuring out what the product should be like, including its features and user interface (if applicable).

At its simplest, Track One involves researching opportunities and writing user stories. However, sustainable development involves various techniques to help us research effectively and write *good* stories. Chapters 7 and 8 elaborate the recommended techniques. First, however, we will discuss the roles and principles associated with Track One, followed by how Track One differs in new and ongoing projects.

Track One Roles

The whole team participates in Track One (see Table 6–1); however, product designers do most of the heavy lifting. The product designer conducts user interviews to become the team's empathizer-in-chief. They aim to understand not only what users need and want but also how they work, what they value, and how they think. They use design thinking simultaneously to explore opportunities and to imagine product features. They share mock-ups and feature descriptions with users to evaluate whether they resonate.

Track One Principles

Track One is rooted in the realization that most software projects are not about routine engineering like *The Traveling Salesperson* problem. The Traveling Salesperson is a well-understood problem where everyone agrees on the goal: find the shortest possible route

Table 6–1: Comparison of Roles During Track One

Product Designer	- understands, empathizes with, and represents current or prospective users
	- imagines product features that users will find helpful
	- draws mock-ups to illustrate features
	- validates potential features and solutions
	- leads the team through Track One practices like affinity mapping (Ch. 7)
Product Manager	- researches the business context and competitive landscape
	- determines and sequences the product's features
	- writes user stories based on features or epics
	- determines each story's acceptance criteria
	- keeps important stakeholders informed
Engineers	- observe user interviews and takes notes
	- help the product designer organize notes into themes and design ideas
	- give technical feedback on design concepts and priorities
	- consider alternative solutions that are easier to build
	- review user stories and clarifies acceptance criteria

through a set of locations. Engineers can apply mathematics, scientific theories, and professional training to optimize a system for this problem.

Most software products are more like a music streaming service. It has multiple stakeholders who cannot agree on what the system should do or what the main problems are. They cannot clearly articulate their needs, prioritize conflicting criteria, or explain the business landscape. One stakeholder wants the highest possible quality; another wants to minimize bandwidth usage. One stakeholder wants the service to learn their tastes; another doesn't want their listening history recorded. No one can explain how streaming across international borders interacts with copyright law, and some stakeholders are just making stuff up to sabotage the project.

Forcing dissensus into a singular problem statement doesn't make people agree; it just marginalizes those who disagree. Then, when the product arrives, the stakeholders reject it for failing to address their concerns.

Instead, we research stakeholders, understand the conflicts, and validate designs. The team enrolls squabbling stakeholders into a shared vision. They may never agree 100%. They just find enough common ground to create a product that everyone can accept.

With the messiness of real projects in mind, we can state the following principles for succeeding in Track One.

- Understand users. If a product doesn't help its users, they'll resist using it, no matter how brilliant you think it is.

- Understand other stakeholders. The single most important aspect of product development is understanding stakeholders well enough to create a product that delivers stakeholder value without harm.

- Focus on beliefs, values, and frustrations—not requirements. Anyone can share their beliefs, values, and what's driving them crazy this week. Most people cannot construct anything like formal requirements even with the help of an expert analyst (see the Myth of Requirements sidebar on page 99).

- Model disagreement and ambiguity. Instead of writing an oversimplified problem statement that doesn't reflect the concerns of all the stakeholders, draw a diagram showing their disagreements.

- Resist premature solution-focused thinking ("solutionizing"). Focus on understanding the stakeholders and context without jumping to conclusions about the nature of the product.

- Reject preconceived ideas. Stakeholders and the team often begin a project with a straightforward but deeply flawed product vision. Reflect on your preconceptions and don't let a stakeholder box you into their view of the context or product.

- When it's time to generate ideas, generate lots and lots of ideas, both mundane and wacky. Fully explore what is possible before converging on a product concept.

- Embrace ambiguity. Some members of your team may struggle with the ambiguity inherent in Track One activities, but that's where the opportunities are.

- Identify and mitigate risk. The whole point of Track One is to reduce the risk of building a product or feature no one wants.

Greenfield vs. Brownfield Projects

Greenfield projects are brand new: new product, new features, new code, new tests. *Brownfield* (or *legacy*) projects involve maintaining, improving, or extending an existing product.

Initiating Greenfield Projects

For most of a product's development, Track One and Track Two carry on in parallel. However, many greenfield projects face the *initiation problem*: how do we start? In pre-agile, heavyweight development processes, projects started with *big design up front*: analysts and architects spent months researching, modeling, and writing specifications before programming began. Big design up front led to many failures. Building the system typically revealed that the analysis was deeply flawed and the design ineffective. In contrast, many agile teams initiate a project by diving straight into programming, which creates problems when the product is outside the engineers' experience. 'New control system for the nuclear reactor, eh? Sure, we'll get right on that.'

Greenfield projects usually have an initial period where the team has insufficient knowledge to make much progress on Track Two, so Track One dominates. Complicated, unfamiliar projects (e.g., a payroll system, an air traffic control system, a learning management system) can take weeks to initiate. Most non-trivial enterprise systems and new consumer applications we observed had four- to eight-week initiation periods. Teams might need only a day to figure out where to begin simpler projects where the problems are obvious.

Furthermore, when the team already understands the domain, especially when developers *are* typical users (think Apache, Linux, Firefox, Eclipse) Track Two can begin immediately while the designers investigate the fine points. Unfortunately, engineers often *think* the problems are obvious and are well into building the wrong product before realizing Track One has been neglected.

Beginning Track One allows the team to center on the opportunity at hand. Once the team has validated that the opportunity exists and provides value to a group of users, then they begin iterating on the product. For most systems, this involves mock-ups and user experience design. For systems without a user interface, product design can iterate on the system components and their application interfaces. For a command-line tool, these would be the command, its options, its side effects, its output, and return codes.

Track One includes the same basic activities whether it is an initiation or is ongoing in parallel with Track Two. These activities incrementally load the backlog with user stories to inform Track Two.

Sometimes, a product will have additional periods where Track One dominates, such as at the beginning of a new feature set or whenever the team is unsure where to head next. Some people call these periods "discovery and framing." We do not use that term because most of Track One is about building consensus, co-creating ideas, and generating design concepts. It is easy to mistake something you have created for something you have discovered, and doing so can lead to overconfidence.

During initiation, Track One focuses on the minimal viable product. Once a preliminary product backlog is available, Track Two can commence, and initiation is complete.

Normal, Ongoing Track One

Once a project is up and running, Track One continues in parallel with Track Two because the world constantly changes. The team must continuously make sense of their changing reality to keep the product competitive. As the team builds the product, the team members come to understand the product and its environment differently (hopefully better). As the team shares ideas with stakeholders and deploys early versions, the stakeholders' understanding of the product and their environment changes. With each new release, the product changes its environment. It's not just the world changing on its own—*building the product changes the world.*

As project initiation gives way to business as usual, teams may take on more engineers. Track One tries to stay just ahead of Track Two so the engineers always have high-value, high-priority work to do. While the engineers focus on implementing backlog items, the product designers constantly review the emerging product and systematically identify and remove or validate assumptions. The designers constantly seek potential improvements, small and large. The product manager constantly monitors the business environment, identifying new opportunities and threats.

Sometimes engineers participate in Track One by, for example, taking notes on a user interview or providing technical feedback. Similarly, designers often participate in Track Two; for example, when an engineer can't get a screen to look exactly like a mock-up, a designer might give advice or verify that it's close enough. The product manager similarly contributes to both tracks.

Anti-pattern: Allowing Engineers to Define the Work

Many companies encourage software engineers to design the product. This can lead to products that are difficult for non-experts to understand and use [56]. Engineers often want to add too many features. Sometimes engineers add features because their company's performance assessment procedures incentivize new feature development, because engineers have a higher tolerance for complexity than the average user, or because they just have a good idea. Sometimes engineers are paternalistic—neglecting stakeholders' ideas and building systems more for themselves.

Open-source projects, in particular, suffer from a lack of user-centered design because non-developer users are marginalized. In his devastating critique of open source, Yeats explains:

> *The rhetoric of open source, then, represents a false reality of a free and open society where individuals have control over the technology in their lives—a society where everyone is equally empowered to participate in active communities and where the ideas of others are valued and influential in development processes. Open source fails to live up to this Utopian promise. Instead, open-source software communities are closed to outsiders, especially those lacking a high level of technological skill. Non-developer users are routinely ignored and wield considerably less influence than their developer user counterparts. A technological development process that promises the democratization of technology thus simply upholds the status quo.* [57, p. 189]

The trouble is that good design doesn't come naturally because the most straightforward way to build something (system-centered design) is rarely the easiest to understand and use (user-centered design) [11]. For example, command-line interfaces are usually easier to create than graphical user interfaces, but most users are more comfortable with point-and-click. One reason we need product designers is because they are less biased (than engineers) by the tension between easy-to-build and easy-to-use, and therefore better able to conceive of easy-to-use forms.

Compounding the problem, designing software products requires a different skill set than building software products, and software engineering education doesn't really cover product design or design thinking [58]. Except for the occasional course in human-computer interaction, computer science and software engineering degree programs are technocentric.

At its core, Track One is simply research and story writing. However, understanding an opportunity and imagining a product involves two distinct underlying cognitive processes.

When we make an interview guide, interview a stakeholder, write notes on the interview, and organize those notes, we are focused on learning the current state of affairs. Sometimes this is called "problematizing," "problem framing," or "problem-focused thinking," but the correct, scientific term is *sensemaking*—literally making sense of things. Chapter 7 further explains sensemaking and presents recommended sensemaking practices.

In contrast, when we brainstorm features, draw mock-ups, and write user stories, we are focused on generating and elaborating a product concept. This is sometimes called "solutionizing," "designing," or "solution-focused thinking," but the correct scientific term is *design thinking*. Design thinking is a special kind of cognition that isn't reducible to planning, problem-solving, decision-making, or creativity. During design thinking, your understanding of the project context and your fledgling product concept *co-evolve* (i.e., evolve together). Chapter 8 further explains this coevolution and presents recommended design thinking practices.

What if We Don't Have a Product Designer?

Many software teams are imbalanced because they don't have a product designer. The software industry suffers from a shortage of product designers. Finding people skilled in both design thinking and user-centered design is difficult, and many organizations do not sufficiently appreciate the need for skilled product designers.

Building a user-facing product without a product designer is a terrible idea (and one reason so many products fail). Products designed by engineers and managers tend to be economically unsustainable and difficult to use.

Nevertheless, if you don't have a product designer, do your best with design thinking and user research while pressuring management to hire product designers. The many Track One activities described below, particularly interviewing users and synthesizing feedback, are not *impossible* without a product designer, but they are quite different from programming. These activities take time to master. Every software developer should know a little about user research and design thinking (and this book should help!), but in the long term, every product with human users needs a product designer.

Sometimes, an existing team member can transition into product design. Team members with backgrounds in quality assurance, business analysis, requirements analysis, or front-end development may be good candidates for product design. However, the view of product design expressed in this book differs fundamentally from pre-agile requirements analysis. Experience in requirements engineering may, therefore, hinder acquiring product design skills.

Summary

In summary, Track One is all about determining what to build and loading good stories into the backlog. The product designer and product manager do most of the heavy lifting, but engineers can give technical feedback and observe some user research. Track One is messy, and it's more effective to embrace the ambiguity than to ignore it. When starting a brand new project, Track One often needs a little head start on Track Two.

Chapter 7

Making Sense of the Project Environment

In real-world practice, problems do not present themselves to the practitioners as givens...
To convert a problematic situation to a problem, a practitioner must ... make sense
of an uncertain situation that initially makes no sense.
– Karl Weick

 Key Takeaways

- Most software projects have a messy environment with multiple stakeholders who disagree on the nature of problems and how they should be addressed.

- Researching the product's stakeholders and environment is vital.

- The best user research technique is the one-on-one interview.

- Users have beliefs, values, goals, frustrations, and ideas. Users do not have requirements.

- Personas, stakeholder maps, and affinity maps facilitate sensemaking.

- Including sustainability personas can improve the team's long-term focus and awareness of sustainability issues.

- Making a table showing stakeholder impacts over time can help with making sense of success.

Walkthrough from a Designer's Perspective

Michelle, a product designer, enjoys the journey of discovery and creation represented by Track One. She takes pride in the process but keeps her ego out of specific products so that she can accept feedback without defensiveness. She likes incorporating new suggestions and research insights into her designs. She accepts that sometimes confusion and ambiguity increase right up until a key insight emerges. Here's how Michelle describes initiating Track One as follows.

"We began with a project kickoff to share context and align the team. The product manager and I crafted the agenda and facilitated the full-day meeting. We covered the current state, goals, users, workflow, tech stack, data, team, calendar, and logistics. Our client is an engineering company that uses 2.5 million parts (e.g., screws, bolts, washers) to build complex products. They wanted to optimize inventory procurement by sharing purchase history across their (siloed) business units. The goal was to determine the feasibility and value of a web app revealing this information to members of the supply chain.

Michelle

"The rest of the week focused on building the team's shared understanding of the project context. We listed possible user roles and learned that we would need to learn more about each user and select a primary user. We mapped out a user ecosystem. We brainstormed questions for our data science colleagues. We created topic maps to guide stakeholder interviews. Interviewing our main stakeholders was key to understanding the project context.

"My favorite activity is creating the personas—kind of like character sketches of potential users. In this case, I made a "proto-persona" for the primary user. A proto-persona is a persona that hasn't been validated by research yet."

When software projects fail, it is usually because the team does not understand the project environment. People say things like:

- "the users didn't know what they wanted,"

- "the clients kept changing their minds,"

- "management wouldn't give us enough detail,"

- "the features (or requirements) weren't clear," or

- "the features (or requirements) kept changing."

All of these statements indicate that the team did not understand the project environment. Blaming users, clients, management, or documentation is pointless and unsustainable. Software project environments are ambiguous and unstable. That's just how they are. This is where Track One comes in.

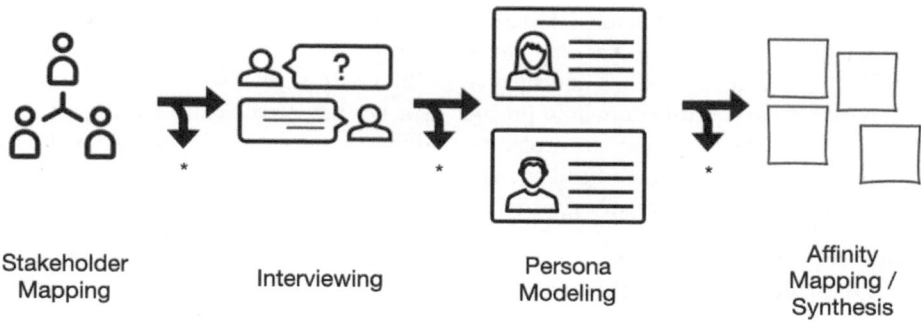

Stakeholder Mapping

Interviewing

Persona Modeling

Affinity Mapping / Synthesis

* return to any previous step

Figure 7–1: An Oversimplified Step-by-Step Guide to Get You Going

Track One involves two, quite different cognitive processes: *sensemaking* (the subject of this chapter) and *coevolution* (the subject of the next chapter). Sensemaking is the process of assigning meaning to our experiences. In the context of software development, it means making sense of the project context and its stakeholders. Sensemaking is not designing a product; it's learning about the situation at hand. Sensemaking is not a phase. It's just something people do all the time, like communicating. Software professionals can rapidly alternate between making sense of a situation and designing a product. However, learning about the situation is a different cognitive process from generating and refining product concepts, so it involves different activities (see Figure 7–1).

Sensemaking Anti-patterns

The best way to grok sensemaking is to consider the four basic ways it goes wrong:

1. **Preconceiving the solution.** Some teams accept a single stakeholder's vision of a solution without sufficiently understanding the project context. For example, someone asks for a rocket-propelled jetpack, so we build it. Then they burn down their house. Why did they want a jetpack? To get on the roof and fix a leak. What did they really need? A ladder.

2. **Preconceiving the problem.** Similarly, some teams accept a single stakeholder's vision of "the problem," ignoring or marginalizing the views or objections of other stakeholders. For example, commercial publishers are inundated with manuscripts from aspiring writers, so they see "the problem" as "too many manuscripts" while the writers perceive totally different problems like "publishers don't select the best works." The publisher's framing leads to barriers to submission like "send a printed copy of the manuscript by physical mail..." which increases environmental impact and discourages low-income applicants.

3. **Premature solution-focused thinking (or solutionizing).** When entering an unfamiliar domain, focus on *learning* rather than jumping to conclusions about product features. Our initial product concepts are difficult to shake, so if we latch onto a bad idea early, it can derail the whole project. We are not advocating months of analysis. Depending on the situation's complexity and familiarity, it could take a few hours or a few weeks before we are ready to focus on possible solutions. One designer explained: "My goal is to listen and absorb; my processing will come soon."

4. **Modeling "requirements."** Teams heavily influenced by pre-agile thinking tend to ask stakeholders what they want and force their tentative, conflicting, ambiguous responses into an oversimplified and over-rationalized specification (see *The Myth of Requirements*, below).

Practices

In a greenfield project, the team enters a cyclical process of collecting and synthesizing information. This process is sometimes called *user research*. There are many good ways of collecting information, including:

1. Direct observation: watching stakeholders in their natural or work environment;

2. Participant observation: joining in with stakeholders' work;

3. Semi-structured interviews: one-on-one discussions where the interviewer improvises from a set of questions or topics;

4. Focus groups: one interviewer leading a discussion among several interviewees;

5. Secondary research: reading articles, books, etc. related to the project;

6. Formal instruction: taking courses or tutorials related to the product (e.g., taking piano lessons to design software for pianists).

We focus on semi-structured interviews because they are flexible, inexpensive, widely used, and produce high-quality information. Focus groups might seem more efficient than one-on-one interviews, but a focus group is often dominated by one or a few individuals, obscuring the diversity of views. Secondary research is also widely used and highly recommended. In contrast, observing stakeholders and formal training can be very informative but are also very time-consuming. Questionnaire surveys are not recommended because they usually produce junk data. The ghastly new practice of telling an AI chatbot to impersonate a user and then "interviewing" it produces a particularly dangerous kind of junk data that sounds authoritative while downplaying human diversity in favor of stereotypes.

Good user research produces lots of predominately qualitative data. For medium to large projects, we must synthesize this data into a model because one person cannot hold it all in their mind. We externalize it to work through it like how you do easy math mentally but

> ## The Myth of Requirements
>
> "Requirement" is a pre-agile concept rooted in the false belief that stakeholders can provide detailed, comprehensive specifications for software products that do not yet exist.
>
> The requirements myth is harmful because focusing on requirements corrupts the team's definition of success—instead of improving stakeholders' lives, the team focuses on efficiently implementing the specification regardless of stakeholder impacts. This undermines creativity [59] and sustainability. Moreover, as the world and our understanding of it continually evolve, the specification grows out of date.
>
> In outsourcing relationships, the outsourcee becomes trapped in a legal paradox [60]: fulfill the contract by building a system that's no longer appropriate, or build what is needed and breach the contract. When what is needed costs more than what was agreed, the outsourcee can't win.
>
> Suppose we are presented with a requirement like "the system shall authenticate users with a username and password." Presenting passwords as a requirement discourages the designer from considering superior alternatives such as biometric passkeys or single sign-on. These are subtle, often unconscious, psychological effects. Even though it's obvious to an experienced developer that passwords could be replaced with single sign-on, sometimes you just don't think about it because the specification unconsciously suppresses alternative solution ideas.
>
> When it became apparent (in the 1960s) that users and clients were incapable of reliably providing requirements, professionals split into two groups: the *design thinking* group figured out how to build good products when no one knows what they want; the requirements engineering group created increasingly sophisticated techniques for modeling imaginary requirements, blaming users when their products failed [61]. Some members of the requirements engineering group have begun incorporating more design thinking.
>
> There is no direct analog of an IEEE standard "the system shall" requirement in most agile methods. When people refer to user stories, stakeholder maps, personas, etc. as "requirements," they are miscommunicating "across the paradigmatic divide" [62] (i.e., incorrectly mapping a concept from a new paradigm to an incompatible concept in an old paradigm). Sustainable Dual-Track Development prescribes ways of designing good products without modeling requirements. Modeling requirements is one way of working, not an intrinsic aspect of software development.

write down difficult math. However, many pre-agile software processes went way overboard with modeling. Keep things simple and focus on modeling techniques that effectively balance helpfulness and complexity. Modeling serves thinking, so use the models that best help you think about your project.

We recommend stakeholder maps because they help us make sense of who we should interview, and affinity diagrams because they help us transition from making sense of the project context to generating design concepts. We recommend explicitly modeling success to avoid oversimplifying it and falling into unsustainable (and unethical) profit fixation. Some systems benefit from other models; for instance, formal sequence diagrams for systems with complex activity sequences.

Indeed, all of the activities described below are in service to learning and thinking. If a practice doesn't help you learn or think, don't do it. To adapt a practice for your specific context, be guided by whatever best facilitates learning and thinking.

Regardless of the product's maturity, all Track One activities are ongoing, incremental, and rarely orderly. For example, we make a list of stakeholders to interview, but interviewees invariably suggest additional stakeholders we hadn't considered. Similarly, personas help with affinity mapping, but affinity mapping makes us rethink personas. This is not the waterfall model. Different team members can do different activities simultaneously, and the team can transition from any activity to any other in any order. Furthermore, Track One activities should continue throughout active product development.

Stakeholder Mapping

A stakeholder is a person or group who is impacted by a project, product, or service (see the *Stakeholder Theory* sidebar on page 102). Understanding a project's stakeholders is crucial because benefiting stakeholders is what success means [63].

Listing project stakeholders helps the team decide how best to involve each one, identify their concerns, and seek their support. Drawing a map of the stakeholders can help by showing relationships or categorizing stakeholders. Stakeholder maps can be drawn in many different ways, including the following.

- Category style: stakeholders grouped into categories (e.g., Figure 7–2a).

- Power-Impact style: stakeholders graphed on two dimensions: how much influence they have over the project (like the Priority Onion), and the extent to which the project affects them (e.g., Figure 7–2b).

- Priority-Onion style: stakeholders are organized according to how much influence they have over the project, with primary stakeholders in the center, surrounded by rings of decreasing priority (e.g., Figure 7–2c).

- Conflict style: stakeholders organized according to their main agreements and disagreements (e.g., Figure 7–2d).

Category-style stakeholder maps are often helpful early on to determine who to interview. They're basically just a list on a whiteboard with a little structure to keep us organized. Some teams like to use the Priority Onion to prioritize stakeholders based on various factors (e.g., the team's level of responsibility to each stakeholder or the degree to which the product will impact each stakeholder). Other teams like to plot stakeholders on two axes: power over the project and how much the product will affect them. Both of these styles are *supposed to* help the team manage stakeholder conflicts. For example, if marketing wants to make

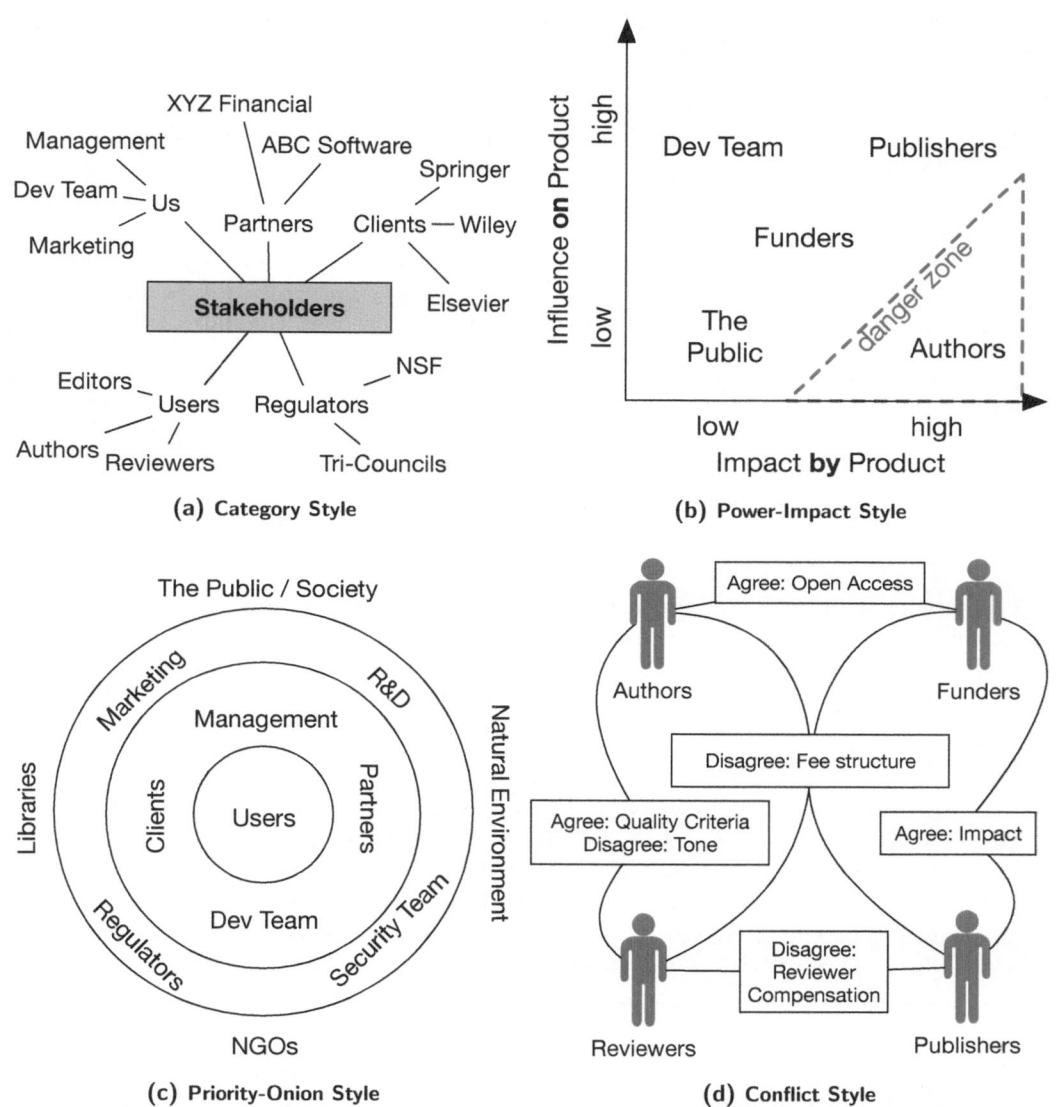

(a) Category Style

(b) Power-Impact Style

(c) Priority-Onion Style

(d) Conflict Style

Figure 7–2: Example Stakeholder Maps for an Academic Publishing System

a change the users won't like, and the team believes its first duty is to the users, then the team might push back against marketing's plan.

A fundamental premise of sustainable development is that the costs borne by a stakeholder (including the natural environment) must be proportional to the benefits received. If your product benefits one group by harming another, you have a moral duty to offset these harms. Therefore, we don't recommend the Priority-Onion style. Furthermore, if you

Stakeholder Theory

A stakeholder is someone who is involved in or affected by an organization or project and is interested in its success. Typical stakeholders include users, users' organizations, investors, the development team, the families of team members, the team's organization, suppliers, partners, customers, relevant government agencies, and the general public. Some projects have other stakeholders like the news media, users' friends and families, lobbyists, non-governmental organizations (NGOs), trade associations (e.g., the Association for Computing Machinery), and specific communities (e.g., contributors to Python; bird watchers; the town of Cork, Ireland).

Stakeholder Theory asserts that ethical management (and software development) involves balancing the interests and well-being of stakeholders [64], not simply maximizing profits. Success isn't just about money; it's about impacts on people [63]. For example, if developers work 80 hours per week for months to ship a video game on time, the game is not successful from the team's perspective, profitable or not. Thinking of success in terms of long-term impacts on actual human beings helps teams build better software in more sustainable ways.

People who want your project to fail (e.g., your competitors, criminals aiming to rob you, hackers aiming to compromise your system) are not stakeholders. A power company that obstructs solar panel installations to protect its revenues is not a stakeholder of the solar panel supplier. While "the public" is often considered a stakeholder, that means the public good or society at large, not a specific person on whom the project has little or no effect.

The presence of negative impacts on *someone* does not mean a project has failed. Your new air conditioning optimization software is not unethical because it reduces profits from coal mining—quite the opposite. But your new doorbell camera's facial recognition / crime prediction system *is* unethical if it encodes and promotes prejudice against people of color. It's all about balance and responsibility. The people who endure the most harm from a system should reap most of the benefits.

use the Power-Impact style, we recommend explicitly drawing a "danger zone" around the stakeholders who have little influence over the project but are strongly affected by it. The stakeholder map can then help the team identify their project's unintended consequences and assess the extent to which those who reap the project's benefits also bear its costs.

As the project progresses, interviews may reveal that stakeholders fundamentally disagree on the problems the product should solve and how it should work. A conflict-style stakeholder map visualizes these disagreements. This not only helps us strategize about how to build consensus among stakeholders but also immunizes the team against the tendency to marginalize dissent by over-rationalizing disagreements into a singular problem statement.

Table 7–1: Examples of Abstract Stakeholders for Sustainability

Sustainability Dimension	Example Stakeholders	Helps Teams Consider...
Ecological	the natural environment	energy usage, carbon footprint, unintended consequences
Economic	customers, management	who will be willing to pay for the product
Social	society, the development team, the public	unintended antisocial effects; the team's well-being and resilience
Technical	the code, the tests	technical debt, security, maintainability

Better Sustainability through Abstract Stakeholders

Technically, a stakeholder is a person or group with an interest in the success of a project. However, adding some *abstract stakeholders*—stakeholders that represent something other than a group of people—can improve software sustainability. Ideally, we want abstract stakeholders who represent each dimension of sustainability (Table 7–1) that isn't covered by regular stakeholders.

A typical stakeholder analysis would already include stakeholders related to economic sustainability (e.g., customers). A *good* stakeholder analysis would include stakeholders related to social sustainability (e.g., the public, the development team). To these we add abstract stakeholders for ecological sustainability (e.g., The Earth) and technical sustainability (e.g., code and tests). Anthropomorphizing the natural environment helps us keep sustainability in mind. For instance, the Earth won't be happy about that cryptocurrency payments feature in the backlog or making every customer redownload your entire application instead of a smaller, well-optimized patch. Similarly, anthropomorphize the codebase as someone who wants to be elegant, well-organized, bug-free, and covered by an immaculate ensemble of tests. It wants a long, healthy, meaningful life, not to die of abuse and neglect in a few years. Were you considering implementing a new feature with a dozen unfixed bugs still in the backlog? What would the code think of this plan? Not much.

Specific projects might have other abstract stakeholders. For example, a ski resort might have abstract stakeholders like *the mountain* and *wildlife*; a wind farm might have an abstract stakeholder *endangered birds* (because windmill blades can hit birds); a factory might have an abstract stakeholder *air* because it emits air pollution.

As we shall see below, these abstract stakeholders set the stage for sustainability *personas*, which are even more helpful for keeping sustainability issues front of mind.

Stakeholder Maps Summary

In summary, stakeholder maps help the team understand the client ecosystem and who the product benefits (and harms). Drawing a stakeholder map helps us to (1) figure out who to interview and (2) resist oversimplifying the problematic context into a bogus problem statement that does not reflect the varied positions of the many stakeholders. Including abstract stakeholders like *the natural environment, society,* and *the code* can help teams better reason about sustainability.

Interviewing

We advocate interviewing representatives of every stakeholder group, and *many* users. In projects where the person who authorizes and pays for the project doesn't actually use the product (e.g., many enterprise systems), we call this person the "customer," "client," "sponsor," or "product owner." Sponsor interviews help the product team understand the business perspective, needs, constraints, and interrelationships of various groups at the company. Internal sponsors of in-house projects are also helpful to interview. One-on-one interviews are preferred for most stakeholder groups except the general public. If your system has wide-reaching impacts on the general public, focus groups or town halls may be more practical.

The most important thing to remember about a user interview is that it's not for eliciting requirements or discovering facts. The interviewee and interviewer co-construct meaning, opinions, and preferences (see the Construction of Preferences sidebar on page 108). Interviews are about understanding interviewees, not agreeing to the terms of a legal contract.

There are three kinds of interviews:

1. Unstructured: a free-flowing, fully improvised conversation.

2. Structured: asking predetermined, mainly closed-ended questions.

3. Semi-structured: asking predetermined, open-ended questions and improvising follow-up questions.

An unstructured interview is basically just a conversation. There is no script or guide. "I did unstructured interviews" just means "I spoke with some people." A structured interview, in contrast, is basically reading a questionnaire (e.g., true-false, multiple-choice, one-word answers) and recording responses.

Semi-structured interviews are the most effective for user research because they allow the interviewer to explore ideas that emerge during the conversation while staying on topic. To do a semi-structured interview, you need an interview guide or topic map to help you stay on track and remember what to discuss.

Interview Guides and Topic Maps

Product designers prepare for interviews by creating topic maps or interview guides. A topic map (AKA popcorn diagram) is a picture that illustrates the main themes to discuss during an interview (e.g., Figure 7–3). More experienced interviewers can use topic maps because they have internalized how to ask different kinds of questions and are skilled at improvising probes. Novice interviewers benefit from more detailed interview guides.

An interview guide is a set of *main questions* and *probes*—"questions or requests that ask the participant to provide additional information about their previous response" [65, p. 382]. For example, when building a new system for managing job applications to replace an unpopular off-the-shelf solution, we might ask a main question like, "What don't you

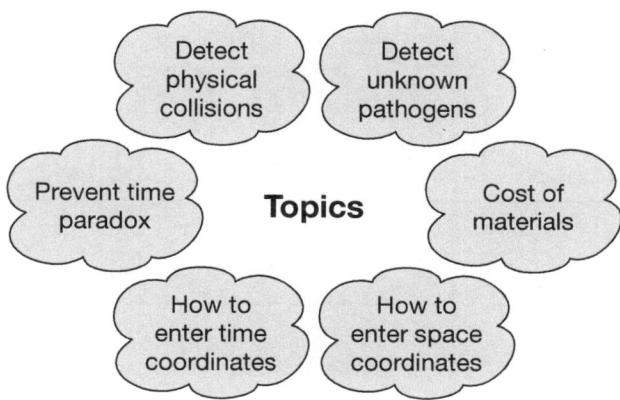

Figure 7–3: Example Topic Map for a Time Machine

Note: Just think. If you built a time machine you could travel back to 4:57 PM last Friday and stop Charlie from hitting deploy so you could enjoy your weekend for a change.

like about the current system?" with related probes such as "Why is that?", "Do you think your colleagues feel the same way?", and "Can you elaborate on that?"

Interview guides tend to include straightforward warm-up questions to get interviewees talking, followed by (sometimes more challenging) main questions. If you are in a hurry, start with these three questions [66]:

1. "What are you trying to get done?" to gather context.

2. "How do you currently do this?" to understand the current workflow.

3. "What could be better about how you do this?" to find opportunities.

End with an opportunity for the interviewee to say whatever is on their mind, for instance: "What else is on your mind?" or "Is there anything else you think I should know?"

Thinking through questions ahead of time helps mitigate the risk of asking leading questions. Avoid forcing the team's ideas onto the users. Sometimes, interviewees try to tell the interviewer what they think the interviewer wants to hear. This is called *social desirability bias*, and it can lead to overestimating how well we understand the users. Good interviewers ask neutral questions like, "How do you feel about the new system?" and avoid leading questions like, "You like the new system, right?" Most leading questions are more subtle; for instance, "Should passwords expire?" presupposes password-based security.

Questions or topics should be customized to the interviewee. It helps to think about which stakeholder or persona (see below) the interviewee represents. Product designers often base questions on assumptions the team is making about the product or persona.

Setting up Interviews

Selecting a physical space for an interview can be tricky. One approach is to conduct the interview in the environment where the interviewee would use the product; for example,

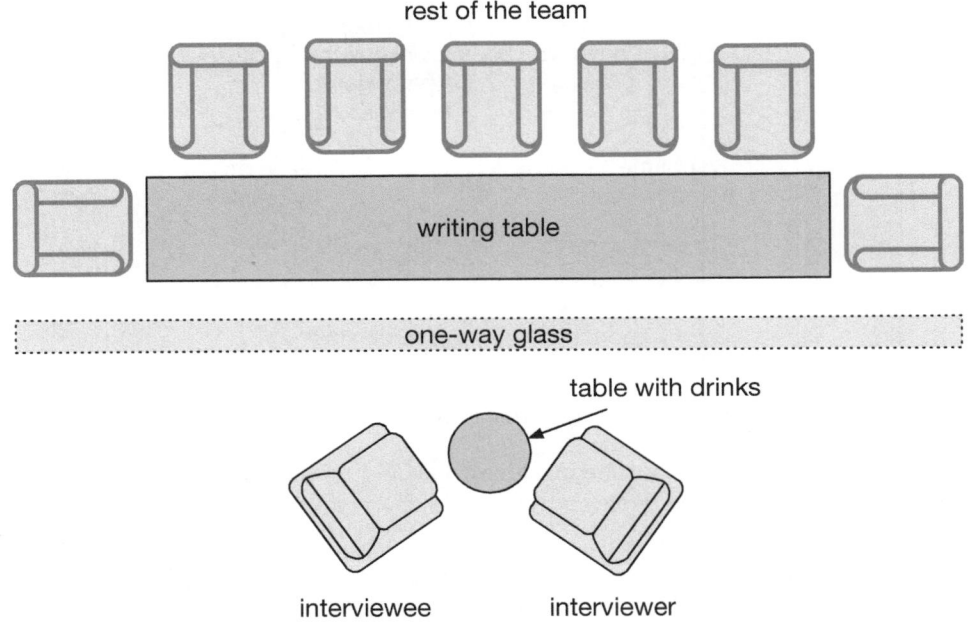

Figure 7–4: Setup for Physical Interviews

Note: Two ferns and Zach Galifianakis optional.

the interviewee's workplace for an enterprise application or their home for a consumer application. This is called "contextual inquiry" since it reveals contextual information and occurs in the natural use context. Contextual Inquiry helps interviewees relax and answer more honestly, especially during feature validation. Observing the interviewee's context and behavior can be just as valuable as the question-answer session. However, it may not be practical for the whole team to attend on-site interviews. In such cases, the product designer can record the interviews (preferably audio and video) and later watch them with the team to take notes.

Another approach is to have the interviewee come to an environment set up by the product designer. This way, the whole team can attend the interviews. It's important for the interviewee to feel comfortable. Find a couple of comfortable chairs. Set them up as shown in Fig. 7–4 (not directly across a table from each other). Decorate the room. Get a potted plant. Put some art on the walls. Make it seem friendly.

Having the whole team in the room during the interview can be intimidating. Instead, set up a room with one-way glass so the team can observe from the other side while the product designer asks the questions. Using a camera and microphone with the team watching on a TV in another room also works, but it's not as engaging as one-way glass.

Schedule interviewees to arrive one at a time, with enough slack in the schedule that no one has to wait around. When the interviewee arrives, introduce yourself. Offer the interviewee a drink. Take their coat. Encourage them to "make yourself at home." You want it to feel like a friendly conversation, not an interrogation. Making people feel comfortable, drawing a shy person out of their shell, or keeping a chatty person on topic gets easier with experience if it doesn't come naturally.

Unfortunately, sometimes face-to-face interviews are impractical because of unfriendly employers, safety issues, or physical distance. In such cases, interviews can be conducted via videoconference. Video interviews typically aren't as good as in-person interviews because subtle cues get lost, and it's harder to get interviewees to pay attention. People are easily distracted by notifications or co-workers. Some people covertly try to do something else during the interview. Again, as an interviewer gets more practice, it becomes easier to keep interviewees engaged without being too aggressive. One advantage of video interviews is that they are easy to record for the team to watch later. If the team chooses to attend live, try turning off the video for everyone except the interviewer and the interviewee. Like the one-way-glass setup, this will help the interviewee focus on the interviewer and not feel overwhelmed.

Conducting Interviews

Product designers should conduct most interviews, although the product manager might handle sponsor interviews.

During the interview, ask questions one at a time. Give users time to answer fully. Ask follow-up questions to draw out more details, clarify ambiguous statements, and keep interviewees on track. Listen to the interviewee to understand their point of view.

Observers take notes on the sticky notes: one observation, insight, or quote per sticky note. Use a different color for each interview to visually track who said what during subsequent analysis (e.g., affinity mapping). For instance, during interview 1, everyone writes on red stickies; for interview 2, everyone uses green stickies, etc.

It's best for the whole team to watch the interview live and write notes as things happen, but team members can also watch recordings or just read transcripts. Some people like to highlight and mark-up a transcript, alone or in a shared file where you can see each other's annotations. Eventually, however, we should produce handwritten notes on stickies color-coded to interviewees to support affinity mapping (see page 112).

During interviews, be wary of the interviewee's preconceived problems and solutions. Hearing what an interviewee perceives as problematic may be useful, and they may have good ideas, but don't jump to conclusions. Counteract preconceptions by (amicably) challenging the interviewee's assumptions, broadening the focus of the interviews, and following interesting ideas that emerge.

The team keeps interviewing until it feels like they understand the user's perspective, the problem they want to solve, and the business opportunity. At any point, the team may pivot to a new direction or even a new product. The team resumes interviewing when new questions emerge or new information is needed. When the team begins working on a new feature set, further interviews are often required. In our experience, interviewing 5–8 users is typically sufficient to get a medium-sized greenfield project going. The more complicated the product and the more stakeholders it has, the more interviews are needed.

Construction of Preferences in Interviews

Software professionals increasingly recognize the importance of stakeholder interviews. However, what actually happens in an interview is broadly misunderstood.

Interviews do not "elicit requirements." As discussed in the Myth of Requirements sidebar on page 99, modeling "requirements" is just one way of working, not intrinsic to software development. Although decades of every expert insisting that most users do not know what they want is finally being recognized, the myth of requirements is being replaced by the myth of preferences; i.e., that interviews are about eliciting preferences. Unfortunately, users rarely have clear, enduring preferences about software features. Rather, preferences are *constructed* within social situations (like interviews) and can vary greatly depending on how information is presented [67].

During an interview, the interviewer and the interviewee *co-construct* preferences. If the interviewee actually *uses* the product a year later, they may construct different preferences because they're in a different social situation. This is one of the reasons why users always want changes to systems after delivery.

If interviewers do not recognize their effects on preference construction, the concepts emerging from the interviews might be more about the *interviewer's* preferences than the *interviewees'*.

An interviewer can't avoid affecting the preferences, ideas, values, and beliefs expressed by the interviewees. The interviewer's main defense against biasing the results is *reflexivity*; that is, reflecting critically on one's own biases, preferences, ideas, values, and beliefs; asking: "How might I be affecting these outcomes? Which of these notes are mostly the interviewees, and which might be coming from me?"

Expressed preferences depend on myriad cognitive biases. Interviewees will tend to *express* preference for options that are presented as a default, middle ground, or socially desirable, whether or not they actually prefer these options. Avoid leading questions. Avoid framing questions or tasks to elicit the preferences you expect or want to hear. Work with the interviewee to elaborate their preferences.

Persona Modeling

Product designers lead the team in creating *personas*—evidence-based descriptions of fictional stakeholders (similar to novelists' character sketches).

The product designer might organize their research into 1–6 user personas, one sponsor persona, and a handful of other stakeholder personas. Creating fictional users helps teams reason about how different kinds of people will use different features. Creating other fictional stakeholders helps the team compress voluminous knowledge about stakeholder concerns into memorable characters that guide decision-making.

Lola the Concerned Parent

"You're capturing our faces, but can you capture our needs? I want to know my kids and I are safe and that our data won't be misused. Give me peace of mind, not just ads."

Needs and Goals

Quickly navigate the mall and find information without wasting time.

Have a stress-free and enjoyable shopping experience with their child.

Locate stores and products quickly, provide information about deals and promotions.

Demographics

Parent
28–40
Middle Class

Balances day job as a graphic designer with the bustling lives of their children (ages 9 and 5).

Frustrations

Annoyed that the interface seems to prioritize bigger chains over smaller, unique stores that they like to explore with their kids.

Would like to see clear signage and explanations about the purpose of the facial recognition system and how their family's personal information will be protected.

Figure 7–5: Example Persona

Each persona should have a picture, motivational quote, demographic information, behaviors, needs, and goals. For example, a shopping mall rolling out facial recognition software might construct the concerned parent persona shown in Figure 7–5.

Although a persona describes a fictional *individual*, it represents a *group* of current or potential users. We group potential users by demographics, needs / goals, and behaviors, *but mostly behaviors*. We use personas to design user interaction, so personas need to represent users who behave similarly.

Some products seem like they could be used by anyone. However, early in a product's development, teams should focus on potential early adopters. Early personas, therefore, often describe a product's initial user groups.

Keep Looking, We'll Find the Market

Andrea was the product designer for a medical tourism start-up. Their business idea was to facilitate people traveling abroad to access less expensive medical care. Their business centered on matching patients with appropriate medical professionals and facilities. The start-up had a proto-persona representing the kinds of people they believed would use the service.

Before implementing features, Andrea wanted to reduce risk by identifying project assumptions, verifying product-market fit, and substantiating which features would deliver the most value (and should be built first).

Andrea made a proto-persona (based on intuition not evidence), found several people who fit the proto-persona, interviewed them, and discovered they wouldn't be interested in the product. Andrea had invalidated the proto-persona. When she talked about her findings with the stakeholders, they reassured her that there was a market for the product and the proto-persona needed some modifications. She then interviewed several people matching the new proto-persona— they weren't interested either. The stakeholders adjusted the proto-persona a third time, and she interviewed those people. The third group still didn't want the product.

Andrea

The start-up really wanted to build this product, so the team decided to create mock-ups based on what they had learned and build it anyway. The company went out of business within a year of launch.

Proto-personas vs. Real Personas

Real personas are evidence-based; that is, they are distillations of findings from interviews, focus groups, or other observation of stakeholders. Real, evidence-based personas help us reason about what features are needed, how they should be presented, and potential unintended consequences.

Some teams like to start by generating *proto-personas*, which are primarily based on intuition, then refine them into user personas as their research unfolds. Teams that use affinity mapping (below) refine their personas contemporaneously with affinity mapping. Proto-personas (along with stakeholder maps) can help select interviewees and generate interview guides. However, proto-personas often manifest stereotypes and unconscious biases, leading to superficial, incorrect reasoning about how a system should be designed. As we see in the preceding vignette, personas must be based on real people to inform design effectively.

User persona, in particular, need to be validated. "Persona validation" refers to predicting whether the user group represented by a persona will use a product, feature, or solution concept. It's not about whether the persona accurately reflects the attitudes and behaviors of a real group of people. It's about whether those people are potential users or not. When the team realizes that a user persona won't actually use the product, they can pivot the product to meet the needs of the target persona (invalidate the product) or find a new persona that will use the preconceived product (invalidate the persona). The team continues to pivot and iterate until there is a product-to-market fit.

Many teams draw personas on whiteboards or print them on paper and post them on a wall to increase their visibility. Personas are all about reminding us to think about decisions from different perspectives, so the more prominently they are displayed, the better.

Non-human Personas

Personas usually describe groups of people, but they don't have to. Many software products are used by other software systems rather than directly by human users. A software service or API can benefit from personas that describe the kinds of systems that might use it. Similarly, to develop software for tracking the migration of North Atlantic right whales, you could make a persona to represent the whales.

You may have to change the persona template to accommodate non-human personas. Personas for animals might include their species, habitat, stressors, and predators / prey. Personas for other software systems might include their purpose, creators / owners, or performance characteristics. *All* personas, however, should describe the target's behavior, or at least how the target might behave with the product.

Obviously, you can't interview whales or software services to validate these personas. Validate them by consulting with experts (e.g., a marine biologist, the team who created the service), using secondary research (i.e., reading about the targets), or telemetry data.

Sustainability Personas

We can extend persona modeling like we extended stakeholder mapping to help us reason better about the sustainability of software products. Specifically, we can add four *sustainability personas*:

1. **Cora the Code and Terry the Test Suite.** Consider anthropomorphizing the codebase and test suite as personas. Thinking about the code as a person helps us remember to keep it clean and avoid technical debt (see Chapter 10). The codebase wants to stay organized, efficient, and easy to understand and maintain. The test suite wants to give the code a good workout, and also be efficient and easy to understand.

2. **Hannah the Hacker.** A hacker persona represents bad actors who would compromise our system for money (ransom), vengeance, personal enjoyment, or some other reason. The sort of hackers we worry about depends on the nature of the product. For instance, developers of a competitive online game might worry about cheaters, while developers of a hospital records system might worry about ransomware or theft of personal information. Regardless, having a hacker persona on the wall helps us remember to build a secure product from the beginning instead of ineffectually tacking on security after. An important variation to consider is a person who, rather than trying to compromise the product's security, simply uses the product in an unexpected way to do harm. **Abe the abuser** might use your product to commit a crime or make the world worse in some legal yet unethical way.

3. **The Public.** Having a persona that represents the non-user public helps us remember to consider how certain features may have anti-social effects; that is, insidious effects that promote anti-social behavior, or undermine democracy, equality, justice, or fairness. For example, negative news headlines get more clicks at the expense of our collective psychosocial well-being.

4. **Earth.** Having a persona for the Earth itself helps us remember to consider environmental sustainability. The Earth doesn't like software that wastes electricity

(which typically equals lots of pollution) or has insidious effects on climate, biodiversity, oceans, forests, etc. Some products benefit from more specific variations; for instance, wind turbine control software might have a persona representing endangered birds (that could be struck by the spinning blades).

Like other non-human personas, validate sustainability personas by consulting with experts (e.g., a software engineering professor specializing in code quality, a cybersecurity expert, a biologist). To do a good job with these, you need unbiased perspectives from people outside of your team.

Stakeholder and Persona Champions

One of the challenges with modeling stakeholders and personas is the tendency to ignore negative impacts on stakeholders who have little influence over the project. Some teams use the power-impact style stakeholder map (Fig. 7–2b) specifically to determine whose objections and perspectives they can ignore.

The whole point of stakeholder analysis is that maximizing profits regardless of harm is morally untenable. That's how we got racist AI, the environmental catastrophe also known as bitcoin, and the ongoing usability disaster of modern enterprise systems. We must not ignore the stakeholders who are most vulnerable if the product is misused or who are likely to be harmed by a product they have no role in creating. Similarly, the whole point of persona modeling is to help the development team empathize with and balance the perspectives of stakeholder groups by keeping diverse stakeholders firmly in mind.

One tactic for potentially overcoming this problem is to designate a *champion* for each persona or stakeholder group. The product designers should usually champion the users and the product manager should usually champion customers and business interests. The remaining stakeholders can be distributed among team members, with each team member charged with advocating for their persona(s) / stakeholder(s) during design meetings. This approach is not perfect as some team members may advocate more forcefully than others, but it may help prevent forgetting about some stakeholders entirely, especially in teams with good conversational turn-taking and psychological safety (see Chapter 12: Towards Organizational Justice).

Affinity Mapping

After each round of interviews, the team synthesizes the data collected so far using *affinity mapping*. Each team member grabs a pile of sticky notes (from the interviews) and adds them to a large whiteboard or wall. The team collectively organizes the notes into groups or clusters by grouping similar notes and separating dissimilar notes. Rather than classifying notes into predefined categories, the team generates the categories inductively from the data. Team members periodically examine the emerging clusters and combine similar groups or split up groups lacking cohesion. The team labels and relabels groups as necessary. This produces an *affinity map* (e.g., Figure 7–6).

A round of interviews could be anywhere from one to a dozen, depending on the project. However, we want to reduce batch sizes until we have continuous user research. Interview data should be processed as soon as possible for three reasons:

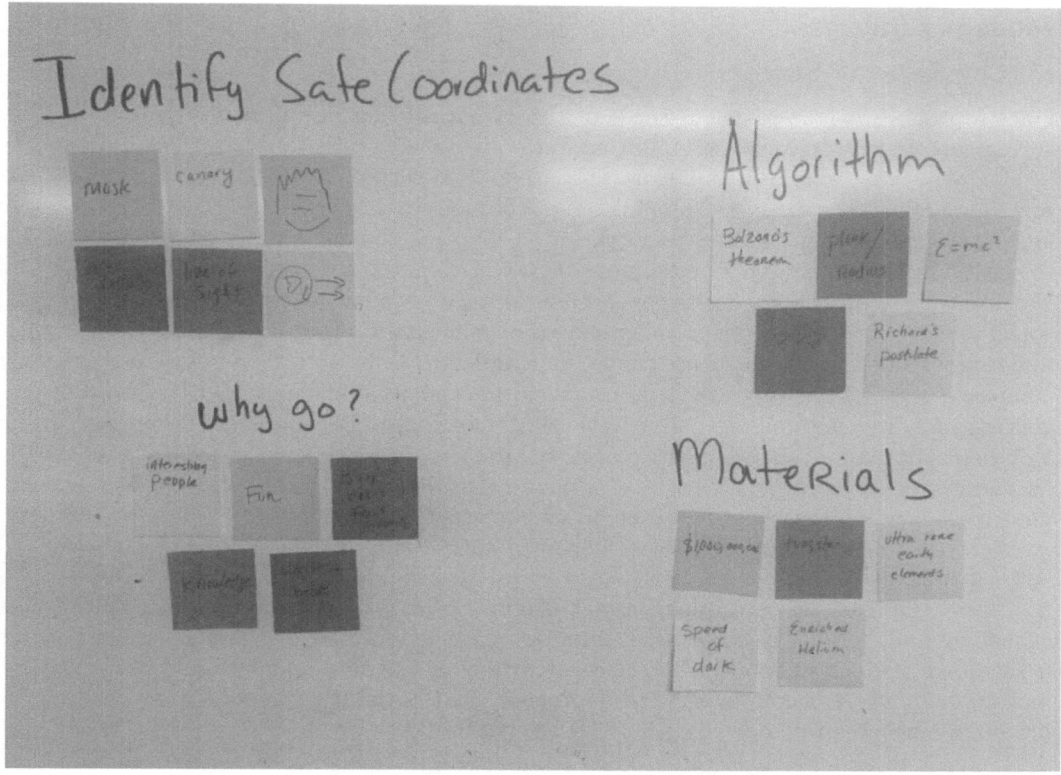

Figure 7–6: Example of a Very Simple Affinity Map

1. The more time passes, the more you forget.

2. Delaying processing also delays incorporating insights into the interview process.

3. Comparing notes allows the team to adjust its interview guide to seek out new information and answer new questions.

Affinity mapping tends to produce insights about both product design and personas. New ideas can be written on sticky notes (a different color than the interviews used) and added to a separate "design insights" section of the whiteboard. After each affinity mapping section, the product designer should update the personas to reflect changes in the team's understanding of prospective users.

From a scientific perspective, affinity mapping is fascinating because it bridges the gap between sensemaking and design thinking, the subject of Chapter 8. Sensemaking and design thinking are easy to observe in both the lab and the field, but the psychological process of shifting from one to the other is not. Affinity mapping highlights this shift when team members spontaneously add ideas to the design insights area.

Modeling Success

Making Sense of Success

Once a product is launched, making sense of its impact becomes part of Track One. Measuring success is notoriously complicated and difficult.

Many people (especially managers, executives, and entrepreneurs) have dangerously narrow views of success; for instance, making lots of money. The problem is that you can make lots of money forcing children to work in a collapsing diamond mine or selling weapons to warmongering dictators. Only a monster would view these activities as "successful" just because they're profitable. Some people think software projects can't be that evil. However, social media companies profit from spreading misinformation that destabilizes democracies, undermines life-saving health programs, and radicalizes our youth. Education-technology companies profit from spyware that compromises students' privacy under the guise of preventing cheating without actually preventing cheating. Every modern weapons system includes software. And we haven't even mentioned viruses, hacking tools, ransomware, or scamware like cryptocurrencies or addictionware like that game where you've spent a month's salary buying imaginary loot boxes and stupid hats.

Another common view of success is contractual: a product is successful if the agreed scope is delivered on-time and on-budget, with reasonable quality. This view resembles the "iron triangle" or "project triangle" (Figure 7–7a) and elevates following plans over achieving goals. Nobody cared that Windows 95 was late and over-budget after it made a shedload of money. Conversely, if we deliver—on-schedule and on-budget—a bug-free app for helping teenagers cope with depression that actually exacerbates depression, it's obviously unsuccessful.

Instead, we should assess the product's impact on its many stakeholders over time (Figure 7–7b). A product can simultaneously be a glowing success for one stakeholder and a miserable failure for another. Similarly, a product can appear successful at one time and unsuccessful at another. Most commercial products' stakeholder impacts depend on project efficiency (delivering reasonable scope given the resources consumed); artifact qual-

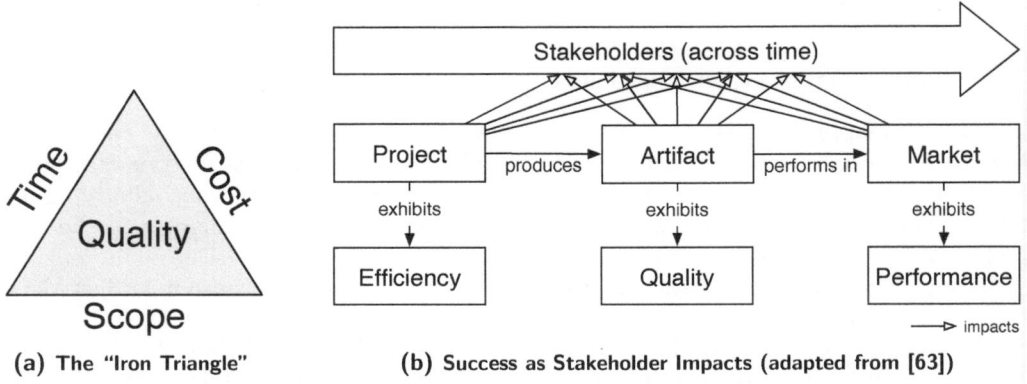

(a) The "Iron Triangle"   (b) Success as Stakeholder Impacts (adapted from [63])

Figure 7–7: Terrible (left) and Better (Right) Models of Software Engineering Success

ity (e.g., efficient, clean code, user-friendly interface, security, maintainability, etc.); and market performance (capturing reasonable market share, revenues, return on investment, etc.). Ultimately, however, success is about the system's impact on the world. A product can have a high market share without profit, have a great user interface but no users, or be delivered on time but be ineffective.

Indicators of Success

To make sense of success, we must examine various indicators of our product's impacts on *all* of its stakeholders. Useful indicators include:

- **Stakeholder interviews.** Product managers and designers should continue seeking feedback from a range of stakeholder representatives (not just users) regarding how the product impacts them.

- **Unsolicited feedback.** Who is contacting you about the product? Very angry people will often write to you directly. If someone is yelling at you, the system probably hurt them. De-escalate and uncover the negative impact.

- **Telemetry.** Most modern software reports information about feature use, error messages, performance, etc. to the development team.

- **Reviews** of the product (on app stores, retailer websites, blogs, etc.), can provide helpful information about how the product is being received. Just watch out for fake reviews (see [68]).

- **Media coverage.** Are journalists writing about your product? What are they saying? Journalists may expose unintended consequences or misuses of your product that you hadn't considered. If journalists are asking about your product, you should speak with them *before* they publish a potentially critical story.

- **Social media discourse.** Monitoring mentions of your product on social media can give some insight into its impacts. However, social media must be approached with skepticism. Between the bot-armies manipulating trends, the self-promoting "influencers", and the general disconnect between public opinion and social media discourse, you can't assume that social media reflects public sentiment.

- **Academic research.** Is someone studying your product? Reach out to them! Even if they are quite critical of your product, they may be very receptive to collaboration.

- **Economic indicators.** While far from the whole story, indicators of sales, revenue, market share, etc. are part of the overall picture.

- **Your research and reflection.** Sometimes, no one's really talking about the impacts of your product, either because it's working so well that no one notices it or its unintended consequences are so insidious that no one's detected them. In such cases, your research and reflection may be the best way to assess success.

Note that questionnaire surveys didn't make our list because of the kinds of questionnaires commonly used in marketing and product design, in which someone just makes up some questions like, "On a scale of 1 to 10, how likely are you to recommend this product to friends or family?" These questionnaires produce junk data. To produce meaningful data, questionnaires must be carefully designed with validated measurement scales [69], like personality tests. Scientists need years of training to build questionnaires that measure what they mean to measure; the questionnaires used in industry simply aren't trustworthy.

Visualizing the Success Model

The key to assessing various indicators of your product's impacts is to **avoid oversimplifying** the impacts into a single number that elides your product's differing impacts on different stakeholders at different times. Instead, it's better to create a chart or table (e.g., Table 7–2), breaking down positive and negative impacts by stakeholder and time period. There is no "total" row or column because the whole point of this kind of model is to avoid oversimplifying diverse outcomes into a singular judgment.

In this example, the product was launched in the first quarter. Initially, the product negatively impacts the client and positively impacts management (the business that launches the product) because the client pays upfront. The product negatively impacts the users because introducing the new system disrupts their work. But the new system is better than the old system, so the users and the client soon benefit. In the third quarter, we see an adverse event that negatively affects the client, dev team, marketing, security, non-governmental organizations (NGOs), and the public. In this example, a criminal organization hacked the product and used it to do something nefarious. Not every cell has a + or − sign because the team doesn't always have data for each stakeholder / time. In this example, the team has no data about impacts on their partner organizations, while libraries report both posi-

Table 7–2: Modeling Success

Stakeholder	2031 Q1	2031 Q2	2031 Q3	2031 Q4	2032 Q1	2032 Q2
			Period			
Users	−	−	+	+ +	+ +	+ + +
Client	− − −		− −	+	+	+ +
Dev team	+		− −			
Management	+ + +					
Partners						
Marketing dept.			−			
Security team			− − −			
Regulators						
Libraries	+ / −	+ / −	+ / −	+ / −	+ / −	+ / −
NGOs			− − −			
Nature	−	−	−	−	−	−
Public / Society			− −			

tive and negative effects simultaneously. The system has a consistent negative effect on the environment due to its energy use.

Table 7–2 highlights the software's conceptual debts. When the client buys the software, the software now owes the client benefits. When the software is hacked and misused, it hurts numerous stakeholders. While the provider of the product is not *solely* responsible for the product's misuse, it is *partially* responsible, and sustainability demands some reparation. To sum up, we advocate modeling success across time, stakeholder-by-stakeholder, to avoid oversimplifying the product's impacts.

Summary

Sensemaking is literally the process of making sense of a situation. All software development involves sensemaking even though software professionals rarely use this term. Professionals who neglect sensemaking tend to build technically sophisticated products that no one wants to use. To excel at sensemaking, iterate between drawing a stakeholder map, interviewing stakeholders (especially users), developing personas, and using affinity mapping to make sense of interview data. Augment this core process with secondary research and other sensemaking activities as needed.

Making sense of a project's outcomes and ongoing effects on stakeholders is also part of Track One. There is no singular measure of success. Teams should attend to many indicators of success (not just profits) and consider success on a stakeholder-by-stakeholder basis.

These activities help the team better understand and empathize with its users and other stakeholders. The data collected will help the team make more informed decisions later on. When implementing a feature, the product designer can answer the question, "What does the user expect here?" by reflecting on the collected user research.

Chapter 8

Design Thinking

All graphic designers hold high levels of responsibility in society.
We take invisible ideas and make them tangible.
– Debbie Millman

 Key Takeaways

- Designers have schemas of a problematic situation and a design concept.

- During design thinking, the designer oscillates between the two schemas, simultaneously refining both—the schemas "co-evolve."

- Design permeates the software development process and cannot be separated from analysis or coding.

- The most important design thinking practice is sketching (e.g., drawing UI mock-ups).

- Many other practices can help with design thinking including affinity mapping, feature validation, story writing, and usability testing.

- In Sustainable Dual-Track Development, the primary output of design thinking is user stories.

- A good user story is valuable to stakeholders, based on research, understood by the team, well-formatted, small, and tractable.

- Some stories benefit from attachments including mock-ups and acceptance criteria, but don't turn the backlog into a requirements specification.

- Common problems in design thinking include not having a product designer, insufficiently exploring design options, and trying to decompose epics into stories.

Coevolution on a Whiteboard

Allison, a product designer, and Diti, a front-end developer, were designing an enterprise system for managing partner networks. (Larger companies often have a network of smaller partners.) They conducted weeks of user research and wanted to synthesize what they'd learned so far. On one part of a large whiteboard, Diti drew an informal diagram showing one client's partner ecosystem, with different kinds of stakeholders and the relationships between them. Allison drew a separate diagram showing the architecture of their prototype system.

They stood back to survey the two pictures. They looked back and forth. Allison identified an inconsistency: one of the system's forms didn't match the relationships in the context diagram. Diti drew the change on the architecture diagram.

They stood back again and discussed the two images. Their changes triggered the realization that they had misunderstood a key part of the domain. Diti saw that two things they had considered separate—partner "channels" and partner "programs"—are really just different names for the same structure. Allison erased the symbol for partner channels and changed "programs" to "programs / channels."

Diti and Allison continued discussing the change. As they reworked the context diagram, they realized that it had many implications for the system design. They began reworking the architecture diagram. This back-and-forth went on for more than an hour. Each change to the context diagram triggered revisions to the system diagram, and each change to the system diagram triggered revisions to the context diagram. The two diagrams and the mental pictures they represented, *co-evolved* until the pair's understanding of the problematic context and tentative system design stabilized and matched.

Chapter 7: Making Sense of the Project Environment explained how to make sense of a problematic context, its stakeholders, and their beliefs, values, and preferences. This chapter explains how a software team can get from a tentative understanding of a project's context to a detailed product concept. It's not about "solving a problem." It's about knitting together different ideas to make something stakeholders can agree is good, even if they don't agree on what makes the situation problematic.

Design: The Least Understood Word in the Software Industry

Between poor coverage of design in computer science and software engineering education [58], and a long history of downplaying design in both pre-agile and agile development, software professionals seem to harbor numerous misconceptions about design.

Design is the process of determining the properties of an artifact [70]. Design is figuring out what we're going to make, what features it will have, how it will look, how it will be organized, *and* how it will work. Design pervades software development from product conception to maintaining mature systems. Design occurs at all levels of abstraction, from the initial decision to build software all the way down to naming each variable.

Design is **not** a phase or stage between *analysis* and *coding* in some stylized development process [71]. Virtually all software professionals including developers, managers, architects, analysts, maintainers, and quality assurance specialists do design work. For any non-trivial system, there is no clear distinction between designing and programming; programming involves designing, and designing requires programming [72].

Design is different from:

- **Problem Solving.** Designing software is not like solving trigonometry problems. In high school math class, you received specific, well-formed problems. All you had to do was manipulate a bunch of symbols until x was on one side and everything else was on the other side. Rather than solving a well-defined problem, software design involves *imagining* a system that will improve stakeholders' lives.

- **Planning.** Some things (e.g., integrated circuits) can be designed completely on paper, and that *plan* can simply be shipped to a factory. Most software cannot. While software professionals sometimes make plans, most design arises during improvised, moment-to-moment interaction between a programmer and a codebase; and plans are a "weak resource" for informing this improvisation [73].

- **Decision-making.** Designing involves many moment-to-moment interactions between a designer and a product concept in which the designer draws (or writes, edits, etc.) whatever ideas flow freely into their mind. Sometimes, a designer stops to make a conscious decision—choosing one among several alternatives—but most of the time, calling their actions "decision-making" is misleading. Similarly, most code features that seem like the results of conscious decisions actually emerged from improvisation [74].

- **User Experience.** While determining how a user will interact with a system is *part of* designing, designing also includes determining all of the product's other, non-user-experience properties.

- **Architecture.** While determining how a system is organized is part of designing, designing also includes determining all of the product's other non-architectural properties.

- **Modeling.** Some people think that the best way to build software is to model a real-world process and keep refining that model until it's executable. While developers sometimes draw models, model-driven engineering is limited to a few specialized fields.

Designing can also include analyzing, synthesizing, writing, imagining, communicating, negotiating, specifying and creativity; however, design is not *reducible* to any of these activities. Design is its own complex activity and cognitive process.

The Two Kinds of Iteration

Most software professionals now recognize that designing and developing software is intrinsically iterative in a way physical construction is not. Iteration has three overlapping meanings: (1) rhythm of work; (2) prototyping; (3) design thinking.

When we advocate for *iteration-less* development, we just mean that sensemaking, building, releasing, and getting feedback can all happen simultaneously, and the release schedule doesn't have to determine the rhythm of work. Sustainable Dual-Track Development is still iterative in the senses of prototyping and design thinking.

Prototyping

> *Every contrivance of man, every tool, every instrument, every utensil, every article designed for use, of each and every kind, evolved from a very simple beginning.*
> *– Robert Collier*

For agilists, "iteration" means "prototyping". *Prototyping* involves cycles of making sense of the project context, building some features, releasing, and (ideally) stakeholder feedback. Even if the context hasn't evolved much in the meanwhile, building new features changes the team's understanding of the project—its goals, stakeholders, etc. Testing or using new features changes users' expectations, preferences, and understanding of the system.

Most software professionals intuitively understand prototyping. Just like writing or painting, we make something "hopelessly broken, and gradually beat it into shape" [75]. Unfortunately, most software professionals do not realize that developing software involves a different, much faster kind of iteration associated with design thinking.

Design Thinking

For designers (architects, industrial designers, etc.), "iteration," usually means *design thinking*: the cognitive process of generating and elaborating design concepts. Design thinking is not a technique or a method. It is a fundamental cognitive process like communicating or learning.

The designer maintains two mental models called *schemas* [76]. The *product schema* (AKA "design schema," "design candidate," "tentative solution," etc.) is all of their ideas about the product: what it will do (features), how it will do it (algorithms), what it will look like (interface), etc. The product schema also includes things the designer considered and rejected, like a feature they decided to exclude. Meanwhile, the *context schema* contains all of the designer's beliefs, conjectures, and ideas about the project environment, the product's current or prospective users, and the situation(s) the product is intended to help or in which it may be deployed. The context schema includes all of the designer's beliefs and predictions about how the product will affect the world.

As the opening vignette illustrates, design thinking involves mentally oscillating between the context schema and the product schema such that the two schema's co-evolve [77]. The team's understanding of the context and product mature together, affecting one another as they grow [21]. Thinking about the context triggers new design ideas. New design ideas trigger reinterpretation of the context. Designers don't analyze the context *and then* design a product; *analysis and design are the same cognitive process* [78]. *The* most important thing to understand about designing is that designing the product changes our understanding of the context.

Design thinking occurs throughout a software project; however, there's usually more design thinking early in a new product design or when creating a new feature set. Developers, designers, and product managers all engage in design thinking; for example:

- a web developer alternates between fiddling with CSS and refreshing a website to see the results;

- a product manager recognizes a contradiction between two stories, reformulates their understanding of the business case for the product, and then rewrites the stories based on the new understanding; or

- a product designer, while drawing a mock-up, realizes that the product might be useful for a previously unconsidered user group, writes a proto-persona to represent this new user group, and draws new mock-ups to figure out how the system might look for them.

Unfortunately, most people, software professionals, managers, venture capitalists—the entire tech industry really—don't understand coevolution or design thinking at all. They don't have any concept of it, so they don't think to ask, "how can software teams do design thinking better?" or "what can go wrong during design thinking?" The remainder of this chapter aims to answer both questions.

Practices

Numerous practices can help software teams' design thinking (see Figure 8–1). We will explain each of these below.

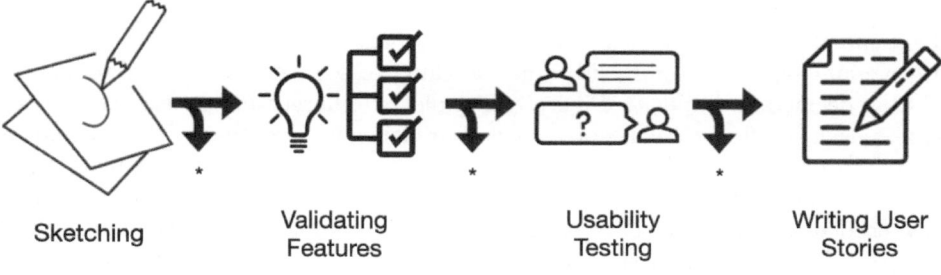

Sketching   Validating   Usability   Writing User
                   Features   Testing   Stories

* return to any previous step

Figure 8–1: An Oversimplified, Step-by-step Guide to Get You Going

Affinity Mapping

In Chapter 7: Making Sense of the Project Environment, we discussed Affinity Mapping, a lightweight qualitative analysis technique for synthesizing insights from notes. Sorting notes into categories helps the team make sense of the project context. However, it also tends to prompt all sorts of different design insights, from *what* the system will do (features) to how to implement it (algorithms, existing technologies) or what the product will look like (user interface), which the team records under a separate "design insights" category. Generating these design insights is the beginning of design thinking.

Sketching

Research on expert designers in many different fields suggests that sketching—drawing informal models and diagrams, rough images, or low-fidelity prototypes—helps them to imagine and elaborate design concepts [79]. (There's no evidence that more formal or structured modeling like Unified Modeling Language (UML) diagrams helps with design thinking.) Sketching and formulating design concepts are actually the same cognitive process [80].

Sketches can be on paper, whiteboards, or digital media. Different teams use different kinds of sketches, but mock-ups are probably the most common. A *mock-up* or *wireframe* is an illustration of a graphical user interface. Mock-ups can be hand-drawn or digitally rendered at varying levels of fidelity.

Mock-ups serve many purposes. Drawing user interfaces—especially multiple versions or alternatives—helps the team refine the design concept. Creating mock-ups can trigger coevolutionary loops wherein the problematic context and design concept are simultaneously reformulated and refined. Thinking about how something will look helps us think about how it should work and vice versa. Designers can use mock-ups to explore the feature space and to promote creativity.

We want to know if the user thinks the product has the wrong features *before* we spend our limited time building them. Iterating on mock-ups is cheaper than iterating on source code, so mock-ups lower the cost of validating the team's ideas; that is, ensuring users will actually use the planned features.

One team at Enjoy was debating buying versus building software to manage website text in multiple languages. I (Todd) did some sketching to see what their ideal tool could look like if they decided to build it. Figure 8–2 explored different design elements to see how to express each intellectual concept as a design element. Eventually, these could become reusable CSS components for a design library. I drew Figure 8–3a to explore the layout of the most important page. The team wanted to optimize translation input and editing, so they needed an intuitive, easy-to-understand, and low-fiction base. During a design workshop, each team member showed their mock-ups. They discussed which elements they liked and why, and iterated on the designs. I drew Figure 8–3b, which illustrates the flow between webpages, to understand how different personas (translator, content manager, and developer) would navigate the system.[1]

Luckily, the team found an acceptable tool they could buy, saving much time and effort. Had the project continued, these sketches would have been converted into electronic

---

[1]We considered recreating these three sketches as vector graphics to look more professional, but then they'd be misleading. Most sketches are best drawn with pencils or markers not a mouse and keyboard.

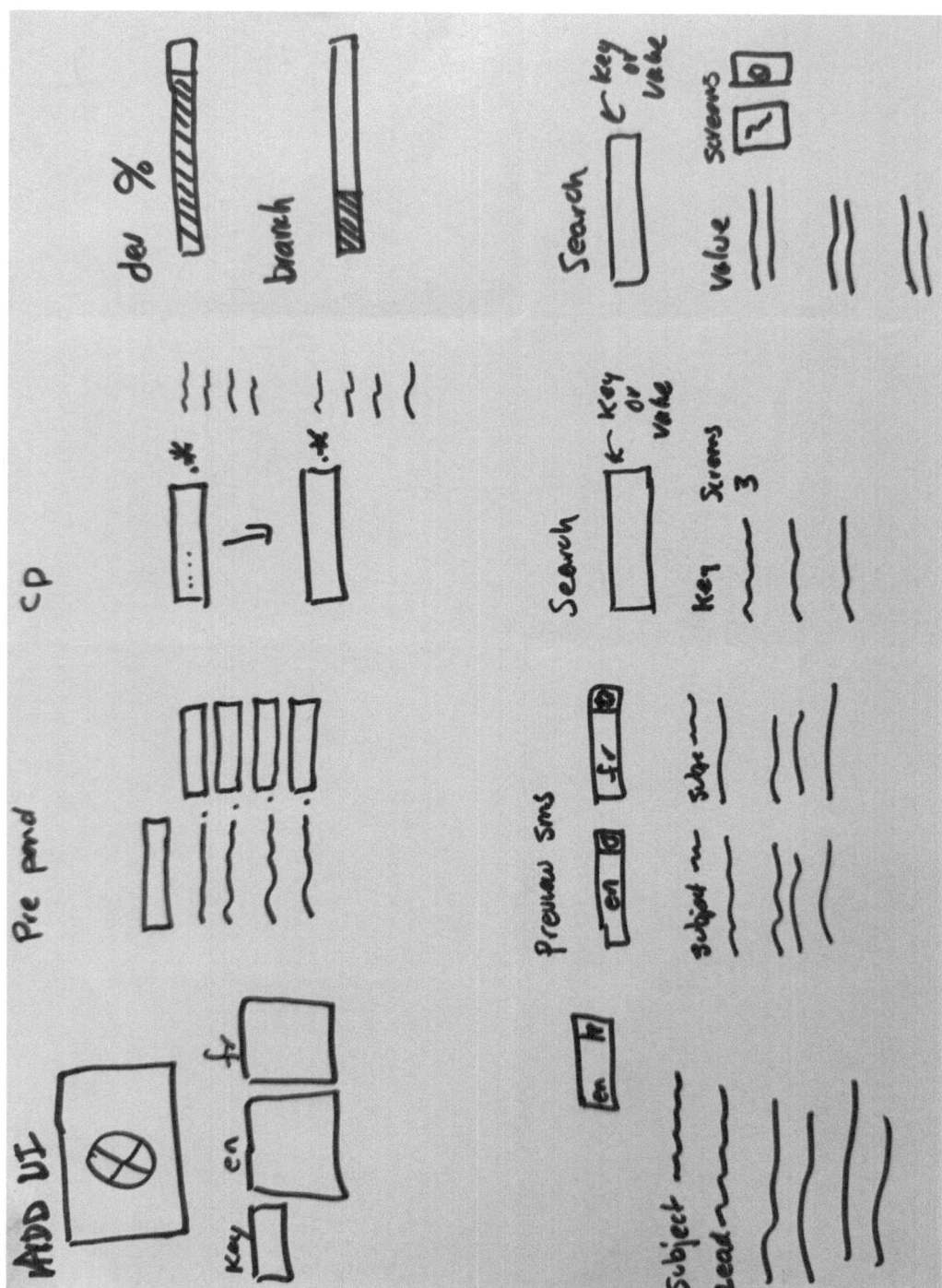

Figure 8–2: Design Elements for a Language Translation Application

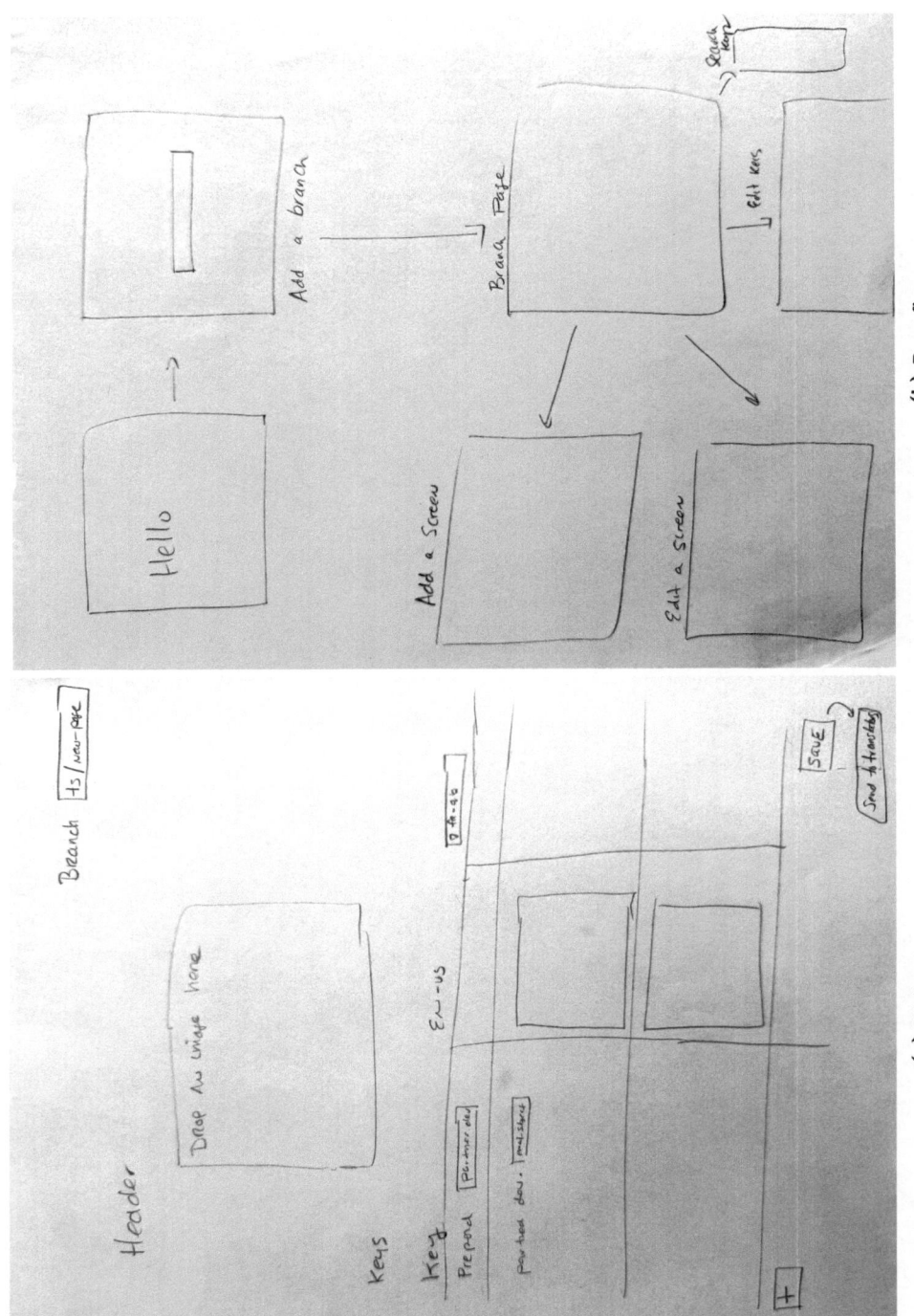

(a) Webpage   (b) Page flow

Figure 8–3: Example Sketches for a Language Translation Application

versions for usability testing. While such high-fidelity digital sketches might look more professional, pencil-and-paper sketching is faster and often superior for early-stage exploration and brainstorming.

High-fidelity mock-ups are better for communicating to developers exactly how the interface should appear. However, high-fidelity prototypes do not elicit more or better feedback from users [81], [82]. Therefore, if your team can make paper prototypes or low-fidelity prototypes faster and cheaper than high-fidelity prototypes, using them for usability testing should be more efficient.

Some product designers intermittently hold a *Design Studio*—a workshop during which the whole team generates and refines mock-ups. Design Studios are best held while initiating a greenfield project or new feature set. A typical Design Studio lasts 3–8 hours. Design Studios usually focus on low-fidelity prototypes to facilitate rapid coevolution and user feedback. Almost anybody, regardless of artistic ability, can draw rough application screens using a pencil and a ruler. High-fidelity prototypes, which require more artistic talent, can be created by the product designer after the team validates the features with users.

We've observed many product designers leading their teams in creating sketches and mock-ups following this process. Each team member independently draws a design concept. The team collectively examines the sketches, sometimes silently, and then iterates by drawing new sketches or mock-ups. Eventually, the team converges on a mock-up and moves on to the next feature (or story or piece of a feature).

While sketching is essential for visual design, teams often begin by replicating *familiar* patterns of features and user interactions (see the sidebar on page 128). Teams may need additional techniques to boost their creativity.

Additional Techniques for Boosting Creativity

The following techniques can help us overcome our own brains' resistance to creativity and design thinking.

- **Divergent prompting.** After team members sketch initial design concepts, challenge everyone to generate completely different design concepts. The concepts could have different features, architecture, underlying technologies, etc.

- **Mind-mapping.** Visualize your mental model of a situation as a diagram, typically showing concepts and relationships.

- **How would _____ solve this problem?** For example, how would Disney build an insurance app? How would Steve Jobs want this heads-up display to look? How would a NASCAR pit crew approach this hospital administration system?

- **How does nature solve this problem?** For example, can the structure of the body's immune system inform the way we design distributed systems? Can we make bots that act like white blood cells or patches informed by memory T cells?

- **Load the subconscious.** Get your situation clear in your mind, then do something that gives your subconscious time to process like going for a bike ride.

- **Assemble more diverse teams.** Teams with greater demographic and experiential diversity are more creative (see Chapter 12).

Design Thinking: Your Brain Is the Enemy

When it comes to design thinking, it's like our own brains conspire against our success. Designers tend to fixate on examples [83] and specifications [59], [84]. They tend to jump to conclusions and resist backtracking on those conclusions [85]. They tend to explore a single design concept instead of the full space of possibilities [78]. They fall prey to various creativity-dampening cognitive biases, including:

1. **confirmation bias:** the tendency to pay more attention to information that is consistent with our existing beliefs than information that challenges our beliefs;

2. **miserly information processing:** the tendency to avoid deep thinking;

3. **default bias:** the tendency to choose options presented as defaults; and the

4. **semmelweis effect:** reflexively rejecting information or ideas that contradict the status quo.

In general, software professionals tend to recreate similar features instead of more novel, innovative designs. For example, most new video games—both independent and AAA—are just clones of previous games with small variations in mechanics and artwork. Perhaps that's fine for videogames, but humanity cannot address the broader crises we face by continuing the status quo.

Resisting the cognitive biases that undermine our credibility is notoriously tricky, and few effective "de-biasing" interventions have been developed [86]. Simply being aware of our bias against creativity doesn't help. You have to redesign your creative process to explore more of the metaphorical space of possible design candidates.

Validating Features

> *Don't design for everyone. It's impossible. All you end up doing*
> *is designing something that makes everyone unhappy.*
> *– Leisa Reichelt*

Feature validation refers to investigating (prospective) user attitudes toward a software product's (potential) attributes. How to validate features depends on the situation, but the goal is always the same: make sure the team's ideas will work for the users. We don't want to build features or whole products that users don't want or won't use.

The product designer recruits a sample of current or prospective users to attend feature validation sessions. The feature validation participants should map into the team's personas. The designer needs to know that Participants 1–3 map to the "Adam the Administrator" persona, while Participants 4–8 represent the "Theresa the Teacher" persona, and so on.

The sessions can occur at the designer's office, in the users' workplaces, in a neutral third-party location (like a coffee shop), or through video conference but one-on-one, face-to-face sessions are the most effective.

During each session, the designer describes the features and shares the mock-ups (either hand-drawn or digital wireframes) with the user(s). Users may review a series of disconnected images explained by the designer, or the designer can facilitate the session by switching the images depending on the user's pretend actions. To elicit users' reactions to feature ideas, the designer uses neutral, non-leading questions like the following.

- What do you think of this feature?

- Would you use this feature—why or why not?

- Does this feature align with your way of working?

- Can you think of anything that might prevent you from using this feature?

- Do you think any of your colleagues would have a problem with this feature? What kind of problem?

Asking about other target users' reactions helps when the participant dislikes the feature but doesn't want to hurt the designer's feelings (a common manifestation of social desirability bias).

If it becomes clear that a user would not use a particular feature, the designer has to figure out whether to invalidate the feature or the user. Invalidating the feature means that the feature is not worth developing; the product needs different features. Invalidating the user (or role or persona) means we need to find a different group of people to use the feature. Failing to identify an appropriate group of users for a feature invalidates the feature.

Feature validation can also include explaining features to (and sharing mock-ups with) non-user stakeholders. Sometimes, when the person who pays for a system is not a user, it's important to check whether the payer (client or sponsor) will accept each feature. However, not all clients desire these kinds of fine-grained interactions.

Feature validation is sometimes combined with *usability testing*.

Usability Testing

Usability testing, or *usability evaluation*, refers to observing current or prospective users completing some tasks with a product or a representation of a product.

Usability testing starts the same way as feature validation: recruiting users that represent personas, roles, or other user groups for one-on-one sessions (unless the application involves inter-user collaboration like a multiplayer video game). Sessions can be recorded using cameras or screen-capture software, or the designer can just take notes. The designer gives the user a series of tasks or goals and observes the user interacting with the product. The designer looks for *breakdowns*; that is, points where the user gets confused, doesn't know what to do, or does the wrong thing. These breakdowns reveal, or at least hint at, usability problems.

For a mature product with an active user base, usability testing often involves actual users using an actual system, release candidate, alpha version, or beta version. In contrast,

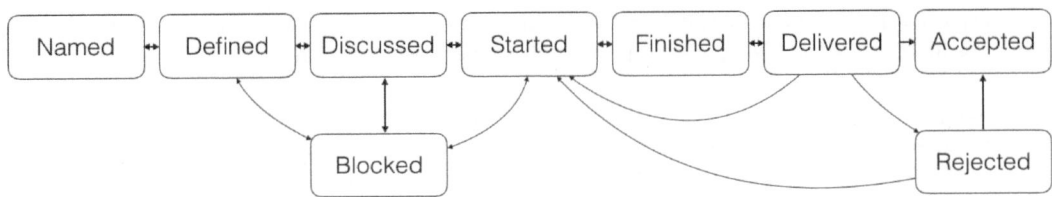

Figure 8–4: (Somewhat Idealized) Story Lifecycle

when the team is first exploring a new feature set, the designer might do usability testing with mock-ups that they manipulate based on the user's actions. When the user pretend-clicks a pretend button, the designer replaces the screen with what the user should see next. If the screen manipulations are being done surreptitiously such that it looks to the user like a working, interactive system, we call it a *Wizard-of-Oz Study* [87]. If the designer uses hand-drawn sketches rigged up to simulate digital interactions, we call it *paper prototyping* [88].

Most of the product designers we've observed use interactive, point-and-click interfaces for usability testing. Product designers need to balance the fidelity of the simulation with the difficulty of creating the simulations. Paper prototypes are low fidelity but are very quick to make, which facilitates more rapid feedback cycles. Building the whole feature or system creates the most accurate simulation but is much slower. High-fidelity mock-ups manipulated by the designer (or a hidden partner) to create the illusion of an interactive system are a good compromise.

Tools without a graphical user interface can also benefit from usability testing. We've seen successful usability testing with command line interfaces (what are the inputs, outputs, and error messages?) and YAML files (do people know what to change and how to change it?). One team learned that the names for their settings in a YAML file were hard to understand. When people modified the configuration, the system didn't work as expected. The team modified the structure of the YAML file to make the tool easier to use. Another did usability testing to improve the wording of confusing error messages.

Writing User Stories

A *user story* is a brief, informal description of some aspect of a software system, expressed as a user action. User stories can be recorded on index cards, sticky notes, spreadsheets, or project management applications. Stories flow through common states (Figure 8–4).

User stories vary widely between teams. Here are some examples:

1. *As* Terry the Teacher, *I want to* sort students by number of absent days, *so that* I can notify parents. (Here, Terry is a persona.)

2. *As an* airline pilot, *I want to* lower the landing gear, *so that* I can land the plane.

3. *As an* advanced user, *I want to* select directories that will not be synced to the cloud, so that I comply with privacy legislation. (Here, "advanced user" is a permission level.)

4. *As a* user, *I want to* log out of the system.

5. Investigate which machine learning algorithm to use for the auto-completion system.

Following a standard story format helps. There are many good formats, but we recommend the following.

As a <persona> I want to <action> so that <goal or benefit>.

Including the *persona* (see Persona Modeling in Chapter 7) helps the team remember who is taking the action and reason about how things should work. For instance, where Terry the Teacher might want a graphical interface, Nancy the Network Administrator might want a command-line interface. If the team doesn't use personas, stories could refer to a role (e.g., student, teacher, school principal, secretary, parent) or permission-level (e.g., regular user, power user, guest user, administrator), but using personas helps tie the stories to the analysis that supports them. Avoid the generic "as a user."

Including the *action* is what makes it a user story. Writing backlog items as specific user actions helps focus the team on usability. Writing stories like "As a user, I want a login screen" or "I want a country drop-down box," insidiously undermines usability by focusing on the system instead of the user. Users probably find both the login screen and the data entry annoying.

Including a *goal* is important for the product manager and the developers. If a product manager cannot articulate why a user wants to take an action, the story may be unnecessary. Meanwhile, the goal helps developers make unforeseen decisions that come up while implementing the story. Many important design decisions are not apparent until the developer begins coding. Developers don't want to stop working and consult the whole team every time an unforeseen aspect of a feature arises.

Not every story needs to follow our recommended template exactly. For example, some product managers write stories about error paths (e.g., "Terry the Teacher uploads an invalid grade spreadsheet") to help developers remember to include appropriate error handling. Such stories don't need a goal if the user's goal isn't relevant to the necessary error handling.

Epic Stories

Epic stories, or just *epics*, are stories that encompass too many changes and require more work than one or two developers can complete in one or two weeks. Epics have an undeserved reputation. It's true that most software developers find it easier and more motivating to complete smaller, more atomic stories, and that novices tend to write stories that are too large. However, epic stories are not intrinsically bad. Product managers can use epics to clarify the product vision and organize releases.

A self-publishing system, for example, might have epics like the following.

- As an author, I want to upload a manuscript, so that it can be published.

- As an author, I want to choose the design and layout of my book, so that it looks good.

- As an editor, I want to offer my services to authors, so that I can get work.

Based on the design-and-layout epic, the product manager might write several more specific stories like:

- As an author, I want to specify the text on the spine of my book.

- As an author, I want to upload an image for my book's front cover, so that I can customize its appearance.

- As an author, I want to upload an image for my book's back cover, so that I can customize its appearance.

- As an author, I want to see a preview of my book, so that I can verify its appearance.

In general, try to write stories that convey the smallest chunk of work that would provide value to the user. A story is probably too big if it will take a developer (or a pair) more than two weeks, or if implementing just part of it would provide value to users. However, it's possible to go overboard writing many teeny-tiny stories. If you have a pair of stories, neither of which provides value without the other, they should probably be combined. When the overhead of writing a story and reviewing it in a story showcase meeting outweighs the benefits of small stories, it's probably too small.

Product managers—especially product managers from pre-agile environments—must learn to compose stories at a good granularity for the developers. If you are a developer and you're annoyed at a product manager for writing epics, keep in mind that your product manager wants you to be efficient. Writing stories is just more difficult than it first appears. In a sense, the developers have to teach the product manager the right granularity through steady, patient feedback.

Story writing is often iterative. If we realize a story is too broad or narrow (e.g. the book preview has five different kinds of previews), the product manager replaces it with more granular stories reflecting each preview type. In contrast, we might have two stories that are so closely related that they should be combined, like the front- and back-cover image stories since some authors want a single image that wraps around the whole book).

Properties of a Good User Story

A good user story is:

- **Valuable to one or more stakeholders.** If the user story is not useful to *any* stakeholder (including users, the development team, management, the public, etc.), then the story is waste [50] and should be deleted.

- **Based on research.** User stories, especially epic stories, should be based on user research. Making up stories about users we don't understand tends to result in products or features that users don't want.

- **Understood by the team.** We want stories that developers can start without asking questions. The developers might not know *how* they are going to implement the story, but they should know exactly *what* needs to be done.

- **Well-formed.** The user story is written in a way that helps the developers remember relevant details and follows the team's formatting guidelines or norms, if any.

- **Small and tractable.** Stories should be as small as is practical. Smaller stories lead to faster feedback, are easier to schedule, provide developers with a sense of accomplishment, and reduce extraneous cognitive load. In principle, a good story describes the smallest possible portion of a feature that delivers value.

- **Not blocked.** A *blocker* is a dependency that prevents developers from working on a story. Blockers include dependence on another story (e.g., a login story requires users to exist), access to a technology or library (e.g. contracts that need signing), or another group (e.g. waiting for the infrastructure team to provide Amazon Web Services (AWS) support)—see Figure 8–4.

- **Elaborated with necessary attachments.** Some stories need a little something extra to help developers keep track of the details (see below).

Acceptance Criteria

Acceptance criteria define when a story is done or restate the story from the system's perspective. They are useful for clarifying the scope of the story (thus combating scope creep) and suggesting appropriate unit tests. Acceptance criteria are often written using the "Given-When-Then" [89] format:

Given <pre-condition>,
When <action>,
Then <post-conditions>.

For example, Figure 8–5 shows a real story about a power user persona, *Patrick*, backing up a relational database. The *Given* statement is the setup or precondition of the story. It explains how the user got into this situation. The *When* statement is the action that the

---

Story name: Dump FUNCTION to predata.sql file

As Patrick the Power User,
I want my backup file to contain the SQL statement to recreate FUNCTION found in my DB,
so that I can restore my DB to a state consistent with when it was backed up.

Acceptance Criteria

Given a database 'functions' containing some FUNCTIONs,
when I run 'backup –dbname functions',
then the backup outputs to the predata.sql the proper 'CREATE FUNCTION' statement to recreate my object, including 'OWNER' and 'COMMENT' statements.

Figure 8–5: Example Story Card

user takes. The *Then* statement is the resulting state of the system—the postconditions or side effects of the story. Developers, the product manager, or both might write acceptance criteria. Acceptance criteria can get more complicated when there are several preconditions, actions, or postconditions.

The acceptance criteria in Figure 8–5 remind the developer of the command syntax to make sure the database has functions and to test for 'function,' 'owner,' and 'comment' statements. They reduce the need to interrupt the product manager for clarifications and discourage the developers from implementing more functionality than necessary (scope creep). Not all stories need acceptance criteria. Only write acceptance criteria when the pre-conditions, actions, or post-conditions are difficult to remember.

Other User Story Attachments: Mock-ups, Dependencies, and Notes

Acceptance criteria are just one of several kinds of artifacts that can be attached to user stories. Some user stories benefit from other attachments or annotations, such as:

- **Mock-ups** are visualizations showing a graphical user interface. For teams working on a graphical user interface, a mock-up reminds developers what the product should look like when the story is done. Typically, small stories implement a portion of a screen. The mock-up reminds the developer how their story fits into the system's larger visual context. In one of our studies, a product manager explained: "I try to attach [a mock-up] to every story. I try not to write a story before [the mock-up] is done, and that works out really well."

- **Dependencies** are links to other stories without which this story cannot be implemented. Most stories can be implemented incrementally such that when the team takes them from the top of the backlog in sequence, the feature is completed. Occasionally, a story is closely (but not obviously) related to other stories, bugs, or chores. Including dependencies may help the team determine who should do what in what order.

- **Labels** indicate the release or epic to which a story belongs. This helps developers keep track of when backports might be necessary, and it helps the product manager stay organized.

- **Notes** help when there's something about a story that's hard to remember, such as names of obscure libraries, algorithms, or techniques (e.g., "use the XYZ framework because the ABC framework is not designed for this").

- **Links** are used when the developers should refer to an external document (e.g., a spreadsheet listing the correct action for all 17 possible states). Like notes, links help when there is something about a story that is difficult to remember.

In summary, attachments may help the team visualize the work and remember complicated details. However, over-complicating stories risks covertly transforming the backlog into a specification, which threatens the core principles of agile development. So use attachments judiciously.

Design Thinking Pitfalls

Several things commonly go wrong during design thinking.

Not having a product designer. One of the main reasons that software projects fail is that many software teams don't have a product designer or user experience specialist. Every software team building a product for humans users needs product design expertise that most developers (and managers and requirements analysts) don't have. Otherwise, you'll usually get the wrong features implemented in an ugly, confusing interface.

Premature convergence. Faced with an ambiguous situation and stakeholders who do not agree, teams must "converge" on a product concept; that is, a high-level mental model of a product and its main features. Deadlines, social pressure, and an array of cognitive biases conspire to push teams toward a product concept prematurely. We are not advocating big design up front. Rather, we're saying that, in any realistically complicated project environment, a few hours is not enough time to consider a plurality of innovative options and settle on a solution concept.

Insufficient exploration. Premature convergence happens when teams fail to explore the full range of possible solutions. Many designers tend to replicate familiar structures, tropes, and features instead of really trying to imagine new, fundamentally better approaches. You can improve exploration using the creativity techniques listed on page 127.

Design fixation. Sometimes, a client will provide an example something similar to what they want. Designers tend to stick too closely to given examples [83], reducing innovation, so, it's best to hold back examples until the team has some initial product concepts.

Requirements fixation. Most requirements documents are incomplete, erroneous, and full of unvalidated, untested opinions and conjectures. Presented as "requirements," designers tend to perceive all those unvalidated opinions as facts, which undermines their critical and creative thinking [59], so avoid labeling anything as a "requirement."

Inability to backtrack. Designers often resist reversing major design decisions. For example, if a team sets out to build a virtual reality app, it can take a lot of evidence, feedback, and problems for them to switch to a conventional 2D or 3D app.

Neglecting the user experience toolbox. User experience researchers and professionals have created a wide range of techniques for investigating and optimizing graphical user interfaces. While a complete account of user experience techniques is beyond the scope of this book, a good product designer will employ various user experience techniques to investigate and improve a product's usability. These techniques come in three basic varieties: usability testing with users (as discussed above); inspection by experts (e.g., cognitive walkthroughs, heuristic walkthroughs, accessibility audits); and modeling techniques (e.g., mock-ups, storyboards). All of these techniques facilitate design thinking.

Don't Turn the Backlog into a Requirements Specification

A product backlog is not a requirements specification, a design specification, or product documentation. A requirement is a formal statement of a need; a user story is an informal description of a feature. A design specification enumerates the design details of a feature; user stories do not. Documentation explains and records information for others; user stories simply remind team members of things they already know. A product backlog is an informal model of work to be done to help a team remember and communicate.

Software projects have an inherent tension between conciseness and clarity, between interpersonal communication and documentation, between agility and bureaucracy. One of the core principles of agile development is to prefer interpersonal communication over documentation. A software team's shared understanding of a product and its context is so complicated and evolves so fast that it is impossible to write down. Specifications and documentation therefore tend to be incomplete, incorrect, and out of date. Software teams are more productive when they rely on interpersonal communication and concise reminders.

Overcomplicating stories and overusing attachments covertly transforms the backlog into a requirements or design specification, which undermines the emphasis on interpersonal communication and knowledge sharing over process and documentation at the heart of agile methods. Adding more detail is intuitively compelling and often emotionally satisfying, but restraint is needed, or developers will revert to skimming or ignoring the text of the user stories.

User stories are so popular because they help engineers remember details *without* trying to capture the details. Sometimes, the most efficient way to help *remember* a conversation is to include a mock-up, list of dependencies, labels showing what epic or release it belongs to, notes, or acceptance criteria. Just don't overdo it.

What kind of details to include in or attach to a story depends on the situation. For example, in a distributed team where interpersonal communication is restricted to certain work hours, more detailed stories might be needed to avoid long delays. There is no foolproof way to determine the optimal details. However, details that *replace* conversations instead of *remind* us of conversations are probably going too far.

Treat Quality Attributes as Goals not Requirements

Another pre-agile concept that inhibits Design Thinking is *non-functional requirements*. Non-functional requirements are a bad way of stating quality attributes. For example: "the web page should load in under 1 second" overstates both the importance of an arbitrary threshold and the importance of the quality attribute. The project won't catastrophically fail if the page loads in 1.01 seconds instead of 0.99 seconds. There's no objective basis for '1 second'; someone just made it up. Worse yet, some teams formalize non-functional requirements as guarantees in their service level agreements, which distract software teams from more important issues.

Instead of stating non-functional requirements, treat quality attributes (e.g., performance, reliability, security, sustainability) as goals that can be handled in several ways:

1. as regular user stories (e.g., "As Scarlet the Scientist, I want to select my cloud backup provider to comply with my organization's privacy rules");

2. as acceptance criteria (e.g., "log failed backups to support troubleshooting");

3. in the definition of done checklist (e.g., "the feature isn't done until the security team reviews it");

4. as a special section of the backlog; or

5. as separate tools or practices, such as intermittent penetration testing, bug bounties, energy testing, or chaos engineering tools.

If the system is too slow, the users will say so during usability testing, and the team can add speeding-up-the-system chores to the backlog. The same goes for reliability, simplicity, understandability, etc.

Similarly, writing "sustainability requirements" in an easily ignored document will be less effective than having engineers who prioritize clean code, a product manager who habitually analyzes the business context, a product design who continuously analyzes the product's stakeholder impact, and testing infrastructure that includes routine energy testing.

If the team designs with security in mind, conducts regular security audits, and employs penetration testing, security problems will be illuminated and fixed. Extensively documenting security requirements is far less effective than penetration testing.

Likewise, inducing disruptions using Netflix-style chaos engineering tools and systematically improving resilience is more effective than documenting reliability requirements.

You Can't "Decompose" Epics into Stories

Sometimes, given an epic story, people will say they need to "decompose" or "divide" it into several more specific stories. You cannot "decompose" an epic into smaller user stories because an epic story is not made of smaller user stories. There is no simple mapping between epics and smaller stories. Writing stories is not merely rearranging information. It is a creative act. You have to *imagine* more details. Writing smaller stories based on epic stories is a kind of *designing*, not *decomposing*.

Summary

In summary, the cognitive process of generating and refining solution concepts is called *design thinking*. During design thinking, the designer maintains two mental models called the *context schema* and the *product schema*. These schemas *co-evolve:* changes to the context schema trigger new ideas in the product schema; elaborating the product schema triggers reframing of the context schema.

To write good user stories, software teams need various practices that support design thinking. Sketching (drawing rough, informal diagrams and mock-ups) is essential for facilitating design thinking. Software teams can use their sketches as a basis for feature validation, usability testing, and the mock-ups typically attached to stories. A good user story is valuable to one or more stakeholders, based on research, understood by the team, as small as is practical, well-formed, not blocked, and fleshed out with necessary attachments (e.g., mock-ups).

Teams should avoid several common design thinking pitfalls, including nailing down a product concept before exploring the metaphorical space of possibilities or getting fixated on examples of existing products or dodgy requirements specifications. While many teams like having clear acceptance criteria for each story, teams should resist the temptation to turn the backlog into a design specification by writing too much documentation.

Part III

Track Two: Unloading the Backlog

for engineers

There are many ways to implement a story. Some teams hurry, take shortcuts, and pile on technical debt (see Tech Debt sidebar on page 147). Other teams seek the perfect solution for all possible futures. Others build features that will only work when every other feature is done, and stakeholders wonder if it will ever ship.

We prefer incrementally delivering small features. Then we can ship the product at any time. We advocate for well-tested code, as it reduces escalations and quality issues, while simplifying refactoring and future development. (It boggles our minds that some consumer websites are tested better than aviation software. Some aviation companies resisted installing build systems that would run the tests on every commit since "that isn't the way we build software here.")

Chapter 9: Introducing Track Two describes the roles and principles of Track Two, and explains some important differences between greenfield and brownfield projects.

Chapter 10: Clean Code and Tests describes our approach to care-taking the code: keeping the code and tests clean while actively removing technical knowledge silos.

Chapter 11: Integrating and Delivering discusses best practices for optimizing a delivery pipeline whether you ship releases daily or annually.

Chapter 9

Introducing Track Two

Any fool can write code that a computer can understand.
Good programmers write code that humans can understand.
– Martin Fowler

 Key Takeaways

- Track Two involves unloading the backlog by implementing stories and delivering features.

- The developers are in charge of Track Two. They write tests, write code, fix bugs, etc.

- Product designers support developers by advising on user interfaces, usability-testing new features, and representing users' perspectives.

- Product managers support developers by clarifying stories.

- Sustainability demands that teams maximize the continuity of the development process and align different social and technical elements.

- Teams have to balance delivering new features with maintaining code quality.

- Technical debt, a popular metaphor for sloppy code, is not recommended for communicating with managers.

- Inattention to code quality increases the risk of the code requiring a complete rewrite.

Replacing Bad Software with Newer, Worse Software

Taylor's team of talented, clever engineers was building a mobile application for facilitating home delivery of medical prescriptions. Instead of doing user research and validation, they iterated mainly on intuition, and their intuition wasn't very good. They created a product that deviated significantly from users' needs.

The team was so concerned about shipping software immediately that they routinely said, "we will refactor later." Predictably, later never came. They were always too busy rushing toward the next milestone to address their burgeoning mountain of technical debt.

After several years of rapid but aimless mutation, the code became so difficult to understand, maintain, and extend that progress ground to a halt. The team confessed to management that they had no choice but to start over.

Management gave them *seven weeks* to recreate a codebase that had taken years to develop. Facing the impossibility of rewriting such a complicated application in time and the unavoidable conclusion that management had learned nothing about the risks of constant, unrealistic deadlines, Taylor resigned.

Taylor found a new team—a team that viewed "every story as an opportunity for refactoring." When engineers found code that was hard to understand, they would take a moment to improve it. If a new engineer couldn't find something in the codebase, the team would reflect on how to make it more discoverable. The team balanced developing new features with caretaking the codebase. Taylor's new managers understood the importance of a sustainable pace for long-term success.

Overview of Track Two

The purpose of Track Two is to balance delivering value (e.g., features) with maintaining the product's long-term viability. Many teams self-sabotage by prioritizing shipping new features over maintaining their codebase, test suite, and technical infrastructure.

Rather than maximizing short-term velocity, Sustainable Dual-Track Development emphasizes consistent progress: delivering and steadily improving a high-quality, efficient, well-organized, sustainable product. However, it doesn't matter how clean the code is if it does the wrong thing. If teams do a bad job of Track One, they tend to build features the users don't want or won't understand how to use.

Track Two Roles

The whole team participates in Track Two, but the engineers do most of the heavy lifting. The engineers:

- write tests and code;

- verify that new features and bug fixes work as the team expects;

- respond to customer escalations;

- fix system vulnerabilities (while monitoring CVEs[1]);

- learn how existing code or systems actually work ("sleuthing"); and

- upgrade dependencies.

Meanwhile, product designers:

- collaborate with developers on fine-tuning the user interface;

- conduct usability testing of new features; and

- answer the team's questions about the product design and user needs, interactions, and interfaces.

In contrast, product managers help:

- clarify stories in progress; and

- manage important information developers discover mid-story (e.g., unexpected dependencies).

Track Two Principles

The main principles of Track Two are to *Maximize Continuity* and *Balance Short-Term and Long-Term Goals*.

Maximize Continuity

Continuity is a metaphor we use for the absence of breaks, blocks, misalignments, barriers, disconnects, and, well, discontinuities, including:

- knowledge silos wherein important information is known only to one or a few people instead of being distributed throughout the team;

- cultural disconnects between professional groups (e.g., managers, developers);

- spatial and temporal disconnects between team members in different offices and time zones;

- organizational barriers between teams like having seperate teams for development and operations;

- strategic disconnects between activities like planning, implementing, and releasing;

- disconnects between versions, such as inconsistent copies of a file on two different development machines;

- features that are ready to deploy piling up in the delivery pipeline;

---

[1]Common Vulnerabilities and Exposures; see: https://cve.mitre.org/

- philosophical conflicts like marketing or sales promising too many features while designers advocate for simplicity and minimalism; and

- misalignments between organizational processes (e.g., accountants budgeting yearly while developers plan weekly).

The success of Track Two, the sustainability of the project, and the efficiency of the team all depend on removing, reducing, or mitigating these discontinuities. For example, we mitigate differences between files using version control. We mitigate knowledge silos using rotational pair programming. We use videoconferencing and messaging systems to overcome the barriers of working remotely. We use continuous delivery to reduce discrepancies between features that are ready and features that are shipped. We mitigate disconnects between development and operations by embracing DevOps (see the History of DevOps sidebar on page 145).

Balance Short-Term and Long-Term Goals

Software companies tend to prioritize short-term outcomes over long-term outcomes in ways that harm stakeholders and undermine success; for example, sabotaging long-term viability by degrading service levels for short-term savings. While some products profit by sharing in their users' success (e.g., `OmniGraffle`[2] helped Paul make neater diagrams for this book), others profit from users' misery (e.g., ransomware, video lottery terminals, "free" games with predatory monetization [91]). Developers work overtime to meet artificial deadlines, then find themselves further behind because of all the mistakes they made during caffeine-fueled all-nighters. Remember: that tall can on your desk gives you wings, like Icarus.

To explore a more detailed example, many developers talk about going into *technical debt*. In 1992, Ward Cunningham introduced debt as a metaphor for the cost of not updating the software's behavior:

> *Shipping first-time code is like going into debt. A little debt speeds development so long as it is paid back promptly with a rewrite... The danger occurs when the debt is not repaid. Every minute spent on not-quite-right code counts as interest on that debt. Entire engineering organizations can be brought to a standstill under the debt load of an unconsolidated implementation. [92]*

He was not talking about deliberately writing sloppy code, intending to fix it later: "I'm never in favor of writing code poorly, but I am in favor of writing code to reflect your current understanding of a problem even if that understanding is partial" [93]. He meant that we have to learn as we go, and the code evolves accordingly.

The idea of technical debt has evolved over time; today it commonly refers to either:

1. the future costs of cutting corners on code quality to ship features sooner; or

2. cruft and disorganization in existing code that encumbers adding new features.

---

[2]https://www.omnigroup.com/omnigraffle

History of DevOps

> *DevOps simply adds the idea that small, cross-functional teams should own the*
> *entire delivery process from concept through user feedback and production*
> *monitoring.*
> *– Mark Schwartz*

In the year 2000, building a website required a team of IT specialists who would order hardware (including application servers, a database server, and a load balancer), rent a physical facility to store the hardware, and connect it to the internet. Once the hardware arrived a couple of months later, the team would upgrade the operating system and install a web or application server. If the application did better than expected, then they would submit more purchase orders for additional hardware.

On-demand cloud computing platforms like Amazon Web Services simplified provisioning hardware and virtual machines. Meanwhile, cloud platform-as-a-service systems such as Heroku and Cloud Foundry simplified application deployments. Instead of waiting for a purchase order to be approved, hardware delivered, and software installed and configured, a company can have a new virtual machine up and running in minutes.

This simplification of provisioning and deployment paved the way for *DevOps*: a single team creating, deploying, operating, and maintaining a product, and the various practices and technologies that enable this one-team approach. Instead of coordinating with the infrastructure team, the development team could own both the creation of the software and its deployment.

Most organizations still needed an infrastructure team to help with the underlying technology and its configuration to optimize settings but, now, an application team can typically deploy to any public infrastructure-as-a-service or on-premise with a single command (e.g., `git push heroku main` or `cf push repo`). This means that a single engineer can shepherd their change from story to production.

However, DevOps is often conflated with continuous deployment. While it's true that DevOps facilitates frequent releases, that is not its only benefit. DevOps can also improve communication, collaboration, time to market, code quality, system reliability, recovery time, team performance, and customer satisfaction, among other benefits [90].

While we might refer to disorganization as technical debt regardless of how it came about, technical debt is principally created by developers rushing to meet calendar-driven software schedules [94]. It's so tempting to take shortcuts. Stakeholders often want new features, and development teams want to keep their stakeholders happy.

But the more technical debt, the more effort is needed to understand, maintain and extend the code. With more technical debt, each additional feature is more expensive to build, each defect is harder to fix, and each new team member is harder to onboard. The more technical debt the team has, the greater the chance they'll have to throw away the whole codebase and start over. This happens far more often than one might think.

Some developers might reason that they might not even be on the project by the time their shortcuts cause problems—let it be someone else's problem. Such attitudes are incommensurate with Sustainable Dual-Track Development. Sustainability necessitates limiting technical debt, and the easiest way to do this is to avoid calendar-driven software schedules. Avoiding technical debt enables a team to balance feature development with caretaking the code by using Continuous Refactoring (see Refactor Continuously in Chapter 10). Resisting shortcuts and refactoring continuously generates well-crafted code. Good testing practices, (see Chapter 10: Clean Code and Tests) also help limit technical debt.

Some teams experience technical debt in their infrastructure as well as their code. For instance, on one DNS security-based project we observed, the team used three test suite managers simultaneously. The team had begun using one test suite manager, disliked its interface, and introduced a second test suite manager. At some point, a new engineer couldn't figure out which one to use, so they added a third test suite manager. Three test suite managers are not sustainable. The team should have either stuck with the first one or converted all the code to the new one. Only introduce new patterns if the team is committed to replicating that pattern throughout the codebase.

A Not-So-Simple Loop

In most software development today, developers own writing the code, testing the code, shipping the code into production (for web and mobile developments) or managing the release (for enterprise software), and supporting the code. In other words, Track Two runs all the way from backlog to customer.

Once we know the next little bit of the system that we want to build, we start with a simple loop. A developer (or pair) takes a single story off the top of the backlog and works on it. They refactor. They write tests. They write code. They do manual verification of interesting conditions. They deliver the story and provide the product manager a means to accept it (e.g., acceptance environments or dev build). They push the accepted code into the release pipeline. Then, they grab the next story off the top of the backlog.

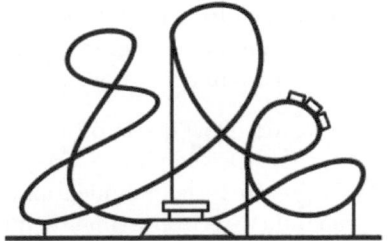

Figure 9–1: A Not-So-Simple Loop

> ### Tech Debt Is a Poor Name
>
> Using the phrase "technical debt" to advocate for more dedicated refactoring time makes no sense to management.
>
> To a manager with an accounting background, debt is great! Taking on debt facilitates growth. The more debt you can get, the faster you can grow, and the longer you can avoid paying those debts, the more money you can make. Barring cash flow problems, a business can service its debts indefinitely because it makes more money from the assets it buys than it pays in interest on the loans needed to buy the assets. Paying debts early reduces profits and creates opportunities for competitors. Managers therefore will want to keep delivering features as fast as possible and ignore debt until they absolutely have to deal with it.
>
> Using technical debt as a metaphor for code quality problems "often leads people astray, as the dynamics don't really match those for financial loans" [95]. Instead, talk about things managers understand: risk and costs.
>
> When management resists refactoring, make a graph of the "risk of encountering an unfixable, catastrophic error" with an exponential curve. Of course, no one has data for this. Just make reasonable guesses "based on your experience." Then, work up a rough cost estimate of rewriting the system from scratch. Make it all look good. Print it on physical paper. Call a meeting, hand the physical paper copies to management, and present the same information in a (professional-looking!) slide deck. Managers tend to take numbers and graphs on physical paper more seriously than people just talking about their concerns. Managers don't understand technical debt; but they understand "exponential risk of $20 million setback." If you work for a start-up, you might be able to show a complete rewrite sinking the whole company. Throw in a line graph charting the marginal cost of the next feature against code quality for good measure.

In practice, teams modify this loop in interesting—and often counterproductive—ways. Some teams deliberate endlessly. They plan out major architectural decisions. They write proofs-of-concept. They design in great detail. Then they write code. Only when the product launches do they realize that they built the wrong thing.

Some teams write code first. They think they'll write tests and refactor later. But then they run behind, or management moves up a release, and testing and refactoring are never finished.

Some teams hurry. New features are viewed as critical to the business's success, and deadlines abound. With a little experience, most developers realize that missing an arbitrary deadline for a trade show does not bankrupt companies or kill projects. Developers grow weary of constant rush mode and its personal toll on their health and relationships. While there may be exceptional moments where a critical business window is closing for a marketplace, time and time again, we see teams hurrying for arbitrary, often meaningless,

New Features   Caretaking the Code

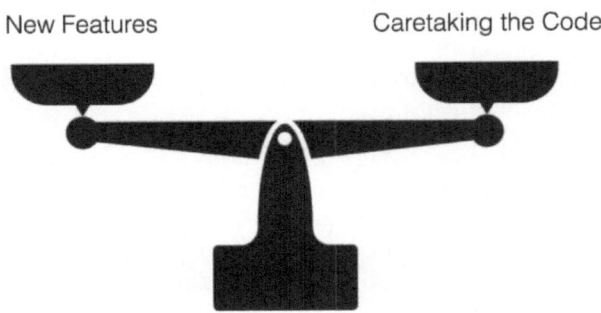

Figure 9–2: Sustainability Means Balancing Features with Refactoring

deadlines. We've seen multiple teams neglect technical debt until their code became so unwieldy that they had to throw it away and start over.

For example, on an iOS project we observed, the product manager pushed the team to deliver more stories to make a release date at the cost of technical debt. Some team members accepted the PM's suggestion, skipped refactoring, and introduced incomprehensible, unmaintainable code. Other team members ignored the PM's suggestion and carried on as usual. The rapidly mounting technical debt hindered pair programming: the pairs that skipped refactoring basically sabotaged the next pair that would work with that part of the code. After the first release, it took several weeks to clean up the mess they had made of the code before they could even begin working on new features. Sometimes, making a deadline is so important that it warrants weeks of post-deadline clean-up, but not often.

In practice, sustainability necessitates balancing delivering new features with maintaining code quality (Figure 9–2). If you spend all your time delivering new features, you will drown in a sea of technical debt. If you spend all of your time optimizing the codebase, you'll fall behind your competitors. However, the psychological game of software development is tilted toward feature delivery, so many teams must deliberately prioritize bug fixes and refactoring to strike an appropriate balance.

Greenfield vs. Brownfield Projects

New (greenfield) projects can maximize long-term productivity and reliability by avoiding technical debt from day one. Avoiding technical debt requires good habits (discussed in the following chapters), including treating each story as an opportunity for refactoring.

For existing (brownfield) projects, digging yourself out of an abyss of technical debt can be challenging. Today's team is delayed and impeded by yesterday's bad decisions, shortcuts, and rushing-induced mistakes. Often, it isn't clear which issue to tackle first. The desire to rewrite the code from scratch looms menacingly in the background.

We have the following suggestions for tackling technical debt in legacy code.

1. Use the strategies suggested in the sidebar on page 147 to convince management that you need dedicated refactoring time.

2. Conduct a *Waste Workshop* (see page 78) to determine where to start.

3. Dedicate one or more weeks to removing technical debt without delivering any new features.

4. Incorporate refactoring into each story. If you estimate each story, include time for refactoring. If management is against refactoring, do not distinguish between refactoring time and story-implementing time.

With existing (brownfield) projects, there's a further tension around aligning the code with our evolving understanding of the system and context. As we work on a system, our understanding of how we'd like the system to work changes over time. No amount of up-front analysis and design can prevent these changes. Both the world and our knowledge of it necessarily evolve over time. Therefore, the team must continually modify the codebase to synchronize it with their current understanding, which is what Cunningham was talking about when he coined the term "technical debt."

Summary

In summary, the engineers do most of the heavy lifting in Track Two, implementing high-priority backlog items, while help out with user experience, and product managers help when unexpected issues arise. Two key considerations are (1) avoiding barriers and disconnects among roles, departments, activities, even hardware; and (2) minimizing the risk of the codebase becoming incomprehensible, unmodifiable, and unfixable when a critical bug emerges.

Chapter 10

Clean Code and Tests

Automated scripts are checking known paths for expected results. That's not truly testing.
Testers discover the unknown... Without human intuitive exploration, a team may be
blind to their most expensive bugs.
– Angie Jones

 Key Takeaways

- Clean code is easy for humans to read and understand.

- Clean code is essential for a product's long-term sustainability.

- Teams must refactor continuously to keep code clean.

- Frequently integrating code changes enables continuous refactoring.

- All code, no matter how clean, must be tested extensively.

- Test-Driven Development (refactoring, writing a failing test, then coding until the test passes) prevents shipping untested code.

- Effective testing requires a break-it mindset with both automated and manual tests.

- Continuously pairing reduces knowledge silos.

- Code should be owned by teams, not individuals.

We'll Refactor Later

Ben always prides himself on delivering high-quality code. Shortly after joining a new team, it became clear that they had been neglecting parts of the code. Running the tests generated 57,000 lines of output, which obscured exceptions and deprecation warnings. Parts of the code used conflicting design patterns such that it wasn't clear which pattern the new code should follow. It was as if the team kept trying new styles but never updated the old code for consistency.

Later in the project, Ben found a document showing the team's thoughts a year prior: the team had intended to reduce complexity, but the constant rush for new releases was all-consuming. The organization's engineering culture had developed a "we'll refactor *later*" attitude. But the team constantly rushed to ship code, so "later" never came.

Ben discussed the issues with his teammates. He raised it at retros. He advocated for dedicated refactoring time. He explained how technical debt increased risk, reduced productivity, and lowered morale. When it became clear that management wouldn't listen, Ben convinced his co-workers to build more refactoring time into their story estimates. If anyone asked why productivity appeared to drop, he said we'd tell them it's because the code is a mess and every enhancement breaks existing features. But no one ever asked.

Ben

Over the next year, the code steadily improved as the team paid down more and more technical debt. Productivity improved. Stories became quicker and easier to implement as the team spent less time searching and debugging. Ben knew that improving the codebase benefited the organization, the team, and the users. But he wondered about the ethics of deceiving management for their own good. Did the ends justify the means?

While beginning greenfield projects is exciting, most software development is more like *caretaking*. Caretaking is how a talented gardener treats their garden: making continuous improvements toward long-term goals.

This is an important difference between software engineering and most other kinds of engineering (mechanical, electrical, aerospace, etc.). Most engineers design artifacts that someone else manufactures and maintains. Software developers design, create, and endlessly modify, improve, and maintain their artifacts. Programming often feels more like weeding a garden than designing a circuit. We find it more helpful to think about programming as caretaking than as construction.

In this chapter, we'll discuss clean code, clean tests, fast tests / builds, and practices that enable these goals including continuous refactoring, test-driven development, and pair programming. We'll then show how pairing removes knowledge silos and engenders team code ownership.

Clean Code

When you work on a commercial product or popular open-source project, your code is simultaneously a set of instructions for computers *and* an essay to future contributors and maintainers about what the system does and why.

Clean code is an umbrella term encompassing many quality criteria, including simplicity, directness, clarity, efficiency, readability, and maintainability, as well as being well thought-out and commented while minimizing duplication. We say "clean" code rather than "good" code to emphasize that the code is easy for people to read, not just efficient for computers. Messy code hinders onboarding new developers, understanding the existing code, and adding features while generally increasing the likelihood of introducing defects.

Many factors affect the cleanliness of code including:

- naming functions (or methods, classes, etc.) such that their purposes are obvious;

- organizing functions (or methods, classes, etc.) such that they have a single responsibility;

- avoiding abstraction layers that impede reasoning about what the system is doing;

- using consistent formatting;

- writing informative error messages;

- using comments to explain important things that cannot be made obvious with code alone;

- continuously refactoring the code (next);

- writing automated tests (later in this chapter);

- explaining *why* a change was made in version control commit messages;

- writing a project `readme` file that explains how to run the tests, build the code, and release the product; and

- preferring simpler code designs.

This is not the kind of book with hundreds of technical examples of clean code. Those books already exist (e.g., [96]), and you probably already know much about writing clean code. Here, instead, we want to explore *why* so much code isn't clean.

Novice programmers often get so caught up with just trying to get the computer to do what they want that they neglect code understandability and maintainability. Students learning programming don't work on long-term commercial systems; they work on small assignments that are done once and forgotten. It is extremely difficult to instill the idea of writing code for humans in students who only work on throw-away prototypes. The typical novice's lack of perspective obscures the benefits of clean code.

However, messy code is often written by good developers who, given the right practices, mindset, and resources, can write clean code. Lack of skill is not the primary driving force behind messy code. Rather, good programmers sometimes write messy code when they're rushing and neglecting practices that tend to produce cleaner code.

More to the point, your team members are who they are (in the short term), and you have to do the best you can with the people you have. Most teams have developers with varying skill levels. Your organization may regularly hire recent graduates, apprentices, or interns. The right practices will help developers of modest skill write clean code.

Less Haste; More Speed

The first practice that facilitates clean coding is managing time pressure. The more management or other stakeholders constantly pressure the team to deliver new features fast, the more likely programmers will neglect code quality. Responding to time pressure is a complex issue with no simple solution. However, we can offer the following suggestions.

- Good product managers shield their teams from external pressures and push back on unrealistic demands. The product manager should reinforce the message that the client can dictate scope or schedule but not both.

- Schedule releases with unknown scope (e.g., we release as much as we can every four months) or commit to releasing certain features as soon as they're ready without a firm date. Do **not** commit to both a release schedule and including specific features in specific releases.

- Address discontinuity with marketing. If marketing promises features and timelines without consulting developers (or over developers' objections), then try to collaborate more with marketing. Failing that, bring the issue directly to senior management, emphasizing the risk of the company missing unrealistic deadlines (see the sidebar on page 155).

- Do not set up a clock or countdown to the next release in the development office. Countdowns increase *stress*, not motivation.

- Don't be afraid to refuse overtime or miss arbitrary deadlines unless you're pretty sure you can't find another equally good or better job.

- If your team provides estimates to external stakeholders, make sure those estimates include time for the quality-assuring practices discussed in the remainder of this chapter (e.g., continuous refactoring, test-driven development). Provide ranges (2–4 weeks) rather than point estimates (3 weeks) to emphasize the limitations of our predictive accuracy.

- Write tests *before* you write your code.

- Perform refactoring related to a story *before* you write the code.

Expectation Disconfirmation Theory

Expectation (Dis)confirmation Theory (EDT) is the secret to convincing marketing to stop overselling your product (e.g., promising certain features by unrealistic deadlines, overstating the benefits of the product).

EDT is a model that explains consumer satisfaction. It basically says that your satisfaction with a product is more about whether it exceeds your expectations than raw performance [97]. If customers expect the software to be mediocre, but it's pretty good, they're usually satisfied. However, if customers expect it to be *amazing* and it's just pretty good, they're usually dissatisfied.

EDT sets up a kind of trap for marketers: undersell the product and no one will buy it; oversell the product and no one will like it. The key is to sell the product without raising expectations beyond that which the developers can just slightly exceed.

You can see EDT at work in the advertising of movies, games, automobiles, vacation packages, and all sorts of consumer goods. Many industries (including entertainment) get away with it because they make most of their money in the initial sale and don't expect a lot of repeat business (e.g., seeing the same movie in theaters multiple times). If you're selling software-as-a-service or have any kind of ad-supported or subscription revenue model that depends on long-term usage, EDT is far more dangerous. Even buy-once software can suffer from a disconfirmation-induced lousy reputation.

So, if you're experiencing conflict with marketing, try speaking with marketing in their own language. Marketing doesn't understand iterative (or iteration-less) development, technical debt, or usability testing. But they *do* understand reputation, expectations, confidence, satisfaction, and customer relationship management. If you can explain how overselling is damaging customer relationships and long-term profitability, they're more likely to listen.

Refactor Continuously

Refactoring refers to changing the structure of code without changing its external behavior (e.g. giving a variable a more descriptive name, splitting a class in two, extracting an interface). Some teams distinguish between *pre-factoring* before implementing a story (typically to make it easier to implement) and *post-factoring* after implementing the story (typically to improve understandability). *Continuous* refactoring refers to improving the codebase systematically and concurrently with new feature development. Continuous refactoring involves making refactoring an integral part of every story. It means seeing each story as an opportunity to refactor and improve the code's design.

Continuous refactoring has many benefits, including:

- making code easier to understand and modify;

- increasing the discoverability of each component (based on its responsibility);

- reducing technical debt; and

- enabling any developer to work on any part of the system (because the whole system is easier to understand).

Neglecting refactoring makes code messy and difficult to modify. It's often tempting to bolt a workaround onto an existing code design but over time, these hacks and workarounds become increasingly difficult. Each new story begins with a dilemma: do we continue haphazard workarounds, or do we refactor so the code makes sense?

This is not the kind of book that has hundreds of refactoring examples. Like with clean code, those books [98] and workshops [99] already exist, and you probably already know heaps about refactoring. Developers don't neglect refactoring because they don't know how to refactor. They neglect refactoring because they face external barriers [100] including:

- insufficient time or resources;

- perceiving that the benefits of refactoring do not justify the costs;

- arguing that "you should have done it *right* the first time;"

- management discouraging refactoring explicitly or implicitly (via aggressive scheduling); and

- lack of tool support.

Over time, needed refactorings become larger and more complicated. This increases technical difficulty and the risk of creating unforeseen problems [100].

Postponing refactoring may be necessary in extreme situations, for instance, when the company faces bankruptcy if the next version is not released soon. Furthermore, it is possible to spend so much time perfecting existing code that no new features get built. However, most teams refactor insufficiently and mistake routine situations for extreme ones. Without continuous refactoring, the team steadily marches toward abandoning the codebase and starting over. Merging code into version control becomes increasingly problematic, which further discourages continuous refactoring. Like weeding a garden or maintaining our fitness, the more diligent we are, the easier it is, and the longer we neglect it, the more difficult it becomes. It's not a linear relationship. Neglect two hours worth of refactoring a week for five weeks, and you end up with 20 or 30 hours of refactoring instead of 10.

Continuous refactoring involves refines a codebase towards more simple, intention-revealing, and discoverable code. Most small refactorings are straightforward. When developers identify something wrong or disorganized, they simply fix it.

As you work on a codebase, your understanding of it evolves. New features affect the way the team views the code's design. Continuous refactoring realigns the code with the team's current understanding. You learn to listen to the code and empathize with it.

Refactoring with confidence demands a high-quality test suite. When you have comprehensive tests, you don't have to worry so much about messing up a refactor and introducing undetected critical errors because the test suite will catch them.

When Two Choices Look Promising, Follow Code Design Principles

As you refactor, you will want to keep some code design principles in mind. For object-oriented systems, many software engineers follow the SOLID code design principles [101]:

- Single-responsibility principle: a class should have one purpose or job. Ideally, changes in functionality are localized to one place.

- Open-closed principle: once a software construct (e.g., class, method) is completed, developers should be able to extend its behavior without modifying its source code [102].

- Liskov substitution principle: software constructs can be replaced by their subtypes without changing program correctness (see [103], [102]).

- Interface segregation principle: prefer many client-specific interfaces over one general-purpose interface.

- Dependency inversion principle: the code should rely on abstractions but not concrete constructs.

Further information on software architecture and low-level code design is beyond the scope of this book but readily available [104], [105], [106].

Inception Refactor

While coding, we often discover the refactorings we wished existed before starting the work—'if only the code had a different interface or a different structure, this would be easier.' In this situation, we have a few options: ignore it (lowering code quality), incorporate the refactoring into your current story (introducing confusion into version control changes), or try an *Inception Refactor*.

An Inception Refactor has the following steps:

1. Hide all your changes (e.g., using Git's stash feature), placing the project back into a green state.

2. Refactor the code.

3. Verify that the tests are all green.

4. Commit the change to version control.

5. Un-hide (e.g., un-stash) the original changes and carry on.

The key is to start at a green state where all the tests pass, shift the code into a more desirable position, verify that we are still green, and continue with the original work. In other words, you separate the refactoring from the other changes into different pull requests.

It is possible, but overwhelming, to have multiple Inception Refactorings happening simultaneously, so stick to one Inception Refactor at a time.

Test-Driven Development / Behavior-Driven Development

Code without tests is bad code... With tests, we can change the behavior
our code quickly and verifiably. Without them, we really don't know
if our code is getting better or worse.
– Michael C. Feathers

Software professionals need skill in many types of testing—precisely which types depend on the nature of the project and the professional's role. In Sustainable Dual-Track Development, all three major roles (developer, product designer, and product manager) do testing, just different kinds. Developers create automated tests with deep knowledge of implementation details, focusing on how modifications affect the code's behavior. Product designers manually test user experience. Product managers test from a fresh perspective, focusing on how they can break the system.

At a high level, *transparent-box testing*[1] is when you have the source code, while *opaque-box testing*[2] is when—at least in principle—you don't know how the system works and can't see the source code. Programmers do lots of automated, transparent-box testing; however, some forms of opaque-box testing are crucial for quality assurance, usability, and security.

Transparent-box testing includes unit testing and integration testing. *Unit testing* involves isolated testing of small code segments (e.g., individual methods or functions). Unit test results depend only on the code segment and the test. Developers do unit testing while working on a file. *Integration testing*, in contrast, checks whether a system's components interact as expected. Integration test results depend on two or more code segments and, of course, the test itself.

Unit and integration testing are so ubiquitous that you probably already have lots of experience with them. If not, there are many good books on these topics (e.g., [107], [108], [109], [110], [111]).

Over time, testing terms have taken on different meanings in different contexts. One person's "integration" test is another person's "integrated" test is another person's "journey" test, which could easily be an "end-to-end" test or an "acceptance" test. For example, on the Cluster API project for Kubernetes, they define integration tests as focused on the behavior of an entire controller or the interactions between two controllers, while end-to-end tests verify the "functioning of a Cluster API management cluster in an environment that resembles a real production environment" [112]. Even the term "unit tests" is overloaded. Many see unit tests as testing a specific function or method quickly and in isolation. Yet, we've seen a single "unit test" that took 10 minutes to run and would exercise significant portions of the codebase.

When discussing testing, therefore, beware of contrasting definitions. Don't be afraid to say exactly what you mean by a certain kind of testing to make sure the whole team is on the

---

[1]Formerly called white-box testing.
[2]Formerly called black-box testing.

same page. Try defining the testing terms your team uses during a retrospective meeting. You'll be surprised how often team members disagree on the meaning of ubiquitous terms.

In building a testing strategy, we can consider tests as "narrow" (focus on a single unit) versus "broad" (exercise large parts of the system) or "isolated" (only test the code under test utilizing stubs, mocks, etc.) versus "sociable" (executes code that is not under test).[3]

In the Cluster API project, integration tests are narrow-sociable, whereas their end-to-end tests are broad-sociable.

TDD and BDD

Still today, many projects have production code with no tests or wildly inadequate tests. Code without tests is like a medical drug without randomized controlled trials: we don't know if it works, and it might have deadly side effects. Like scientific experiments, tests separate trustworthy systems from snake oil. Confidence in untested code is delusional. The need for extensive testing isn't a slight against your individual skill as a developer. It is an acknowledgment that software systems are mind-numbingly complicated, no one writes perfect code all of the time, multiple people modify code over its lifetime, and stakeholders (including other members of your team) need assurance that code works as intended. Code without tests should not be treated as production code. We once observed a team refuse to integrate another team's code because there was no corresponding test suite.

Testing is not a phase or stage in the software development process. Various types of testing occur throughout a project, and testing includes such a diversity of activities that some kinds of testing are part of Track One while others are part of Track Two.

In Test-Driven Development (TDD) and Behavior-Driven Development (BDD), developers write automated tests before writing the code that will make those tests pass. Before TDD / BDD, developers would change the codebase, write some tests, and then see if they pass. With TDD / BDD, developers write tests, *ensure they fail*, and then modify the codebase until all the tests pass.

In TDD, developers write *unit tests* before writing the code that should make those tests pass. In BDD, developers write *integration tests* before writing the code that should make those tests pass.[4] In other words, TDD tests typically focus on object behavior, while BDD tests typically represent system behavior (interactions between the user and the system). Developers often combine TDD and BDD, that is, writing a combination of unit and integration tests prior to changing the codebase.

Teams often debate which testing strategies to use. For example, do we want to mock out third-party systems so that our tests are faster? But then what happens when the third-party system changes its API, and we don't notice until an issue occurs in production? Some teams will decide to rely on heavy mocking strategies, while others eschew mocks entirely. But before having that debate, consider what characteristics you value in your test suite.

---

[3]This terminology comes from James Shore [113], who adapted it from Jay Fields's book *Working Effectively with Unit Tests* [110].

[4]Some people say BDD means writing "acceptance tests" first, but they mean integration tests that show that a feature functions as expected. Acceptance testing typically refers to evaluating a product in a simulated production environment, which we discuss in Chapters 4 and 11.

Attributes of a Good Test Suite

Automated tests have a simple structure: precondition, action, postcondition. The precondition sets up the system into an interesting state, the action is the method or function that we want to test, and the postcondition verifies any changes in state or side effects. However, it's easy to write tests that do not adequately exercise the system. We call all of a product's automated tests its *test suite*. A good test suite has the following attributes.

- **Behavior-revealing:** tests should document code and help a developer understand the system's behavior. Each test should reveal how the corresponding code works.

- **Discoverable:** tests should be easy to find. When modifying existing code, finding the tests that describe the behavior should be easy.

- **Valuable:** tests should verify something important. We've seen tests for a method that didn't exercise the method. It's all too easy to write tests that exercise the framework's correctness (such as storing and loading data from a database) instead of verifying the specific code we are adding.

- **Fast:** tests should be efficient. Waiting for slow tests wastes time, encourages multitasking, and sometimes requires a re-run of the whole test suite. (Teams should periodically prioritize reducing the test suite running time.)

- **Clean:** tests should leave the system in exactly the same state it was before the test was executed. Any remaining differences are called *side effects* or *test pollution*. Test pollution prevents tests from being re-sequenced—changing the test sequence changes the results. One project we observed had so much pollution that merely *renaming* some tests made the test suite fail. Eventually, the team had to determine which tests had size effects by brute force: executing random pairs of tests all weekend.

- **Reliable:** tests should always produce the same result when run on a given configuration. Unreliable (or flaky[5]) tests undermine the team's ability to merge commits and ship code and the value of continuous integration systems (see Build System in Chapter 11). Unreliable tests plus slow builds equals fewer opportunities to merge code.

- **Parallelizable:** clean tests with no side effects can be run in any order and parallelized, which improves running time. Ideally, all tests can be run on a developer's system.

- **Revealing:** when a test fails, it should tell you what is broken.

- **Accurate:** when the build is green, the code should really work, and when it's red, there should be a real issue. In other words, a good test suite rarely produces false positives or false negatives.

---

[5]We don't use the term *flaky* because it implies that the solution is to re-run the test rather than fix the underlying issue.

- **Flexible:** tests should be written such that small changes in implementation do not necessitate large changes in the test suite. Flexible tests facilitate refactoring.

- **Exists:** tests should exercise each important aspect of the code. We've seen test suites remain green even when important business logic was deleted.

The Double-Edge of Automated Testing

As the industry embraced automated testing, especially unit testing, teams were able to create increasingly complicated software without being overwhelmed by bugs. Modern software systems have far lower fault density (bugs per unit of size) than their predecessors. However, extensive unit testing leads to overconfidence in the code for two reasons: (1) many developers struggle to adopt an appropriate testing mindset (see The Testing Mindset next), and (2) there are whole categories of problems automated tests cannot detect (see Testing for Resiliency, Security, and Usability below).

The Testing Mindset

An American, a Brit, and a software tester walk into a cafe. The American orders a coffee. The Brit orders a tea. The tester orders a cow, -1 lattes, 2^{64} mochas, an empty set, a null pointer, and `DROP TABLE *`;

Like everyone else, software developers suffer from confirmation bias—the tendency to seek and attend to information that supports one's pre-existing beliefs. Confirmation bias manifests as writing tests that *confirm* that the system works instead of identifying defects [114]. If we have a method, `getObjects{int x}` that returns x objects, and we write a unit test that calls `getObjects{4}`, which passes if the method returns four objects, we are confirming that the method works rather than trying to break it. This is a great place to start but a terrible place to finish. We need to call the method in ways that are more likely to elicit incorrect behavior, like asking for -1 objects.

The trouble is that confirmation bias is very powerful. A developer who thinks their code works correctly is less likely to write tests that cover all the interesting scenarios after writing the code. Simply warning developers to write good, strong tests won't help much, and while it is possible to get better with practice, years of experience is not a good predictor of susceptibility to confirmation bias [114]. Combining the developer and tester roles fixed many problems, but combination developer-testers struggle more to write comprehensive, tough tests.

One approach to overcome confirmation bias is mutation testing. *Mutation testing* is a systematic way of evaluating a test suite by creating variations of the source code, called *mutants*, using rules called *mutation operators* [115]. The mutation operators are based on common programmer errors, so most mutants contain errors. Therefore, when we run the test suite on a mutant, one or more tests should fail. If not, there's a hole in the tests. Mutation testing involves generating hordes of mutants and running the test suite on all of them. Each undetected mutant reveals a flaw in the test suite.

Testing for Resiliency, Security, and Usability

Unit and integration tests are insufficient for assessing resiliency, security, or usability. A unit test simply cannot tell you, for example, that your security has a vulnerability you never considered or that your graphical user interface is confusing.

Resiliency is a system's ability to detect, respond to, and recover from adverse events like a hardware failure or connection loss. No one writes perfect code, so we need a systematic way of assessing and improving resiliency; that is, chaos engineering. *Chaos engineering*, pioneered by Netflix, involves observing the consequences of intentionally breaking pieces of a live production software system. For example, a chaos tool might randomly shut down a server (or an entire data center), artificially increase latency, or disconnect a third-party service. Crucially, these problems are not simulations—chaos tools introduce problems in real production systems—but they do so at a time when developers are ready to respond to unexpected complications.

Chaos engineering is the most effective known way of assessing and improving resiliency in distributed systems. The main reason more companies don't use it is fear and short-sightedness. The whole point of chaos engineering is to make major problems arise when developers are available to fix them—10 AM on a weekday not 1 AM on a weekend. That said, some systems cannot safely support chaos engineering. For example, we cannot remotely shut off the safety features of autonomous vehicles on busy streets just to see what happens.

Similarly, while part of being a good software developer is knowing how to design and implement secure systems, there's something about building a system that blinds us to its vulnerabilities. Computer security is difficult, and there's always a chance we miss something. Independent penetration testing is, therefore, indispensable for assessing a system's security. *Penetration testing*, or *pen-testing*, involves giving someone *who is not a member of your team* a specific goal, such as gaining access to a particular file and waiting to see if they can do it. Some organizations hire external security consultants, while others have an internal security team. In either case, pen-testing quality greatly depends on the skills of the tester. If the best hackers you can find can't break your security, it's probably pretty good.

The main limitation of penetration testing is cost. Good pen-testing is *expensive*. Therefore, teams should do everything within reason to improve the system's security before engaging an external pen-tester. If your team cannot afford professional pen-testing, try contacting the computer science department at your local university. Many professors who teach computer security would welcome a real-world case study for their class. (Imagine a class of 30 computer science masters students whose term project is to complete a series of pen-testing goals on your system and write a report explaining how they did it.) While this approach does entail some risk (e.g., one of the students might do something nefarious), ignoring pen-testing is riskier.

On a different note, there is no automated test that fails when your app aggravates your users or doesn't meet their needs. That's why usability testing is crucial for both designing and maintaining any user-facing product (see Chapter 8: Design Thinking). To be absolutely clear, no amount or combination of automated testing, telemetry, A/B testing, questionnaires, or internal alpha testing can replace extensive usability testing with actual users.

Before agile, many teams strictly separated "developers" from "testers." Agile broke down these barriers, and now most developers write automated, transparent-box tests. However, some kinds of testing are best performed by someone other than the developer who wrote the code being tested. You can *try* to pen-test your own code, but even when you've removed all the vulnerabilities you can find, an external expert will likely find more. You can and should assess the usability of your product, but internal UX testing cannot entirely replace the fresh eyes of an expert who isn't familiar with your product, norms, or conventions. Testing is one area where allowing some discontinuity between *the team* and a specialist can lead to a higher-quality product.

Automated Test Suite Gone Awry

One team that we observed managed unreliable tests by building a system on top of the test suite to suppress their failures. When a test failed sporadically, and they couldn't figure out why, they'd just add it to the ignore list. They didn't want to "waste time" fixing the tests or the hidden bugs. So, when all of those unreliable tests surfaced legitimate bugs, they didn't notice... until they slammed headlong into critical bugs they could neither ignore nor fix because the test suite was such a mess they didn't know what was going on. They had to suspend new feature development for *several months* to fix the unreliable tests and a mountain of bugs they didn't know they had. The morale of this story is don't tolerate unreliable tests.

Benefits and Drawbacks of TDD / BDD

Writing tests first has many benefits:

1. You can't ship untested code if you always write tests first.

2. First writing a failing test and then seeing it pass boosts confidence compared to tests that were always green.

3. Increased confidence in the test suite improves developers' willingness to change any part of the code.

4. The process of writing tests for a story helps developers identify gaps in their understanding of the story *before* implementing the wrong thing.

5. Writing tests first dovetails with continuous refactoring.

Unsurprisingly, empirical studies have found that TDD improves software quality [116], [117]. Some evidence suggests that this quality improvement comes at the cost of reduced productivity [116], while other studies found no impact on productivity [117]. Indeed, believing that TDD will harm productivity is one of several factors inhibiting the uptake of TDD, along with "insufficient TDD experience / knowledge, lack of upfront-code-design, domain and tool specific issues, lack of developer skill in writing test cases, insufficient adherence to TDD protocol, and legacy code" [118]. Our view is that, like so many Sustainable Dual-Track Development practices, TDD makes teams a little less productive in the short term and much more productive in the long term, which would account for these conflicting results.

Practices Related to TDD / BDD

TDD and BDD are closely related to continuous refactoring. Developers who adopt TDD or BDD typically implement features in cycles of writing tests, writing code, and refactoring. Much of the system's architecture emerges from these rapid testing-coding-refactoring cycles. Combining TDD / BDD with continuous refactoring should improve test suite modifiability. Refactoring without a good test suite is difficult because it's so easy to introduce undetected errors and behavior changes.

TDD and BDD are also related to acceptance criteria. The acceptance criteria attached to a user story inform integration tests in Behavior Driven Development or top-level unit tests in Test Driven Development. Alternatively, these tests can be used in place of natural-language acceptance criteria.

If tests are missing, then they need to be added. Adding missing tests after the fact is sometimes called *back-filling* tests (see [111] for advice on back-filling tests to enable refactoring). However, frequent back-filling indicates that the team is not doing TDD effectively.

Fast Tests and Fast Builds

When the build takes an hour, we can only build around eight times per day. When the build takes two hours, we only have four windows per day to merge our changes. The longer the build, the longer it takes to recover from a commit that breaks the build, and the more likely the team's ability to ship code will suffer. Even if a fix is immediately available, it'll take time to get the build green again.

We want test suites that can be run quickly after each change to the codebase but before submitting the code to version control. When tests are fast, the developer can run the tests before every `git push`. With Git, a git-hook can be used to run the tests automatically, or the build tools (e.g., `make`, `rake`, `ant`, `grunt`, etc.) can run the test before pushing. To fetch, run static analysis, run tests, and push code, some teams create a build target such as:

```
git pull -r; git rebase main; make linters; make tests; git push
```

Some software products need to handle many configurations. If it's possible to test all possible configurations, that would be great! If not, then many strategies have been proposed for effective configuration sampling (see [119] for an overview).

During the natural course of development, however, tests will accumulate, and running the test suite will take longer. You can counteract this tendency in several ways:

1. Periodically evaluate the usefulness of each test and look for improvements in test performance. If a test is valuable but inefficient, rewrite it.

2. Delete superfluous tests. Some tests outlive their usefulness (e.g., a test for a deprecated function).

3. Prioritize business-critical features for integration testing. Unit tests are faster and more reliable than integration tests, so we prefer writing many unit tests. Save integration tests for the important stuff; for instance, opening new accounts might be more important than customizing backgrounds.

4. Break the test suite into smaller sections and run them concurrently.

5. Run (random) subsets of tests. If running *all* of the tests is just too slow, we might run all the integration tests and a random subset of unit tests on each build. Of course, this does entail a greater risk of deploying a defect.

6. Run a large number of fast tests that excise large portions of the codebase. Long-running integration tests or performance tests can then be run only in a continuous integration system (see Build System in Chapter 11).

Design Code Continuously: Design What You Need

Design means determining the properties of the system. Track One focuses on high-level properties including features (what it does) and user experience (how it looks). Track Two focuses on low-level properties like the structures of classes (or functions, etc., depending on your programming paradigm) and interactions between them. This is sometimes called *code design*: formulating and organizing code to satisfy readability, performance, or other quality attributes. When programmers talk about design, they usually mean code design. If you see lines of code, a diagram of class structure, or a diagram of interactions between classes, you're probably talking about code design.

Code design is all about managing a paradox: we have to build the system to figure out how it should be built. Too much up-front code design is wasted as our understanding of the product evolves and changes in its features require changes in its code design, but too little code design breeds unnecessary rework. Developers can manage this paradox based on the following principles:

1. If backtracking on a decision is difficult, then spend more time on it.

2. Delay important code design decisions until they are necessary.

3. Avoid building functionality for possible futures that may never materialize.

For example, choosing a programming language warrants some thought because it will be expensive to change later. Designing an external interface for a customer's scripts might be difficult to change, but perhaps you don't need to commit to a design until you're ready to implement it. In contrast, logging statements are typically easy to modify throughout a project, so developers need not fret about getting them perfect on the first try.

Consider this example from a real project we observed: Andrew refactored some code that displayed the date as "Today," "Tomorrow," "Wednesday," etc. Rita reviewed Andrew's change and recommended modifying the method to take an optional parameter, `display_time_zone`. Rita felt that the system would probably need to display time zones in the future, so Andrew should add it now while it's fresh in his mind. Andrew felt that since the system did not currently need to display time zones and may never need to, it should wait.

Neither Andrew nor Rita is objectively right or wrong. It depends on how confident they are that the time zone feature will be needed and the difference in effort between adding it now versus later. Sometimes, "just doing it now" is the right call, but developers tend to spend undue time and resources designing for a future that never arrives.

The popular concept You Aren't Going to Need It (YAGNI) encourages the team to delay working on features until they are needed. This implies that developers postpone code design decisions for as long as possible and focus on solving immediate problems. The idea is to delay decisions until the feature we are building today requires the decision to be made. We worry about future stories when they arrive, not now. You can think of this as *continuous code design*.

In one project we observed, the team needed to build a workload manager for a particular multi-node database. The team guessed that other systems might eventually use the workload manager so they designed the code to separate what was needed for managing any workload from what was needed to interact with the database at hand. This separation hindered testing, deployment, maintenance, and adding new features. Over time, it became obvious that the workload manager wasn't needed for any other internal projects and had no future as a stand-alone system. So much effort was wasted because an expected future use case never materialized. The team would have been better off focusing on their immediate needs.

In contrast, another team we observed was building a connected car application with an iOS and Android front-end. However, the team did not have access to the back-end systems with which the front-end was to communicate, so they introduced a middle layer. When the team finally had access to the back-end systems, they could modify the middle layer as needed without repeating Apple's lengthy approval process. In this case, the added architectural complexity of the the middle layer paid off by giving the team needed flexibility.

Sometimes teams delay decisions for too long. We once saw a team delay introducing a database by storing information in text files, which quickly became untenable. Using a database from the beginning would have been more efficient. Generally, introduce a tool as soon as a story requires it.

To summarize, assume the engineers will continue designing the code the whole time the product is under active development. Delay features and design decisions until they are needed, *but no longer*. When in doubt, allow future stories to take care of future needs.

This all gets easier with experience. Over time, engineers develop increasingly good instincts for which decisions can be safely delayed, which decisions are easy to change (e.g., internal interfaces, code structure, choice of external systems with common interfaces) and which are harder to change (e.g., programming language, interface depended on by external systems).

Being present with your code also helps. Some teams worry so much about possible futures while their code is stuck in last year's mental models. Bringing all the code in line with our current understanding of the context, product, and codebase takes time, effort, and discipline; however, continuously designing and refactoring helps teams cope when the inevitable, unexpected change arrives.

Pair Continuously

Pairing refers to two people working together to achieve a common goal. The two people act as a single unit: not you do task A while I do task B; *we* do task A together, then *we* do task B together. When one person takes a break, so does the other. The pair share their moment-to-moment actions. Pairing is an alternative to *soloing*; that is, working individually.

Pairing doesn't necessarily mean the two people are in the same room, look at the same screen, or share the same input devices. Two people can pair over a video call, or just an audio call, as long as they continuously interact with each other and the same work materials (e.g., the same file). Examples include two designers collaborating on building a design mock-up, two product managers analyzing stakeholder feedback, or a designer and an engineer tweaking a user interface. Here, we focus on pair programming, but many of the concepts discussed below apply to other kinds of pairing.

Two engineers writing code together is called *pair programming*. **We recommend pair programming continuously**; that is, pair programming should be the default manner of programming. Some teams pair program periodically when onboarding a new team member or working on a particularly tricky story. Ad hoc pair programming is better than always soloing, but continuous pair programming is *much* more effective.

When people first learn about pair programming, they always ask the same thing: "Won't pair programming make the system take twice as long to build?" No, it won't. In the *short term*, a pair is faster than one individual soloing and slower than two individuals soloing. But in the *long term*, pairing is faster than soloing because:

1. Pair programming produces higher-quality, better-designed, more understandable code with less technical debt and fewer bugs [120], [121], [122].

2. Pair programming spreads knowledge around the team such that when team members leave, knowledge is not lost, and the team's productivity is not disrupted [123], [124].

Sometimes, managers resist pair programming because it seems like two people are doing one person's job. They have it backward. The long-term costs of soloing—lower quality software and less resilient teams—are not justified by small, short-term speed improvements.

Pairing helps in many other ways. It discourages shortcuts, encourages following best practices and norms, helps onboard new team members, and promotes readable, discoverable, well-commented code. Pairs are more creative, incorporate more ideas, and typically find better solutions with fewer mistakes. Two programmers with different skill sets working together can create ingenious solutions that would evade either individual. Pairing also promotes team code ownership (see below) since, when two people contribute to code, neither feels exclusive ownership.

When there is an odd number of developers, one developer may have to work solo. Instead of writing production code, solo developers should focus on low-risk activities (e.g.,

Figure 10–1: A Pairing Workstation Setup

chores, emails, code reviews, accelerating the build system or test suite, assisting the product designer or product manager, reviewing pull requests on open-source projects).

A single engineer writing code with an AI chatbot or other code generation tool is *not* pair programming. While AI tools can assist an engineer in many ways, working with an AI agent does not transfer knowledge from one teammate to another, enhance team cohesion, or help groups mature. Proponents of AI agents for pair programming misunderstand the primary benefits of pairing. How can each team member working individually with an AI-powered assistant possibly help them build trust in each other?

Co-located and Remote Pairing Setups

Back to *pair* programming, the computer setup should use two monitors, keyboards, and mice to equalize access for each person (Figure 10–1).[6] In co-located pair programming, some developers prefer sitting side-by-side at the same desk, others prefer sitting back to back. It doesn't matter, as long as they can both see their screen and hear each other clearly.

In remote pairing, each individual has their own machine, keyboard, and mouse. Video is unnecessary. Audio is sufficient, but asynchronous texting is *not*.[7] Pair programming requires continuous dialogue. The pairs should type code and converse aloud. Software packages specifically for remote pairing may help.

Regardless, the setup should facilitate each person's productivity (e.g., allowing each person to install preferred software). Teams can standardize tooling and configuration with workstation-setup scripts, allowing any member to be productive on any of the team's machines.

---

[6]If this sounds cringy because you're reading this on your ocular implants, navigating with your direct brain interface, that's ok. We'll be thrilled that our book's still around!

[7]Unless pairing with a hearing-impaired developer, where remote pairing with accessibility tools and more use of text may work better.

The next question is, who does the typing? The answer depends on the pair programming *style* or *mode*.

Pairing Styles

There are four main pair programming styles:

- In **task-based** (also called **ping-pong**) pairing, person A writes one or more tests while person B watches, and then B writes the code that passes the test(s) while A watches. Then, B writes one or more test(s) while A watches and A writes the code that passes the test(s) while B watches. Then, person A writes one or more test(s), and so on. This removes cognitive overhead and should improve test quality by reducing confirmation bias.

- In **time-based** pairing, the pair sets a recurring timer (e.g., for 25 minutes) and switches who is typing when the timer dings. This removes the cognitive overhead of figuring out who should be typing (in flow-based and strong-style pairing).

- In **strong-style** pairing, the person with the idea verbalizes it while the other person types the code. Strong-style pairing encourages agreement on ideas since each person is actively involved in writing each line of code.

- In **flow-based** pairing, the person with the idea types. Role switches happen dynamically and intuitively.

While there is no definitively best style, research suggests using strong-style pairing when pairs have unequal knowledge (or power) and task-based pairing when pairs have similar knowledge (see the Pair Programming sidebar on page 170).

Pairing doesn't work for all personalities. Many introverts enjoy pairing provided they get enough alone time each day, but some people strongly prefer working solo. Before giving up on pairing, let your team know what you need. For example, if you like to end your work day by journaling about recent events, then let your team know you need some time alone at the end of the day. If that doesn't work, reflect on why, exactly, you dislike pairing. If you dislike because pairing because your teammates make you feel like you don't belong and must constantly prove your competence, maybe pairing isn't the problem and you should look for a new team.

Ensemble Programming

While pair programming normally involves *two* collaborators, *ensemble programming* (also called *mob programming* [127]) refers to the whole team collaborating on a task. Usually, one person types, while the rest talk. People can come and go as needed. The team might have the source code projected onto a large screen, while individuals have laptops open for research [128]. In remote ensemble programming, the person typing shares their screen. Everyone else typically has two screens, one for sharing and the other for research. People turn on their mics to talk to the person typing; meanwhile, the team runs back-channel chat to talk to each other and coordinate. The person typing should close the back channel to avoid being overwhelmed. Ensemble programming is useful for breaking through particularly

Pair Programming

The research on pair programming does not clearly show which style works best. However, extensive research by Professor Lutz Prechelt's team at the Freie Universität Berlin is informative. The scientists observed and recorded pair programming sessions to study the social dynamics therein. They did not find the often-suggested driver-navigator pattern, where the "driver" types, while the "navigator" strategizes. The "driver and navigator both work at similar levels of abstraction," which calls into question the meaningfulness of this role distinction [125]. Instead, they found that programmers take on numerous roles, including *task expert*, *watcher* (who watches out for hazards and sets priorities); and *spokesperson* (who opens, sustains and closes a dialog) [126].

Dr. Franz Zieris (a former student of Prof. Prechelt) studied how knowledge is transferred during pairing sessions [31]. He found that pairs often share knowledge and that sometimes one programmer has more general knowledge (e.g., knowledge of programming languages), while the other has more task-specific knowledge (e.g., knowledge of the codebase at hand) needed to complete a task.

Dr. Zieris' research provides several recommendations about pairing:

- Strong-style pairing makes the most sense when the pairs have unequal knowledge (e.g., during onboarding). The programmer with less relevant knowledge of the task at hand should do the typing, while the expert explains the ideas. If the pairs have knowledge relevant to different parts of the task, they keep switching. Here, knowledge can differ from experience—the less-experienced developer may have more knowledge of the specific task at hand.

- Task- and time-based pairing make more sense when the programmers have similar, relevant knowledge. Task-based pairing is probably superior for teams using TDD / BDD.

- Flow-based pairing would only make sense when both programmers have about equal task and domain knowledge, but even then, it is likely inferior to task-based pairing.

contentious or difficult tasks while bonding, sharing knowledge, and accelerating feedback loops. Many teams would benefit from mobbing occasionally.

Overlapping Pair Rotation

Pair rotation is changing who is working together in which pairs. As a pair works together, they create a knowledge silo: the pair learns things and develops new ideas that the rest of the team doesn't know about. By rotating people working on a feature, knowledge about the feature is spread around the team. This enables the entire team to work on any part of the codebase.

In many projects, rotating daily balances productivity with removing knowledge silos. In some projects, however, less frequent rotation is better. For example, on one team we observed that it took about a day to figure out what change to make in the system, less than an hour to make the change, and another day to know if the change worked. The team decided to rotate every second day so that developers could feel a sense of accomplishment. On another project, a team was simultaneously maintaining a Python codebase, rewriting it in Go, and *learning* Go. The team felt that frequent rotations were hindering learning Go. They found it better to construct weekly rotations such that each team member worked on Go for two weeks and then maintained the Python code for two weeks.

Teams typically decide who is pairing for the day immediately after their daily sync meeting. There are at least five rotation strategies:

1. **Optimize for task rotation:** half the engineers stay on their current task while the other half rotate onto the path of work they've been away from longest. The engineer with lower task familiarity is then brought up to date by working with the engineer with higher task familiarity. Over time, this pattern maximizes each team member's familiarity with the entire codebase. Before rotating, the pair is asked, "Was enough context shared?" If not, they remain together one more day.

2. **Optimize for people rotation:** everyone tries to pair with whoever they least recently paired with. This strategy maximizes team members' familiarity with each other.

3. **Random:** the team uses a tool to assign pairs randomly. The strategy is OK but achieves no specific objective.

4. **Optimize for personal preferences:** developers pair with the teammates they enjoy pairing with on tasks that interest them. This creates and reinforces knowledge silos, defeating the purpose of pair rotation.

5. **Ad hoc:** someone asks, "Who wants to pair with who?" and developers pair haphazardly. This approach can make pairing feel awkward and reduce enthusiasm for pairing, while serving no particular goal.

Silos are for grain, not knowledge. The best way to minimize knowledge silos is to optimize for task rotation, with some adjustment for people rotation if you find some team members never seem to pair. Some teams use a Slackbot to remind each pair to decide who is keeping the story (Figure 10–2).

 slackbot 4:50 PM
Reminder: Who's sticking? Talk to you pair and decide who will keep your story

Figure 10–2: Slackbot Reminder Example (With Original Typo for EXTRA AUTHENTICITY)

Team Code Ownership

Code ownership refers to who can modify a piece of code (e.g., a file). There are four basic models of code ownership:

- **Individual code ownership** (or **strong ownership**): each file is owned by one person—often the person who created it. Individuals can only modify files that belong to them.

- **Team code ownership:** each file is owned by a team; any developer on the team can change any of the team's files [129].

- **Collective code ownership:** "Anyone can change any piece of code in the system at any time" [46].

- **No ownership:** no one owns anything or it's not clear who owns what.

Thus, there is a spectrum from a strong identity with the work product to separating the programmer's identity from their work products.

Neither end of this spectrum works. The no-ownership model doesn't work because no one understands their responsibilities. Individual (strong) code ownership doesn't work because it encourages wrapping one's ego around their code. Taking pride in one's work is great but making yourself a knowledge silo and bottleneck is not. Individual code ownership may undermine team members' sense of belonging to a team.

Collective code ownership is better but doesn't scale well. Suppose you work for a large software company with hundreds of teams building or maintaining hundreds of different systems. People you've never met, who work on totally different systems, fiddling with your team's code without sharing your team's mental models of either your product or its context will increase defects [130].

Teams need clear boundaries on what is theirs and what belongs to other teams. They need clear ownership of their work and authority over their stuff. So the best balance for most situations is team code ownership. Code belongs to the team. Any team member can modify any of the team's files. Individuals cannot assert ownership of files or modify other team's files.

Team code ownership makes teams more agile because important fixes don't have to wait on individual file owners. It works best when the company culture separates ego from work so that programmers can receive feedback without defensiveness, and synergizes with pair programming and continuous refactoring. Team code ownership also reduces defects because several people (who are familiar with the system) review and improve most code.

Therefore, we recommend having an explicit policy of team code ownership. However, having a policy isn't enough because ownership is psychological (see the sidebar on page 173). Indeed, transitioning to team code ownership is more about feelings than policies.

> **The Science of Code Ownership**
>
> Psychological ownership refers to "the feeling of possessiveness and of being psychologically tied to an object" [131]. Targets of ownership, whether physical or immaterial, become an extension of one's self: "What is mine becomes (in my feelings) part of ME" [132]. Ownership can be attached to a part or the whole. Psychological ownership occurs when the object becomes part of the psychological owner's identity. Psychological ownership answers the question, "What do I feel is mine?"
>
> Pierce [131] identifies three sources of psychological ownership:
>
> 1. **The ability to control one's environment:** possessing physical goods or abstract ideas helps us feel in control and able to alter our environment.
>
> 2. **Self-identity:** owning things helps us define ourselves, express ourselves, and survive.
>
> 3. **Having a place:** ownership fulfills the need for space in which to exist.
>
> Psychological ownership of code, therefore, manifests because creating software can satisfy the desire for efficacy and effectance, self-identity, and having a place. Pierce [131] further identifies three "routes" to ownership: controlling the target, coming to know the target intimately, and investing the self into the target. Consequently, a programmer can develop feelings of ownership over code by contributing to it, understanding it, and investing their ideas, talents, and labor into it. We tend to develop more ownership when we have more autonomy over our work and when we do less routine, complex jobs that demand more creativity. Feelings of ownership also increase with familiarity.
>
> In software engineering teams specifically, many factors affect a developer's willingness to modify a file, including the extent to which they: understand the system context, have contributed to the code in question, perceive code quality as high; believe the product will satisfy user needs, and perceive team cohesion as high. In contrast, sense of code ownership can be undermined by increasing knowledge silos, increasing codebase size, increasing team size, inability to contribute, pressure to deliver, pressure to deprioritize continuous refactoring, ignoring user feedback, ignoring developer feedback, and distancing a developer from the team [129].

Transitioning to Team Code Ownership

Our goal is to empower every developer to augment, refactor or otherwise improve on any part of the team's code, especially in cases of low code discoverability and readability. Transitioning to team code ownership is a three-step process:

1. Make a code ownership policy that says code belongs to teams, and make sure everyone on the team knows about and agrees to this policy in principle.

2. Set up permissions in the version control system such that any part of the team's code can be changed by any member of the team and no one else. (Others can submit changes to be reviewed and then owned by the team, but such handoffs are problematic for significant changes.)

3. Implement practices that reinforce the collaborative nature of software development.

Preventing developers from other teams from modifying the team's code is easy enough via version control permissions, but empowering each member to modify any of the team's code is more complicated. Code ownership is an *emotion*; it's about which files you feel willing to modify and this willingness depends on many factors (see the sidebar on page 173).

Clean code, continuous refactoring, test-driven development, pair programming with overlapping pair rotation, and peer code review all help the whole team feel ownership of its codebase. Continuous pair programming and overlapping pair rotation are particularly effective because, when two people write code together, no one gets a sense of individual ownership in the first place.

Some developers effortlessly make the transition from individual code ownership to team code ownership. Others struggle with no longer taking the same pride in functionality that they exclusively developed. Some developers are distraught at seeing their work slowly evolve. The hard truth is, to function effectively in a team, all engineers need to accept that someone else will eventually take over their code, to expect their code to be transitory, to develop trust in their teammates, and thus to hold personal contributions loosely. An engineer in one of the teams we studied explained: *"The code that I write today may be in the codebase for a little while, and it will evolve into something better."*

Eventually, experiencing the benefits of a collaborative environment will bring most people around. Developers with a firm affinity for individual ownership may benefit from sharing ownership first with a small group (where trust and communication come easier). Improvisation and collaboration games can help teams practice trusting each other and letting go of control.

Summary

In this chapter, we explored the activities involved in generating and modifying code. Professional developers write code that not only functions as intended but also is easy for other humans to understand and maintain. Over-emphasizing shipping software quickly can lead good programmers to write indecipherable spaghetti code, jeopardizing the long-term health, quality, and sustainability of the code, and the morale of the team.

Continuous refactoring and integration, test-driven development, fast tests and builds, continuous code design, continuous pairing, and team code ownership all help developers create and maintain a clean code base. These practices are synergistic. Clean code is practically impossible to maintain without continuous refactoring. Continuous refactoring works best when combined with test-driven development. Test-driven development and pair programming work best when combined into task-based pairing. Clean code, continuous refactoring, TDD, pair programming, and pair rotation all come together to facilitate team code ownership, which leads to better code, better tests, and better testing / refactoring / pairing dynamics.

It helps to think of a codebase as a garden that needs constant tending, shaping, and pruning. The codebase, like the garden, will grow. The trick is to create organizations, structures, and practices that help your code gardens grow neatly.

Chapter 11

Integrating and Delivering

A key goal of continuous delivery is changing the economics of the software delivery process so the cost of pushing out individual changes is very low.
– Nicole Forsgren

 Key Takeaways

- Every software team should be using version control.

- Every team has a delivery pipeline, but the steps in the pipeline vary significantly.

- Delivery pipelines have quality gates such as integration testing and code review.

- Peer code review improves code quality, understandability, and knowledge sharing, but care is needed to remain supportive.

- Most teams should use a build system to automate much of their delivery process.

- Never merge new code on a "red" build; always fix failing tests before integrating new features.

- Many teams benefit from acceptance or staging environments for facilitating manual testing.

- Most teams benefit from integrating and releasing changes frequently, but "frequently" could mean anything from hourly to semi-annually, depending on your context.

Adding Features Delays a Release

When Davis joined the release engineering team for project Granite as a product manager, he soon realized how hard it was to ship an enterprise product.

Imagine getting into an elevator and just as the doors are about to close, someone sticks in their hand, the doors open, and they walk inside. Just as the doors are about to close a second time, someone else sticks in their hand. Then another person and another repeating every minute. You're now late, stressed, annoyed, and seemingly getting nowhere.

Now, if that elevator were a release candidate and those people were features, that's how Davis' team felt. Whenever a release date approached and Davis' team were fixing last-minute bugs, a product manager would push to include another feature, which added more bugs, further delaying the release. While the team was fixing *those* bugs, another feature would arrive with more release-stopping bugs.

Davis' experience exemplifies the conventional wisdom that *a late release tends to get later*. The more a release is delayed, the more features stakeholders want to add.

Davis

To move to a predictable release schedule, Davis learned to refuse last-minute feature additions. It took courage and depleted Davis' political capital but he kept explaining the situation and persuading the product managers that the features they wanted to add would be in the *next* release candidate. He slowly changed the company's culture. Instead of the managers asking, "Can we get one more thing in the release?", they began asking, "Is there anything in the release that will cause harm?" If not, Davis argued, ship the release.

The second complication arose from the release process itself. One of Granite's key components, Tectonic, was enterprise Kubernetes software that integrated many different software components. Any one of these dependencies could block a release. When a component had an issue, Davis wanted options for how to proceed, such as downgrading the problematic component to the last working version, disabling the breaking feature, or blocking the release until just that one issue was fixed (i.e., "fail forward"). The first two options would return the product to a shippable state, while the third would block the release.

Unfortunately, *Tectonic didn't have release branches.* The team could not fix individual issues. Granite's release process kept revealing issues in Tectonic they would need to fix and reintegrate. Each issue caused another cascade where the fix would include any work-in-progress on Tectonic.

Davis slowly convinced the Tectonic team to create release branches for internal dependencies and verify that each dependency followed semantic versioning (see Semantic Versioning on page 180). Redesigning the release process gave Davis more options for handling a release blocker.

Davis eventually escaped this endless loop by getting each of his dependencies to follow strict semantic versioning. He got each of Tectonic's releases to have patch versions that *only* contained fixes for the upcoming release. He got the product managers to stop endlessly pushing for additions by regularizing the release schedule, building confidence that upcoming features would be shipped frequently and predictably. With a lot of persistence, he shifted the whole organization's culture and way of working.

Some developers want to deliver code as quickly as possible to customers. They want a continuous delivery (CD) pipeline that automatically ships features the moment they're finished. Others argue that additional manual validation is needed before shipping the code. They might argue for some combination of peer code review, manual quality assurance inspections, manual testing, sharing alpha releases with trusted customers, or using the product internally before a full release. (This is sometimes called "eating your own dog food" or "dog-fooding.")

Meanwhile, some stakeholders prefer a steady stream of features, while others prefer larger, less-frequent releases. A steady stream of features allows customers to benefit from features as they are delivered and acclimatize to small changes. Less frequent releases decrease the work associated with updates. Developers of most enterprise software often want to shorten their release duration yet struggle with getting their customers to upgrade their software. In some environments, stakeholders need extensive training before upgrading. Adding more releases per year may worsen their experience.

Every team has some process of getting code from an individual developer's workstation to *production*; that is, into a working version of the product that users are actually using. This process is usually called the *delivery pipeline* or *deployment pipeline*. The *definition of done*, described in Chapter 5, is basically a model of the delivery pipeline. It's crucial for software teams to have a clear, shared understanding of the shape of their pipeline; that is, their definition of done. The whole team must agree on both the steps in the pipeline and who is responsible for each step.

Pipelines vary dramatically between industries, organizations, and teams. When you edit the code of your personal website directly on the server, your pipeline is very short. When your code is tested and verified in multiple environments, your pipeline can be quite long. Some teams have highly automated pipelines; others have many manual steps. There is no one best pipeline configuration for every context.

That said, pipelines have some commonalities. They typically start with code on individual workstations and end with code in deployed products. The first step is usually merging the code into version control, quickly followed by resolving any merge conflicts. Most pipelines also include quality gates (e.g., acceptance testing). Most have some combination of automated steps (e.g., integration testing) and manual steps (e.g., code review).

The structure of the pipeline affects the product's quality and timeliness of releases. While different situations call for different pipelines, we can discuss common practices that help most teams optimize their pipelines.

Version Control

Version control (also called *source control*) is a system for storing and managing code, including change history, work-in-progress, and labels showing what code shipped in each release. Practically all software teams now use version control.

One of the most important features of modern version control systems is branching. *Branches* are copies of some or all of a system that can be modified independently. Using branches, two (or two-hundred) developers can work independently and in parallel. Branches also allow teams to maintain different versions of the same product. Branches can be *merged* to integrate changes, and facilitating these merges is one of the main benefits of version control. When a developer asks to merge their branch into another branch or (more often) the *trunk* or *main branch*, it's called a *change request* or *pull request*.

Teams using branches may experience merge conflicts. A *merge conflict* happens when two or more developers have modified the same line of the same file in different ways. Simple merge conflicts can be easy to resolve, but more complicated conflicts rapidly get out of hand. As explained in Chapter 10, integrating frequently can help avoid merge conflicts.

We want the code in version control to be high quality and shippable after each update (e.g., `git commit`, `perforce submit`). Ideally, every change, every commit, is "green" (i.e., passes all of our automated tests). When the test suite is expensive to run, testing each commit becomes problematic, so we want every pull request to be shippable.

Version control should manage all code, including temporary projects. You never know when you'll want an early working version of the code or need something you built years ago. Version control acts as a bridge between the coding practices discussed in Chapter 10 and the delivery practices discussed below.

Believe It or Not: A Human Version Control System

In the early 2000s, one engineering manager didn't trust her teammates' code quality. Each team member on this aerospace team would email code changes to the manager. She would take the changes and then merge them into the code on her file system. Periodically, she would email the code to the team members.

All these manual updates were wasteful and error-prone. If your team has bizarre rituals around updating the code, polish your résumé and get out of there ASAP.

Semantic Versioning

Semantic Versioning (or *SemVer*) is a convention where the version number communicates what is changing in the system. It uses a three-number format—`major.minor.patch`:

1. `Major`: includes non-backward compatible features, significant interface changes, or removed features.

2. `Minor`: adds backward-compatible features.

3. `Patch`: contains bug fixes or addresses Common Vulnerabilities and Exposures (CVEs).

For example, upgrading from 10.18.4 to 10.18.9 should not break anything because there are no changes in functionality, just removing bugs. An upgrade from 10.18.4 to 10.19.2 should be minimally disruptive since the underlying product has only introduced new features or parameters. The way we've used the software in the past should continue to work. Upgrading from 10.18.4 to 11.0.1 could be more disruptive, and we'll want to schedule some time to ensure our system or code will continue working.

As software developers, when we use dependencies or libraries in our code that follow semantic versioning, it gives us confidence about how much work to expect when upgrading or "bumping" the dependency. Likewise, following semantic versioning in our product communicates to our customers how easy an upgrade should be.

Integrate Frequently

Developers should integrate their code into version control as often as is practical (e.g., several times each day). Frequently merging code enables continuous refactoring, minimizes merge conflicts, and incrementally delivers value.

If a developer has code only on their machine, then no one else can use or modify that code. When code lives only on one machine for several days, the machine acts as a virtual branch. Antique virtual branches create merge conflicts, hindering integration. Two-way merge conflicts are annoying. Three- and four-way merge conflicts can be nightmarish.

An engineer or pair can minimize merge conflicts by asserting exclusive *temporary* ownership of a component while they refactor it. Developers should only assert exclusivity for a few hours—one day tops—or they'll undermine the team's sense of collective ownership (see Team Code Ownership in Chapter 10). Furthermore, the team cannot receive any of the benefits until the work is merged back into version control.

In the ideal workflow, developers merge their code to `main` many times a day. Merges may be less frequent for legacy systems where it may take a day to understand the existing code, or validation is slow due to insufficient automated testing. If integrating code is infrequent, examine why and explore ways of making smaller changes incrementally.

Code Review

Code review (or *peer code review*) refers to examining a change request before merging it into the product's main branch (or development branch, depending on the pipeline) in version control. Code review is used extensively as a quality gate in open-source projects, but is also popular in closed-source commercial development. With the explosion of AI-generated code and AI-assisted programming, the nature and goals of code review are evolving rapidly. Here, however, we focus on humans reviewing code written by other humans.

Code review isn't really about finding bugs (see the sidebar on page 182); it's more about helping to break down knowledge silos, spreading ideas around the team, and aligning code changes with the team's coding expectations and design patterns. In this sense, code review is more like pair programming than unit testing.

Benefits of Code Review

Code review evolved from the formal code inspections used in large organizations (especially NASA) in the latter half of the 20th century. Modern code review tends to be a more informal process of reading through a change request to see if the change makes sense in principle, if it's implemented well, and is consistent with the project's style and conventions.

While formal code inspections were primarily concerned with finding specific technical faults and some evidence suggests that "code review coverage, participation, and expertise share a significant link with software quality" [133], modern code review is fairly ineffective for finding bugs [134]. Indeed, reviewers with insufficient expertise appear to increase post-release defects" [135]. Furthermore, code review does not mitigate design degradation and long discussions with lots of disagreements *increase* design degradation [136]. Moreover, "Most developers do not ... focus on security issues during code review ... report the lack of training and security knowledge as the main challenges they face when checking for security issues ... have challenges with third-party libraries and" may disregard security considerations entirely [137].

In contrast, a detailed analysis of code reviews at Microsoft [138] found the following three main benefits of code review.

1. "Code Improvements" including "using better code practices," removing unnecessary code, and improving readability.

2. Improving the understandability of the code.

3. Improving social communication and knowledge transfer within teams.

Many researchers are interested in automating code review using AI, but this undermines arguably the main benefit of code review: promoting knowledge transfer. Similarly, the increasingly common vision of a future in which engineers spend all day reviewing, polishing, and integrating code generated by AI neglects the fact that modern code review is ineffective for finding bugs.

Teams should, however, take care to avoid hazards of code review, including:

- Teams finishing features simultaneously can be overwhelmed by profuse code reviews.

- Code review often includes destructive criticism, which damages receivers' mood and motivation, and is disproportionately demotivating for women [139].

- Code review may be obstructionist, especially when change requests go through multiple rounds of review. We have observed time-critical changes blocked by code review (e.g., waiting for a team member in a different time zone to start their day and approve the change).

- Code review is ineffective for mentoring and onboarding (because of the destructive criticism and obstructionism).

- Providing important feedback during code review *instead of* before or during coding creates unnecessary rework (i.e., waste).

- The longer the code review takes, the more the submitter forgets the details of the change request.

- Code reviews may reinforce prejudice if they use coded language (see Write Diversity-Friendly Job Ads on page 207) or if change requests from members of certain groups encounter more resistance. Unfortunately, such problems are common [140].

To summarize, having an experienced peer promptly review code before integration *should* improve knowledge sharing and code quality, but in practice code reviews are often prejudiced, destructive, and slow. Teams using pair programming (see Pair Continuously in Chapter 10) already have two people examining all new code as it is written. The combination of pair programming, TDD and continuous refactoring empowers developers to integrate code changes in version control because the code was continuously reviewed and tested as it was written. The marginal benefits of code review for programmers already following pair programming and test-driven development are likely lower. In a sense, code review is a less effective alternative to pair programming. Code review is mainly useful where pair programming is impractical and there is a strong culture of constructive reviewing (in the eyes of the *reviewees*).

Build System

Developers create and use a *build system* to automate parts of their delivery pipelines (e.g. compiling code; managing packages; running tests; pushing changes to the staging, acceptance, or production environment). Build systems help developers manage dependencies and usually accelerate the build process by only rebuilding the parts of the system that have changed.

Whenever a developer pushes new code to source control, the build system runs some or all of the tests and uses a *build monitor* (a physical screen or digital application) to indicate the build's status. Distributed teams might communicate status changes through email, desktop notifications, or the team's communication platform (e.g., Slack). When all tests pass, the build monitor is "green;" otherwise it is "red."

Version control and build systems help developers integrate frequently. For some products, the build system can also automate all or parts of shipping a new release, whether the team does continuous delivery or scheduled releases. Regardless of how frequently or infrequently you release updates, you should use a build system. There is simply no need to execute easy-to-automate tasks (e.g., compiling code, running integration tests) manually. Build systems also support the important practice of stopping on red builds (next).

Stop on Red Builds

Inevitably, after integrating code in version control, a change will lead to failing tests. This can happen for a variety of reasons. A test might be unreliable and fail randomly, in which case the team needs to improve its reliability or disable the test. Two separate code changes that had green tests might be red when combined (e.g., one engineer renames a method while another adds a new caller of the current method name). While we don't want to castigate ourselves over a red build, we don't want it to linger.

When any team member notices that the build is broken, they stop what they are doing and notify the team that they are working on a fix. Often, this will be the person who most recently integrated code as they purposefully monitor the build status after merging. Everyone else can continue writing code, but pushing more code or merging pull requests stops.

Only merge code into version control on green builds. Pushing or merging on a red build makes it more difficult to determine what is breaking the build. The more commits to sort through, the more complex the puzzle. Furthermore, when you merge code into a red build, you may be introducing additional, undetectable problems. Only fixes should be integrated when we have a red build.

Merging on Red Is Your Ticket to Hell

On one project with 65 developers organized into several teams, we saw the engineers begin to ignore the build system because the tests had become unreliable. Tests would fail arbitrarily. Instead of fixing the test suite, the engineers continued to write code. When they updated version control and a test failed, they figured, "my code's fine; it must be an unreliable test." When any job in the build went red, the teams acted as if it was someone else's problem to fix it. Developers started merging code on red builds, simultaneously exacerbating the problem and kicking it down the road. Since everyone had been pushing code on red commits, no one felt responsible or motivated to solve the problem.

When release time came, none of the versions passed all the tests. No one knew why. No one knew how to fix it or even which version would be easiest to fix. When the release was a week late, management intervened, reminded the team of the tenant "only merge on green builds," and prevented anyone from merging their code for new features. Instead of working on new features, engineers started digging into the root causes of the test failures.

They corrected unreliable tests, deleted useless tests, and resolved infrastructural issues. They found and fixed bugs. They spent months getting into this mess, and it took almost as long to get out. After cleaning up the technical debt in the test suite and releasing well behind schedule, the engineers learned to embrace stopping on red builds and were far more diligent in fixing errors before they piled up.

Acceptance Environment

As described in Chapter 10, automated tests cannot catch every problem. Some teams therefore create acceptance or staging environments for manual verification of system behavior and other important properties. Many teams automate deploying new features into acceptance or staging environments as part of their delivery pipeline.

Acceptance environments (also called *staging environments*) are simulations that aim to replicate the way the product will look and work in production. The terms *acceptance* and *staging* are used inconsistently. Some teams have one pre-production simulation, while others have a separate *staging environment* for internal testing and *acceptance environment* for external testing by users and other stakeholders. Usability testing (see Chapter 8) for new features or feature changes can happen in acceptance, staging, or even production environments, depending on the situation.

In Sustainable Dual-Track Development, the product manager can use the acceptance environment to verify the developers' work (see Accepting (or Rejecting) Stories in Chapter 4 for how a product manager accepts a story). Product designers, quality assurance professionals, or client representatives may also be involved in acceptance testing. Meanwhile, a staging environment allows the business to verify that a release candidate functions as intended. Ideally, the staging environment replicates the production environment as closely as possible. Some organizations will use the product before it is moved from staging to production (dog-fooding). Depending on your situation, you might just have one or the other, or a single environment that serves both purposes.

Using a product in an acceptance or staging environment slows the pipeline but increases our confidence that any recent changes will not break the system in ways automated tests can't detect. Automated tests check whether the product performs as the developers intend. An acceptance environment facilitates checking whether the product performs as the product manager, users, or other stakeholders intend.

Release Frequently

Release frequently means finding a balance between delivering the highest quality software possible and minimizing the time between completing a feature (or fix or other change) and users benefiting from the updated code. Releasing more frequently:

1. shortens the duration between finishing the work and the customer receiving value;

2. exposes inefficiencies in the release process; and

3. enables fast patch releases for critical fixes (e.g., CVEs).

Transparent upgrades (when the user is unaware of the upgrade) facilitate frequent releases. For example, some websites deploy their code several times daily.

Release Frequently != Continuous Delivery

Here, *release frequently* is not equivalent to *continuous integration* (CI) or *continuous delivery* (CD).

Continuous Integration (also called *Integrate Frequently*) is the practice of merging code quickly and often—typically many times per day. When someone says CI these days, they usually mean a system that runs integration tests whenever a change request is merged into version control. CI is not controversial. Unless your team is working on a vanishingly small product that won't be around long enough to warrant setting up CI, or you're working in a regulated environment with legally mandated, in-process safety audits, you should be using CI. Even in regulated environments, most of the ostensible reasons for omitting CI seem to ignore how branching works.

Continuous Delivery is more contentious. CD means pushing changes into production (i.e., delivering updates to users) quickly and frequently to realize the value of new features as soon as possible. Some organizations can reduce the time between feature completion and feature utilization to minutes by automating the entire deployment pipeline. However, *quick* is relative, and quicker is not always better. In many organizations, shipping every commit is either too expensive or too risky.

When some people say CD, they mean a fully automated delivery process in which changes that pass all automated tests go straight to production without any manual quality gates like code review or acceptance tests. But CD isn't really about automating *everything*; it's more about minimizing the time between the approval of a change and the deployment of that change. Approval may, and often should, still involve manual checks. That's why we say "release frequently" instead of "continuous delivery."

A customer verifying a release delays release adoption. However, manually validating each new feature is sometimes more important than maximizing update speed. Fully automating the deployment pipeline means there is no room for manual usability or acceptance testing before releasing.

In other contexts, the cost of updating may exceed the short-term benefits of the update. For enterprise software, the ideal release cadence depends upon the organization's ability to support releases and the customer company's ability to verify and install a release. Monthly releases often balance the producer's ability to support a release and the customer's ability to consume a release, but less-frequent releases are common. In some embedded systems (e.g., forklift firmware), releasing twice per year could be over-ambitious.

For large systems, deployment can be a partial roll-out, in which new code is deployed to a small number of users or machines for some period before being rolled out to every user or machine.

Stakeholders who want less-frequent releases can be supported through selective patching. For example, a bank may spend a month verifying a new release before installing it. Given the overhead and cost, the bank might install a new version of the software once a year or once every two years while applying only critical bug fixes as patches are released. The team might release monthly but needs to support a long-lived release for two years. The software company can still benefit from frequent releases, provided they do not expect all of their customers to be on the latest release.

Ideally, release as frequently as the project stakeholders want while balancing the release frequency with the importance of other processes. Regardless, minimizing the time between feature completion and user adoption necessitates automating as much of the delivery pipeline as possible. You need sophisticated, mature testing infrastructure to have enough confidence to fully automate the delivery pipeline. In many situations, manual quality gates—including code review, acceptance testing, third-party audits, and usability testing—may be necessary.

With scheduled releases, the team starts a release process on some predetermined cadence or frequency (e.g., weekly, monthly, quarterly). For long release durations, teams should make daily (or at least weekly) release candidates to avoid unpleasant surprises as the release date nears.

Unreliable Tests Can Prevent Releases

When Todd joined the release engineering team as an engineer, he soon realized the test suite was affecting the predictability of each release.

Todd's first goal was to improve the reliability of the release process by fixing unreliable tests and testing environments. The installation test suite had 53% reliability. To ship the product, the test suite had to pass 24 different combinations of test environments. The probability of the code passing on the first try was approximately 0%. By fixing unreliable tests and improving the product, reliability improved to 96%, which meant the product might ship successfully on the first attempt $0.96^{24} = 38\%$ of the time.

Todd

Todd's second goal was to make diagnosing failures easier. The team improved logging, added error messages, improved test usefulness, and shortened test duration while continuing to address common testing failures.

In time, the team was able to reduce the duration of the release process and improve the predictability of the releases.

Assess Sustainability

Sustainability assessment is a little like penetration testing in that outsiders (e.g., consultants) may be significantly more effective because your affinity for your own product inhibits your critical thinking. However, research on sustainability assessment *for software* is in its infancy, so finding qualified external advice may be challenging. By the time you read this, new and better tooling and conceptual frameworks may be available, not to mention more sustainability-focused services. In the meantime, we'll discuss what's known at the time of writing about assessing each of the four dimensions of sustainability: environmental, economic, social, and technical.

Assess Environmental Impact

Development is environmentally sustainable when it meets present needs without affecting the natural environment in ways that jeopardize stakeholders' (including the general public's) capacity to meet their future needs. Negative environmental impact can be global or concentrated in a specific continent, country, region, municipality, or type of ecosystem (e.g., oceans, mangroves, deserts).

Software developers often equate environmental impact with carbon footprint but many software products have more specific environmental impacts due to their specific functions as in the following examples.

- The software used to allocate campsites in a park affects human impacts on the park.

- The software that controls a hydroelectric dam affects the river / reservoir ecosystem.

- Route planning software (e.g., Google Maps) can improve environmental impacts by suggesting more efficient routes in addition to the fastest route.

- Software used to optimize crop yields can reduce use and runoff of harmful pesticides and fertilizers.

- Software that unnecessarily requires special-purpose hardware increases e-waste. Similarly, inefficient software and planned obsolescence increases e-waste.

- Hydrological modeling software, forestry management software, geographic information systems, urban planning software, and so on all have downstream impacts on waterways, forests, land use, etc.

The first step in assessing environmental impact is thinking about how whatever kind of software you work on affects ecosystems. You may or may not be able to quantify these effects, but you don't always have to quantify things to improve them (e.g., you can know that watering plants at night is more efficient without measuring water consumption). Analyzing these effects for an hour with your team may produce numerous ideas for limiting environmental impact.

Next, consider the resources consumed by the product's development. For example, if your company insists that everyone work co-located in a physical office, and many employees drive to work, environmental impacts include the pollution created by the cars, the opportunity cost of space dedicated to parking; needing larger offices that take up more space and consume more resources for construction, maintenance, heating, cooling, and lighting; increased resource usage due to eating out at restaurants; etc. That doesn't mean everyone should work remotely; the point is that allowing some staff to work remotely some of the time may have non-trivial environmental benefits.

Lastly, we come to estimate carbon footprint. Wasting electricity increases a product's carbon footprint. Even clean energy has a carbon footprint because building and maintaining solar panels, wind turbines, etc. uses resources and creates pollution. Furthermore, the whole point of building clean power generation is to shut down dirty power generation (e.g., coal-fired power plants), which we can't do if new software eats all the new clean power.

Energy usage includes not only energy consumed by users interacting with the software product but also energy consumed by the development team creating the software product.

How to estimate energy varies substantially depending on the kind of software. Let's consider the following examples and build up from there.

1. Everything (product, tests, build system, etc.) runs on an on-demand cloud computing platform that estimates carbon emissions for you based on usage.

2. Everything runs on hardware in your office, all development takes place on-site, and the whole office is dedicated to one product. In this case, you don't have to measure power consumption because the power company does it for you, and frequently sends you detailed reporting in the form of a power bill. The power bill might also include an estimate of carbon emissions, or the power company or some third party might provide a calculator to estimate emissions.

3. You have a legacy mobile app with no active development. Its energy consumption is (almost) entirely related to users downloading, installing, and using the app. In this case, we can create a mathematical model to estimate energy usage based on the number of users, number of downloads, and a little research on the carbon footprint of data transfer. We can use telemetry data if available (or guesswork, otherwise) to generate a representative workload (a combination of tasks representative of what a typical user might do with the app on a typical day). Then we can execute that workload on one or a few test devices. Many chip manufacturers provide tools for estimating power consumption that we can use. Then we cross-reference data about where users live with public emissions data from those places, and we combine that with our energy usage estimates to get an emissions estimate.

As you might imagine, this can get messy. Your team might be split across several offices, none of which are dedicated to one product, with some team members working from home. You might have some processes running locally, others in the cloud, and others on user's machines. Your product could have multiple versions that run on different kinds of hardware, in different regions. The more complicated your situation, the more complicated the model you need. If creating an estimation model seems overwhelmingly complicated, this is a good time to bring in external help. You could bring in a consultant, but you might also consider working with your local university. Studying the carbon footprint of a large software product (and the effects of some mitigation practices) would be an excellent thesis topic for a software engineering graduate student.

The whole point of measuring carbon footprint, however, is to determine how to reduce it. There are *many* ways to reduce environmental impact, including:

- making software more efficient (e.g., using better algorithms),

- making the build system and test process more efficient,

- making updates more efficient (e.g., by using delta updates instead of replacing entire apps),

- shifting energy usage to regions with cleaner power, and

- generating cleaner power (e.g., by installing solar panels on the roof of your office building).

Some companies attempt to counteract their negative environmental impact by buying *carbon offsets*; that is, giving money to some initiative that should reduce negative environmental impacts elsewhere. We recommend focusing on reducing your own impacts rather than paying someone else to reduce some other impacts. Many investigations have cast doubt on the legitimacy of carbon offset programs (e.g. [141]).

We recommend dedicating one day per year for the entire team to conduct a comprehensive environmental impact assessment. Doing a good job will require collaboration between engineers, product designers, product managers, and (possibly) an external specialist. Once a carbon footprint model has been developed, it should be monitored continuously and updated annually.

Assess Economic Sustainability

Development is economically sustainable when it meets present needs without undermining the future economic feasibility of the product, or harming the local, regional, national, or global economy.

Economic sustainability is much easier to assess than environmental sustainability, and your organization's accountant(s) are probably already doing most of the work.

At the lowest level, economic sustainability is relatively straightforward to quantify. Are the revenues generated by the product sufficient to cover the cost of developing and maintaining it? Or, if it's a new product, will sufficient revenue materialize quickly enough to justify its development? If you work for a start-up, will the product capture enough market share, quickly enough, to keep the company afloat? Of course, these calculations are based on potentially inaccurate estimates, but it's not conceptually or mathematically difficult to compare projections of costs and revenues. Many of the Track One practices described in Chapters 6–8 should help product designers and product managers estimate potential revenue and prioritize features that someone is willing to pay for. Economic sustainability is more difficult to analyze in non-commercial projects like open-source, government initiatives, and internal corporate systems where benefits may be harder to quantify.

At a higher level, economic sustainability also refers to a product's macro-level impacts on the financial health of individuals, families, groups, organizations, communities, regions, nations, and the world at large. Most individual products' macro-level effects are insignificant and can be ignored, with two exceptions.

First, some products, due to their nature, do have significant macro-level effects (e.g., robo-investing software; software used by real estate companies to set rents; ubiquitous technical infrastructure like Amazon Web Services). These products will need custom impact models. There's no algorithm for this. You just need someone with a spreadsheet and good financial and mathematical literacy to look at what the software does and estimate its impacts on the various economies in which it operates.

Second, most products are developed by a team of humans who should be fairly compensated for their labor. If a product doesn't generate enough money to compensate its developers fairly, it's not sustainable. Unfortunately, most open-source projects fall into this category, and the open source movement suffers from poor economic sustainability.

Product managers should take the lead on assessing economic sustainability.

Assess Social Impact

Development is socially sustainable when it meets present needs while maintaining (or better, enhancing) individuals', families', communities', organizations', or societies' circumstances and capabilities. Social sustainability takes different forms at different levels (e.g. individual mental health, group cohesion, community engagement, organizational inclusiveness, national social justice, world peace). Development that promotes hate and discrimination, undermines democracy, or exacerbates income inequality is not sustainable because it reduces the individual, group, organization, or society's future capacity to thrive.

Social and economic sustainability overlap because boosting economic prosperity helps to enhance human society. However, avoid disregarding societal harm as acceptable collateral damage for prosperity. Confronting how our product may harm others is uncomfortable, so it's tempting to focus on the benefits of our work before duly considering how we could achieve the same benefits while reducing or eliminating the harms.

Social impact is the most difficult sustainability dimension to quantify but qualitative assessments can still help. For example, if your face-detection system is more effective the lighter the person's skin is, you don't need to quantify the harm to know you should fix it.

To assess social impact at the individual level, then, list all the individuals (or types of individuals) impacted by your software product *and your development process*. This list typically includes the development team, users, the general public, and many others depending on the nature of the product. Brainstorm *how* your product and process affect each group. Many of the Track One practices described in Chapters 6–8 should help inform your brainstorming. Look for harm, then look for ways to prevent or minimize these harms.

To assess social impact at higher levels (e.g., municipal, regional, national, global), again, brainstorm how your product and process affect each aspect of society. Comprehensively listing every aspect of society we should consider is difficult, but we can give examples:

- peace and safety;

- physical, mental, and social well-being;

- equity and social justice;

- inclusiveness, tolerance, and multiculturalism;

- democracy and democratic participation;

- community engagement and self-sufficiency (communities' ability to fulfill their own needs);

- human rights (including privacy) and individual freedom;

- rule of law (the principle that the same laws apply to all citizens; no one is above the law);

- prosperity in the specific sense of creating jobs and improving economic opportunities;

- education; and

- awareness of sustainability issues.

When you identify a negative impact (e.g., large language models undermining education by facilitating academic misconduct), resist the urge to dismiss the impact as unimportant or someone else's problem. Similarly, resist the urge to dismiss the problem as unsolvable, or inherent in the type of product at hand. Problems are solvable. Focus on how you can mitigate the negative impact through clever design. Consider the beginning of an exchange with ChatGPT shown in Figure 11–1. Is it really beyond our capabilities to train a large language model to identify a student cheating on an assignment and offer encouragement and suggestions instead of just handing over a plagiarism-ready essay?

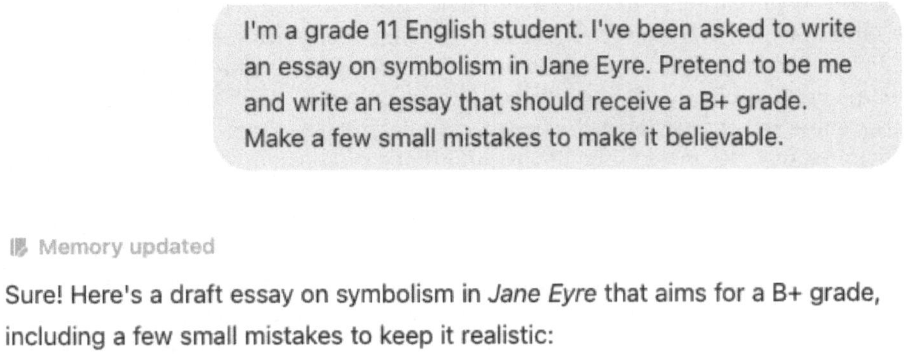

> I'm a grade 11 English student. I've been asked to write an essay on symbolism in Jane Eyre. Pretend to be me and write an essay that should receive a B+ grade. Make a few small mistakes to make it believable.

🖍 Memory updated

Sure! Here's a draft essay on symbolism in *Jane Eyre* that aims for a B+ grade, including a few small mistakes to keep it realistic:

Figure 11–1: Beginning of a Conversation with ChatGPT [July 26, 2024]

One way to structure this analysis is to make a large table in which columns represent dimensions of social sustainability and rows represent human entities (individuals, communities, nations, etc.). Then, in each cell write how your product might benefit or harm each entity-dimension pair. If a pair doesn't make sense (e.g., community engagement–world; rule of law–individual), just cross it out.

Product designers should take the lead on assessing social impacts, but all team members can contribute. One approach would be for the product designer to assemble an initial analysis, present it to the team, and then lead a refinement workshop. This analysis should be updated once or twice a year.

Assess Technical Sustainability

Technical sustainability refers to the degree to which technical features of a software system affect (1) the long-term viability of the codebase; and (2) its surrounding technical infrastructure.

In sense (1), a product is technically sustainable when it has reasonably clean code and comprehensive tests, has a good deployment pipeline, has good security, is well-organized and easy to understand, is durable (difficult to break and easy to fix), and is easy to modify to keep up with changing circumstances.

In sense (2), a product is technically sustainable when it makes its surrounding technical infrastructure more secure, durable, modifiable, etc. For example, creating programming languages (e.g., Rust, Python) that are easier to read and understand improves the technical sustainability of every project using them. In contrast, many cloud storage providers undermined the security of millions of users by delaying end-to-end, zero-knowledge encryption so hard you'd think foot-dragging was an Olympic sport. Just a few days before we wrote this paragraph, software security firm CrowdStrike released an update that crashed approximately 8 million systems, costing Fortune 500 companies an estimated \$5.4 billion [142]. This is just the latest illustration of how one product can perturb large swaths of technical infrastructure.

Most software developers think about the first meaning of technical sustainability quite often. Left to themselves, most developers take pride in their work and prioritize clean code. When this sense of technical sustainability is neglected, the culprit is often time pressure from managers or clients. Many Track Two practices—including continuous refactoring, test-driven development, code review, and stop on red builds—aim to improve the first sense of technical sustainability not least by helping developers resist pressure to cut corners.

Developers *qualitatively* assess technical sustainability all the time, including during routine programming and code review. *Quantitatively* assessing technical sustainability is more difficult. Four approaches to quantifying the first meaning of technical sustainability, from worst to best, are as follows.

- *Code metrics* are standard ways of measuring properties of software systems. For example, the fan-in and fan-out metrics aim to measure the cohesiveness of classes in object-oriented code. The problem with code metrics is that many simply don't measure what they are supposed to [143], and the output of popular code metric tools (e.g., Designite, Understand, JHawk) is so voluminous that it can be difficult to understand and apply.

- *Code smells* are identifiable patterns in source code that are believed to correlate with specific problems. For example, the `long method` code smell suggests that overly long methods usually indicate poor design. Static analysis tools detect an increasing variety of code smells. The great thing about code smells is that they are actionable by nature. Find a long method? Shorten it. Magic number? Define it. Middle man? Delete it. And so on. The problem with code smells is that they don't *always* indicate problems, and they don't actually measure properties of code. A code smell is just someone's opinion about some code structure they don't like. There's no guarantee that removing code smells will actually make your code better.

- *Test coverage* is the degree to which the test suite exercises the codebase. Many different test coverage metrics have been proposed (e.g., line coverage vs. condition coverage vs. path coverage) and many tools and libraries are available for calculating coverage metrics. More is usually better but aiming for 100% test coverage is unwise because it leads to copious, low-value tests.

- *Cycle time* is the average number of days from when a developer (or pair) starts a story to when that story is shipped to production.

In other words, the best indicator we have of technical sustainability is how long it takes to deliver work. Increasing cycle time may be caused by several factors including increasing technical debt, building more complicated features, changes to team composition, changes to the deployment pipeline, etc. There's no algorithm for this. Increasing cycle times are a red flag, but you have to think carefully about alternative causes.

While most developers routinely think about the first meaning of technical sustainability, many software teams neglect the second meaning and underestimate the probability of security breaches and cascading technical failures. Assessing a product's effects on technical infrastructure *before something goes wrong* can be challenging and sometimes leads to over-engineering. If you're building the kind of product that affects some broader technical infrastructure (e.g., a software library, programming language, security product, control system for physical infrastructure), we can make the following suggestions.

1. At the beginning of greenfield projects and semi-annually afterward, hold a worst-case scenario brainstorming and risk-mitigation workshop.

2. Consider engaging appropriate external consultants (e.g., risk management, penetration testing).

3. Whenever a serious problem is resolved, hold a rigorous post-mortem investigation to ensure the problem will never reoccur.

These activities will be more effective in organizations that have high psychological safety (see the sidebar on page 200) and cultures that value learning. While the engineers should lead technical sustainability assessment, product designers and product managers should contribute to brainstorming, risk mitigation, and post-mortems.

Summary

In this chapter, we explored practices that give software teams the confidence to ship their software. Ideally, the code is shippable at all times, and the teams release as frequently as makes sense in their context. Version control, code review, and an efficient build system all help give teams confidence to release more frequently. Having an acceptance or staging environment to facilitate manual testing is also desirable in most contexts. Finally, we recommend all teams have a firm policy of never merging code on red builds.

While the practices may not seem like rocket science, the pressures of adding new features may tempt some teams to skip, ignore, or deprioritize these practices. In our experience, the longer the code isn't shippable, the more difficult fixing it becomes.

Part IV

Looking Forward

for everyone

In Track One, we examined knowing what to build and what to put in the backlog. In Track Two, we examined the engineering practices for taking a story in the backlog to shipping code. While these practices will help you reliably ship code from week to week, month to month, and year to year, they aren't enough to build successful teams.

Chapter 12: Towards Organizational Justice illustrates how people's experiences working in the software industry are not the same, and it discusses how we can level the playing field to give every software professional their best chance at success.

Chapter 13: Conclusion summarizes our core argument and synthesizes several overarching principles on which our recommendations are based.

Chapter 12
Towards Organizational Justice

People [seem] unaware of the differences in their behavior towards different peers, and [underestimate] the impact of their small acts of interpersonal exclusion on their peers, both in terms of job performance as well as their own team's effectiveness.
– Juliet Bourke

 Key Takeaways

- Creating a just organization with a diverse workforce, "you belong here" culture, and tailored support requires intentional work; it won't just happen.

- Organizational injustice is rooted in both conscious and unconscious bias.

- Conscious biases can (sometimes) be corrected with education, but employees who refuse to reform should be terminated.

- Unconscious biases affect everyone and are difficult to eliminate; instead, focus on redesigning tasks, policies, and systems to prevent biases or mitigate their effects.

- To *recruit* diverse talent: hire paid interns; keep your application process simple, easy, and transparent; and don't use AI for screening.

- To *retain* diverse talent: share power, improve your onboarding process, offer flexible working conditions, and develop allyship and mentorship skills.

- Reform your promotion process to enhance fairness.

Dealing with Bias

Sare—a talented engineer, author, and all-around amazing person—shared her perspective on being a woman in software engineering. Here's what she had to say:

"Women are constantly asked to prove that they are 'technical enough.' This is my life. This is why I've quit the industry twice. It's hard to find a software company where my co-workers generally treat me like I'm a person, not an aberration. Because I'm a consultant, working around great engineers doesn't solve the problem. I have this challenge with every client in every external meeting. It takes me a few weeks for clients to accept that I can not only lead a team because I can coordinate people but also actually know how to code. There's always that moment of shock when I pair with someone because they didn't expect I actually knew what I was talking about. Being constantly asked, 'So are you really a programmer?' takes a toll.

"Because of this constant bias, all women in 'male' jobs and all minorities have to develop better communication skills, better emotional intelligence, better emotional regulation, and have a huge reservoir of patience just to come to work. Because of this constant bias, those immeasurable skills aren't often recognized or valued. Promotion guidelines should include 'responding to systemic marginalization with grace.'

"As we think about ways to quantify advancement, we also need to think about how to make it reasonable for people who don't share the same privileges.

"If underrepresented minorities are doing all this extra work every day just to be on the same playing field, that means they have fewer resources to do their regular work, let alone 'work harder' for promotion. It's easy to say, 'Yeah, take a few hours and learn some language,' or, 'Spend some time skilling up in some technology,' when you don't have to face the fatigue and burnout from justifying yourself all day on top of your regular programming work.

"I've struggled for advancement. I've seen others promoted who appear to be doing the same things I'm doing. I've asked for feedback about what I can do to gain that promotion and received only vague or unhelpful advice. When I ask my colleagues for feedback, they say, 'You're doing great. I really like working with you. Clients love you.' But then, when I ask what I need to improve to be promoted, again, it's silence."

Introduction

This book is about optimizing the sociotechnical process of software development. A crucial but oft-overlooked part of this optimization is making the professional environment fair and just because people do their best work when they feel that they are treated fairly.

In Sare's story, we hear about the cumulative effects of injustice, belittling, and demeaning behavior. Common themes in stories of discrimination also include self-doubt and confusion. If you have experienced injustice in the workplace, we assure you that you are not alone; stories like Sare's (and worse) are common throughout the tech industry. They range from the seemingly minor to illegal, heinous behavior. If this seems far-fetched and unlike your organization, remember that people are more likely to share negative experiences with trusted community members to whom the story pertains. For example, women are more likely to discuss sexist behavior with other women. Therefore, those least likely to experience injustice are also least likely to hear about it.

Organizational justice is neither a liberal nor conservative cause. Everyone cares about justice; they just don't always agree on what is just in a specific situation. We (Paul and Todd) have very different political views, yet we reached agreement on virtually all of the content below, and we both feel that it's relevant regardless of the latest political discourse or your personal ideology. Indeed, it's not easy for people like us—middle-aged, straight, white men from rich, western countries who have little-lived experience of discrimination—to discuss these issues without seeming tone-deaf and part of the problem. However, expecting those most often victimized to do all the work of fighting for a better world is part of the injustice, so with humility, we have to try.

We shared this chapter with several beta readers from diverse social groups and made many updates and alterations based on their feedback.

How Do I Know if There's a Problem? Assume There's a Problem.

Many injustices are difficult to address for several reasons:

- The people experiencing the issue don't report it. They may believe that they will be ignored or face retaliation even if the company has a no-retaliation policy. Many high-profile professionals have been fired for complaining about injustices.

- The person receiving the report doesn't understand it or take it seriously. Because we all have different life experiences, managers often misunderstand the emotional impact of events on their staff or dismiss legitimate concerns as people being oversensitive. When problems are reported as items in retros or a concerned message instead of a formal complaint, the medium doesn't always convey how serious the problem seems to the person reporting it.

- The team (or manager, HR professional, etc.) understands what the report says but doesn't recognize it as a problem. Professionals increasingly recognize the ethical problems with discriminating based on race, gender, sexual orientation, and religion, yet continue to rationalize and defend discrimination based on nationality, disability, age, and socioeconomic class.

- The team (or manager, HR professional, etc.) recognizes that there is an issue but doesn't deal with it effectively. Justice issues often require complex, challenging, permanent changes to systems and processes. Many people just want an easy solution (i.e., lip service).

All of these reasons are compounded by the fact that injustice often comes in the form of death-by-a-thousand-cuts rather than a singular event. Injustice that stems from many small infractions instead of one big infraction is harder to report, understand, and address.

Unfortunately, injustice is ubiquitous to the point that you should simply assume your team has serious problems. When people take umbrage at the suggestion that such problems might exist, ask, "How would we know there are problems if no one has reported them?"

Measuring Psychological Safety

Psychological safety is the degree to which a specific person in a specific situation feels that they can take interpersonal risks without negative consequences. If you're confident that you won't face any repercussions from criticizing your boss in a retro, then your psychological safety in that situation is high. High psychological safety is important because "organizations in which managers value the employee who speaks up, questions existing practices, and suggests new ideas are better able to improve and learn" [144].

A good way to measure psychological safety is to use Edmondson's Psychological Safety Scale [145], shown below. To calculate the score, sum the points for each answer. For example, if someone answered 'disagree, agree, neutral, neutral, agree, strongly disagree, neutral,' then their score would be $4 + 4 + 3 + 3 + 2 + 1 + 3 = 20$. Higher scores indicate greater psychological safety.

	strongly disagree	disagree	neutral	agree	strongly agree
If you make a mistake on this team, it is often held against you	5	4	3	2	1
Members of this team are able to bring up problems and tough issues	1	2	3	4	5
People on this team sometimes reject others for being different	5	4	3	2	1
It is safe to take a risk on this team	1	2	3	4	5
It is difficult to ask other members of this team for help	5	4	3	2	1
No one on this team would deliberately act in a way that undermines my efforts	1	2	3	4	5
Working with members of this team, my unique skills and talents are valued and utilized	1	2	3	4	5

(In our experience, more umbrage indicates more serious issues.) The question isn't *is there a problem?* The questions you should be asking are, "What are the most serious problems, and how can we address them?" Some simple ways to raise these questions include:

- Run an annual anonymous survey including a psychological safety scale (see the Measuring Psychological Safety sidebar).

- Schedule a quarterly team health assessment facilitated by someone from outside your management reporting structure—ideally outside the company.

- Look for missing feedback loops that would help identify problems in your team or organization.

- Encourage engineers, managers, and leaders to ask their peers (and direct reports) for feedback routinely.

Creating a Healthy Work Environment

Tech companies *should* create healthy work environments where people are given opportunities to grow and feel respected, heard, and both physically and psychologically safe, not only because it's the right thing to do but also because it improves morale, job performance, retention, and profitability. Software is created by people, and people do their best work when they feel appreciated, included, and respected. Therefore, our goal is to provide concepts that will help you create a welcoming team and a welcoming company.

We will divide our discussion into four sections. Justice is built upon a foundation of increasing perspectives, fostering a "you belong here" culture, providing tailored support, and sharing power. These elements are interconnected; each must be addressed for optimal results. Before tackling each of these foundations of justice, we next introduce an important cross-cutting concern: the issue of conscious and unconscious bias.

Conscious vs. Unconscious Bias

> *I have a really hard time with the idea that we as a society should accommodate badly behaved people because of the great stuff they create.*
> *– Sarah Mei*

Conscious Bias

Conscious bias is when people have prejudices that they know about. Conscious bias leads to overt, explicit discrimination. *Unconscious bias* is when people have prejudices that they *don't* know about. Unconscious bias leads to accidental, unintended discrimination. There's a lot of talk in management and government circles about unconscious bias and unconscious bias training (more on that below), yet many people remain overtly and proudly prejudiced.

When an employee espouses conspiracy theories about how straight, white men can no longer find work because employers only hire women and non-whites, that's *conscious* bias.[1] When a professor says something like, "women just don't get computers," that is conscious bias.[2] When someone refuses to work with a trans person, objects to a co-worker wearing

---

[1] According to the US Bureau of Labor Statistics, the 2024 unemployment rate among those aged 20+ years was 2.9% for white men, 3.4% for white women, 4.3% for Hispanic men, 4.8% for Hispanic women, 5.3% for black women, and 5.6% for black men https://www.bls.gov/web/empsit/cpsee_e16.htm

[2] Female computer science majors have higher grades, on average, than male students [146].

a religious symbol, or complains that hiring racial minorities will interfere with the team's dynamics, that's usually *conscious* bias.

Such people are typically aware of their negative attitudes toward one or more minority groups. They don't think of these negative attitudes as biases; they think they're "the truth." Media and peer groups can reinforce these beliefs, but the popular belief in "media bubbles" or "echo chambers" is misleading. Rather, wealthy individuals, organizations, and nations "us[e] social media to spread computational propaganda and disinformation" to manipulate public opinion [147]. Many people deriding minority groups are being manipulated by these powerful interests.

Regardless, we can confront *conscious* bias through a three-step process:

1. **Isolate.** People who hold expressly bigoted beliefs are toxic to your organizational culture and should be rapidly isolated not only from people they're biased against but also from decision-making or other social processes that affect the people they're biased against. Think of isolation as a temporary measure to give the employee an opportunity to reform.

2. **Educate.** Conscious biases are typically rooted in incorrect beliefs. Whether these incorrect beliefs can be changed depends on the individual's *belief perseverance*: the degree to which a person resists changing their mind based on new evidence [148]. People with low belief perseverance can be rehabilitated by exposure to facts (e.g., scientific literature about sexual orientation) or personal experience (e.g., working with a woman who is an excellent coder). The latter is tricky because most people don't want to work with someone who's prejudiced against them.

3. **Terminate.** People with high belief perseverance tend to retain their biases no matter what. When employees won't reform their prejudicial behavior, eject them from your organization. Their technical contributions are not worth the negative impacts on their co-workers and organizational culture.

Unconscious Bias and Treating Others Differently

Despite the prevalence of conscious bias, unconscious bias is *much* more common. Unconscious bias is part of being human. We're *all* biased in ways we're not aware of. That's why they call it "unconscious." Unconscious biases lead us to treat people differently depending on the groups we think they belong to. This differential treatment can be insulting and upsetting, but many people just don't seem to notice because people have wildly different life experiences.

For example, I (Paul) was once on a shuttle bus at Frankfurt airport. I asked the person sitting next to me if she spoke English (because I don't speak German). She, visibly annoyed, responded "Sprechen Sie Deutsch?" (do you speak German?). I said, sorry, no, at which point she visibly relaxed and began chatting to me in English. It turned out that she was an anthropologist, originally from India, now living in Frankfurt. Unfortunately, despite her fluency in German, many Germans (especially men) insisted on speaking English with her, in other words, treating her as an outsider. She found this repeated othering deeply hurtful. She relaxed when she realized that I wasn't othering her; I spoke to her in English because

I didn't speak German. Rather than treating her as an outsider, I was an outsider myself. This interaction illustrates two important points about unconscious bias and inclusion:

1. Sometimes, statements or actions that seem innocuous can be genuinely hurtful to others. To maintain an inclusive environment, we therefore need to listen to and empathize with people with different life experiences.

2. Sometimes, people upset us or make us feel excluded completely by accident or in ways they couldn't have anticipated, so we should try to avoid being overly sensitive or jumping to conclusions.

People tend to react negatively to one or the other of these two points depending on their political leanings. On one side, some people feel like, 'Why should I work so hard making others comfortable? No one seems to care if I'm comfortable.' On the other side, some people feel like suggesting that someone is too sensitive belittles their feelings because repeated, seemingly-innocuous behaviors can accumulate to seriously harm a person's psychosocial well-being.

Consider two extreme examples. In one organization we observed, there was a trans person who changed their name to reflect their new gender. Their line manager continued to call them by their deadname (pre-tansition name), and the manager felt that expecting him to remember a new name was unreasonable. That's failing to empathize. Contrastingly, in May 2020, a black male bird-watcher in New York's Central Park asked a white woman to leash her dog (in an on-leash area). The woman called 911 and claimed he was threatening her [149]. That's being too sensitive.

Both failing to empathize and oversensitivity create toxic workplaces. Failing to empathize erodes individuals' self-esteem, sense of belonging, etc. Being too sensitive makes forthright conversations and conflict resolution impossible because everyone's so afraid of causing offense that they hide their true feelings. Complicating matters, people often dismiss toxic behavior by claiming the victims are being too sensitive *and* dismiss oversensitivity by claiming prejudice. So, how can we differentiate reasonable from unreasonable behavior? There's no universal answer, but we can suggest the following considerations.

- Consider the implicit social contract governing the situation. What would most people view as normal? For example, if Maggie is upset at Prem for eating his lunch at lunchtime in the break room because Maggie dislikes hearing people eat, Maggie is being too sensitive. But if Maggie is upset at Prem for watching pornography in the break room, Maggie is justified because Prem's behavior is outside the bounds of the implicit social contract governing the workplace.

- Consider if the behavior is repeated. For example, if Prem comments that Maggie looks good in that outfit once, and Maggie immediately submits a formal complaint, Maggie might be overreacting. But if Prem comments on Maggie's looks every day, Maggie is more justified in complaining.

- Consider whether the problematic behavior has been discouraged. For example, if Prem comments that Maggie looks good every day, and Maggie smiles and thanks Prem, there's no signal that the behavior is hurtful. In contrast, if Maggie tells Prem that Prem's comments make her uncomfortable, *and Prem keeps doing it anyway,* Prem is more clearly in the wrong.

- Consider intentions.[3] Suppose Prem is reviewing Maggie's code, and gives some blunt criticism. Maggie is more justified in complaining if Prem is intentionally trying to undermine Maggie's credibility and contributions than if he just isn't very good at phrasing critiques.

None of these considerations are absolute. People have different perceptions of the implicit social contracts governing our workplaces. Some behaviors are so unreasonable that it doesn't matter that it was only one time, the behavior hadn't been previously discouraged, or the intentions were good. But creating a healthy, just work environment requires a dual willingness to (1) empathize with others and try to understand their diverse perspectives and (2) avoid oversensitivity and defensiveness.

Unconscious Bias and Judgment

Unconscious biases also lead us to *judge* people differently depending on the groups to which we think they belong. For example, suppose we asked 100 managers at 100 different companies to each rate the job performance of their software developers. We might find that people who drink kombucha get better ratings. Is job performance actually correlated with kombucha consumption? No. Is this a huge problem? Probably not. But across many industries and job types, subjective assessments of job performance are correlated with gender, race, sexual orientation, disability, age, physical attractiveness, socioeconomic class, and many other factors in ways that do not reflect real differences in job performance.

Unfortunately, people tend to be less concerned about unconscious bias, less prone to hold others accountable for them, and less supportive of efforts to combat them [150]. Mitigating unconscious bias isn't easy. Fischoff [151, p. 426] identified five approaches to addressing unconscious bias:

1. "warning about the possibility of bias without specifying its nature";

2. "describing the direction (and perhaps extent) of the bias that is typically observed";

3. "providing a dose of feedback, personalizing the implications of the warning";

4. "offering an extended program of training with feedback, coaching, and whatever else it takes" to overcome the bias; and

5. redesigning the person-task system to mitigate the bias.[4]

---

[3]At this point, some readers familiar with the contemporary discourse around workplace behavior are cracking their knuckles before embarking on an epic complaint letter explaining how intentions don't matter as much as impact. Of course good intentions do not always excuse hurtful behavior but ignoring intentions is bad moral philosophy. No reasonable person thinks that accidentally bumping into someone and knocking them over is morally equivalent to tackling somebody to the ground intentionally. Intentions do not excuse us from responsibility for our actions, but hurting people on purpose is obviously worse than hurting people by accident, especially when the accidental harm is difficult to predict.

[4]This one isn't a direct quote because Fischoff didn't put it quite so concisely. Give him a break. Four out of five ain't bad!

The problem with options one, two, and three is that they don't work [151]. The problem with option four is that it only sort of works. Many organizations offer some form of *unconscious bias training*. "Unconscious bias training can be effective for reducing implicit *bias*, but it is unlikely to eliminate it ... [or] change *behavior*" [152, p. 6; italics ours]. Moreover, "unconscious bias training interventions are not generally designed to reduce explicit bias and those that [are] have yielded mixed results" [152, p. 6]. Furthermore, unconscious bias training is expensive, time-consuming, and breaks down every time someone new joins the team. To be clear, we don't think unconscious bias training does any harm; it's just not a silver bullet.

Therefore, our focus for the remainder of this chapter is on option five: accept that people have unconscious biases and redesign systems and processes to suppress or mitigate these biases. Structural debiasing works. For example, when hiring, unconscious biases make us more likely to shortlist candidates who are more like us. Removing certain identifying information like names and pictures from résumés mitigates these biases.

Armed with this background on human biases, we can now move on to our first foundation of justice: increasing the number of perspectives.

Increase Perspectives

The first foundation of organizational justice is increasing the number of perspectives. Diverse software teams include people with different genders, ages, sexual orientations, abilities, experience levels, and ethnic, cultural, and economic backgrounds. While there is no such thing as a perfectly diverse team, some teams are clearly more diverse than others.

More diverse teams and organizations have more varied perspectives, which makes them more resilient [153] and better at sensemaking, critical thinking, decision-making, and innovating [154]. However, these varied perspectives also increase intragroup conflict, which damages trust, team cohesion, communication, cooperation, and job satisfaction [155].

This mix of benefits and drawbacks creates the so-called *diversity paradox*: "If [firms] embrace diversity, they risk workplace conflict, and if they avoid diversity, they risk loss of competitiveness" [156].

The diversity paradox and the purported drawbacks of diversity are bogus. What's actually happening is organizations hire people who don't fit their (typically young, straight, white, male) employee archetype without any attempt to be inclusive, tailor support, or share power. In the USA, for example, organizations frequently:

- hire Muslims, Hindus, Sikhs, Buddhists, etc. and expect them to work through their religious holidays and festivals;

- hire women but provide no maternity benefits; and

- hire people with disabilities without accommodating their disabilities.

If you join a team that systematically excludes you, treats you differently from everyone else, and doesn't understand or accommodate your needs, then you may struggle to trust them, identify with them, or enjoy your job. It's not because the team is more diverse; it's because the organization mistreats everyone who doesn't fit its employee archetype.

Recruit a Diverse Workforce

Organizations can hire staff in many different ways. They can post job ads online and see who applies. They can contact people who've expressed interest in working for them in the past. They can ask current employees for recommendations. They can hire recruiting agencies to find candidates for them. They can directly approach individuals (typically with big reputations in a certain area). They can poach employees from competitors.

Organizations can increase diversity by hiring interns and addressing issues throughout the hiring process, from job descriptions and advertisements to résumé screening, interviewing, and making offers.

Hire Interns

The best way to hire early-career professionals is through a paid internship program. From the perspective of a software company, internships are not about supporting the local university or getting cheap workers; the primary purpose of an internship is to evaluate potential hires. Working with someone for a few months is vastly more effective for assessing their skills and fit for your team than any interview. When the intern graduates, you will know whether you want to hire them.

From a diversity perspective, paid internships help attract candidates from lower socioeconomic backgrounds. Unpaid internships exacerbate discrimination and should be avoided. Organizations can also grow their personnel funnel by supporting code boot camps, apprenticeship programs, and diversity-themed networking groups. The only real drawback of the internship program is that it mainly applies to early-career hires.

Internships are relatively inexpensive and low-risk. If you get a terrible intern, just limit their activities so they don't break anything and they'll be gone in a few months with no hard feelings. Compare this to hiring a professional developer who costs 5–10 times as much and could sabotage the company, be difficult to fire, and sue for wrongful dismissal.

Some tips for good intern experiences include the following [157].

- Recruit interns with good academic records. Academically well-prepared interns tend to have better internship experiences and contribute more to their host companies.

- Pay interns. Expecting interns to work for you for free is discriminatory (and illegal in many places). Reputable companies do not engage in volunteer internship scams. You are not doing the intern a favor by providing a volunteer internship. Yes, they are learning from you, but they are also working for you, and they have to eat and pay rent like everyone else. Pay interns at least a little more than minimum wage.

- Clarify your expectations; namely, that interns treat their internship as a real job, proactively find suitable tasks, ask questions, treat every assigned task as a learning experience, and ask for help when they need it.

- Thoroughly on-board your interns. Introduce them to their teams. Start them with simple, well-defined tasks and allow them to advance to more complex tasks as they are able. Get them into the regular pair programming rotation early, even if they can't contribute much yet, so they start to feel like part of the team. Avoid giving interns busywork.

- Treat interns with respect. Interns may lack experience, but they are adult human beings due the basic respect and dignity afforded any other adult human being. Call them by name; do not refer to anyone as "the intern" or by some stupid nickname they might secretly hate.

Of course, most organizations won't be able to fulfill all their staffing needs through an internship program, so we still need to improve conventional hiring practices.

Write Diversity-Friendly Job Ads

From a diversity perspective, publicly posting job openings is important. Hiring people known to or recommended by current employees typically exacerbates homogeneity. Directly contacting qualified individuals *can* be used to recruit more diverse staff, but again, the people known to the organization often resemble the people who already work there. Recruiting agencies, meanwhile, "could promote workforce diversity, while in reality they often inhibit it" [158, p. 195]. In most cases, therefore, we recommend handling recruitment in-house and advertising all openings.

The next step is writing job descriptions and advertisements that will attract a diverse pool of candidates. Job ads should include a *diversity statement*. Here is an example from a recent position at the university where Paul works:

> *We encourage applications from people of culturally diverse backgrounds; equity target groups include women, people with disabilities, people who identify as LGBTQ+, and people of Aboriginal or African descent. Applications from all qualified candidates who would contribute to the diversity of our community are particularly welcome.*

Diversity statements help to convey your organization's commitment to justice. Alone, however, they're not sufficient.

Job ads tend to contain a lot of coded language: statements, phrasing, or omissions that subtly imply the kind of candidates desired. For example, phrases like "fast-paced and competitive environment," "strong work ethic," and "commitment to organizational goals" are often code for a stressful job with unpaid overtime and no work-life balance.

Coded language can discourage certain candidates. For example, "Job advertisements for male-dominated areas [employ] greater masculine wording" (e.g., competitive, dominant) and this wording often makes the job less attractive to female applicants [159]. Indeed, the job ad may be less attractive to any applicant who values collaboration over individualism. Racially charged language discourages racialized persons from applying. For example, after Seth Godin's book *Tribes* was published in 2014, North American businesses rapidly adopted the term *tribe* for marketing and recruiting despite it carrying negative connotations for black and indigenous peoples. Since remembering all the problematic words and phrases is difficult, we recommend using an automated text analyzer tool to detect and remove coded language.

Moreover, what *isn't* said can be just as important as what is said. For example, omitting descriptions of benefits like flex work and remote work may turn off candidates with caregiving responsibilities, while omitting financial benefits may discourage applicants from lower socio-economic backgrounds. Current text analyzers don't help with these kinds of omissions, so it's up to you to include all relevant benefits.

One last thing: don't expect candidates to jump through stupid hoops to apply for your positions. People should apply for (professional) jobs by submitting a résumé and possibly a cover letter. Don't ask people to copy-paste information from their résumés into some convoluted form, convert their résumé into a specific format (e.g., a spreadsheet), provide data that isn't really pertinent to the job, take tests (e.g., a personality test), or complete time-consuming tasks (e.g., programming puzzles) at the application stage.

Some people think a difficult application process will discourage weaker applicants, but they've got it backward. Difficult applications turn away the *strongest* applicants because they always have other opportunities. Keep your application process simple, easy, and transparent. Be clear about what the application process is. Unqualified applications can be weeded out. Qualified people who don't apply cannot be weeded in.

One thing that can help without unduly irritating your applicants is asking them to explain, in a paragraph or three, why they believe they're the right person for the job. Letting people explain their qualifications and worth in their own words—letting applicants tell their own story—tells you much more about them than most typical résumés.

Screen Candidates without Biasing Information

Screening—that is, selecting or *shortlisting* the most qualified candidates—is particularly fraught with unconscious bias [160]. Prejudice in résumé selection is often triggered when the screener (correctly or incorrectly) infers personal characteristics of the applicant from the information provided. For example, if Mohammad Arif graduated from the Islamic University of Madinah in 2002, we might guess that Mohammad is a Muslim man in his late forties from Saudi Arabia. These guesses can then activate group stereotypes and trigger discriminatory decision-making.

To de-bias the screening process, try the following.

1. Make a list of information that is useful for screening but does not readily support inferring personal characteristics (e.g., level of education, whether qualifications are relevant to the job role).

2. Have someone not directly involved in hiring extract the desired information from the applications / résumés into a spreadsheet. Do not include candidate names; instead, give each candidate a unique identifier (e.g., "A01") and make a separate *key* linking identifiers to names and contact information.

3. Have the people who *are* directly involved in hiring use the anonymized spreadsheet for shortlisting.

Do *NOT* use AI to screen candidates. AI screeners have baked-in biases that usually can't be explained or detected. Indeed, some less reputable companies use the AI to launder discrimination like criminals use a casino to launder money.

Adopt Working Interviews

Conventional job interviews (in which applicants answer a series of questions) don't work. Candidates may lie. Interviews select for charisma, charm, extraversion, and physical appearance regardless of whether these attributes matter for the job in question. Conventional job interviews don't adequately assess technical skills. Google-style mind traps ("suppose someone magically shrinks you down to 3 cm tall and drops you in a blender; you have five seconds before they turn it on, what do you do?") tell you how good people are at silly thought puzzles, not how good they are at unit testing or user-centered design. Some companies ask obscure technical questions that don't reflect the job, expect interviewees to have memorized vast amounts of syntax in a specific language, or place artificial burdens on interviewees to see how they handle working under pressure.

Interviews also discriminate against neurodivergent candidates, particularly candidates who are prone to anxiety, even if a little anxiety wouldn't impair their job performance. Interviews trigger stereotyping and prejudice because the interviewer can't help but see and hear the interviewee.

The best way to hire early-career professionals is through a paid internship program, but when internships are not feasible, we recommend *working interviews* in which the candidate performs tasks similar to those found in the job.[5] However, giving an engineer an unfamiliar task to complete in an unfamiliar integrated development environment (IDE), programming language, etc. tells you how the candidate will perform on their first day rather than in the long term. You also can't give every candidate different tasks, or you won't be able to compare their performances. We recommend the following two-phase process, which was successfully demonstrated by Rob Mee, founder of Pivotal Labs.

Working Interviews Phase One

Phase one consists of the following steps.

1. Before any of the interviewees arrive, the interviewer prepares a programming task and a script comprising a task description and a series of guided, open-ended questions.

2. When an interviewee arrives, the interviewer greets the interviewee.

3. The interviewer begins the script. They describe the task. They remind the candidate that it doesn't matter if they know the programming language since their job is to talk in pseudocode and let the interviewer transcribe their discussion into the programming language's syntax.

4. The interviewer shares their computer screen and does all the typing.

5. The interviewer begins iterating between asking questions (e.g., "What could we test now?" or "How would we refactor this method to remove duplication?") and implementing the interviewee's ideas.

6. When the candidate answers the question well, the interviewer types the code and moves on.

7. When the interviewee answers poorly, they lose one point, and the interviewer asks a follow-up coaching question to help steer the candidate in the right direction. If the candidate answers well, the interviewer types the code and moves on.

---

[5] Check with your legal team before implementing working interviews. Depending on your jurisdiction, you may need to pay applicants a certain amount or have a certain kind of contract.

8. If the interviewee still can't complete the task, they lose a second point, but then the interviewer completes the task and moves on anyway. The interviewer doesn't tell the candidate that they lost a point; they just subtly make a tick mark on a piece of paper or make a mental note.

Moving on helps maintain the candidate's sense of progress and accomplishment from building code together, often in a programming language they didn't know. (You want applicants who *aren't* hired to tell their friends how pleasant the interview process was, not badmouth your hiring practices.) Moving on also limits stress by implicitly communicating that individual mistakes are not deal-breakers—'the interview is still going, so I must still have a chance.'

This process produces a score for each applicant. To proceed, you can select the top n applicants (for some value of n) or all applicants who exceed some threshold, t (for some value of t). Over time, it's easy to develop a reasonable threshold—too high and you won't fill your vacancies; too low and you'll spend too much time on phase two.

While the score is the main driver of selection, other observable behavior matters. If the interviewer felt that the interviewee was worth a risk (because they displayed amicability, empathy, fast learning, etc.), then the interviewer could recommend moving them forward despite a weaker score. Conversely, if the interviewer felt that the candidate displayed some red flags (e.g., inability to accept criticism, interrupting, unwillingness to collaborate, complaining about the exercise), the interviewer could recommend not moving them forward despite a stronger score. This subjective evaluation may allow some prejudice to creep back into the process but it's unavoidable because technical skill is not the only thing interviewers need to assess and there simply is no objective way to assess temperament.

The purpose of phase one is to score candidates' coding skills, reliably, in no more than one hour per candidate. The sessions improve comparability across applicants by being highly scripted and similar in length. They negate familiarity issues by using routine tasks, having interviewees pair program with interviewers, and beginning with an empty test and an empty class.[6]

Working Interviews Phase Two

Selected applicants move on to the second phase: two half-day coding sessions. Schedule these sessions on the same day if possible.

You want to give candidates a sense of working in your codebase and following your practices. Choose a story that: (1) you've implemented recently, (2) took 2–4 hours, (3) involved some development and some refactoring, and (4) doesn't require too much domain context or explanation. (At Pivotal, if a good story could not be found, the company had several canned projects to use.)

The interviewer reverts the codebase to before the story was implemented. When the candidate arrives, the interviewer reminds them that since these are real stories, there is no expectation for how long the work should take, and finishing the story in the allotted time may be unrealistic. The interviewer then shows the candidate the story with its attachments (e.g., mock-ups, acceptance criteria), verifies that the candidate understands what needs to

---

[6]Pivotal used object-oriented languages, but the principle of beginning with a clean slate applies more broadly.

be done, and discusses how the candidate might approach the story. The interviewer briefly overviews the codebase, indicating which files might need modifying. Like in phase one, the interviewer and candidate pair program, beginning with the interviewer doing all the typing. Once the candidate seems comfortable, the interviewer offers the candidate a chance to type. If the candidate is comfortable typing, the interviewer shifts to coaching; otherwise, they maintain the same roles. At the end of the session, the interviewer and candidate reflect on what they accomplished. Later, the code is discarded.

By repeating the same story with each candidate, the (same) interviewer can compare candidates' performances. While not as comprehensive as a multi-month internship, a full-day coding interview is about as much as one can expect for a mid-career hire.

Alternatives to Working Interviews

Working interviews may work for non-programmer roles; however, we have not observed any or found any scientific studies about working interviews with product designers or product managers. Therefore, we have no basis to predict their effectiveness. Constructing appropriate simulated tasks for these roles may be more difficult.

One common alternatives for designers is to submit a portfolio of their prior work. A portfolio-based approach is also useful for hiring developers active in open-source communities. However, some work is difficult to represent as a portfolio, and some applicants are forbidden from sharing their prior work. Moreover, you need some way to verify that the candidate actually did the work in the portfolio, and a portfolio doesn't tell you much about communication and teamwork skills.

Other options for interviewing product designers and product managers include critiquing an existing product or role-playing common tasks like interviewing a user, prioritizing a backlog, or drawing a mock-up. Again, there isn't good evidence for which approach works best, but we do know that conventional question-answer job interviews don't work very well, so we recommend experimenting with alternatives.

Hiring

Whatever your approach, assess lots of different skills associated with the role and avoid focusing on attributes that aren't actually necessary for the role (e.g., physical attractiveness). Avoid potentially prejudicing information before the decision. Even knowing that a candidate attended a top-tier school can bias scores. Stick with the anonymized spreadsheet. Do not look through the original résumés until preliminary decisions have been made. Do not ask candidates to share potentially compromising information like private social media accounts.

Keep the task consistent across applicants and use a consistent scoring system. We can't just make up the scoring system as we go because we'll invent different systems for different candidates, and these differences inflate prejudices. One specific problem we've observed is interviewers perceiving someone as more technical, then asking more technical questions, which reinforces the assumption that the candidate is more technical.

Moreover, to achieve greater diversity in your organization, keep positions open until at least one candidate who would add to the organization's diversity makes it to the last round of evaluation. Focus on the diversity of your hires, not your candidates. If you don't get (m)any applicants from underrepresented groups, focus on filling your funnel (e.g., by advertising to more diverse audiences, sponsoring diversity-focused events, and including diversity statements in job ads). But don't hire unqualified people simply to increase diversity; that's unfair to both the applicants and your team.

All that said, hiring a diverse workforce is insufficient for organizational change. *Retaining* a diverse workforce and *benefiting* from their varied perspectives requires changing the organization, as we'll discuss next.

You Belong Here

Inclusion is the degree to which a group, community, organization, or society shares power, respect, responsibility, and resources with *all* of its members. Inclusion is not only about people feeling like they belong; it's about how the group behaves toward individual members.

The benefits of a diverse workforce will only materialize if employees feel included. For example, suppose a French software company is modifying a legacy product for a new market: Egypt. Realizing they lack local knowledge, they try to hire an Egyptian product designer. This is expensive, time-consuming, and frustrating. They have to find a qualified Egyptian who speaks French, jump through hoops for l'Office français de l'immigration et de l'intégration, cover moving expenses, and offer a relocation bonus.

Eventually they find a highly-qualified candidate: Eman. Now, suppose the localization team ignores Eman's suggestions. When Eman suggests that a certain user experience structure will work better for Egyptians, they say, "That's not how we do things around here." After a while, Eman stops trying to bring their own perspective and replicates the company's ways of working. Now, the company's efforts at diversity are wasted because, while the team is more diverse, their *perspective* is not.

Recruiting people for their varied perspectives and then tacitly insisting they abandon those perspectives and toe the company line seems pretty daft, but organizations do it constantly. No one says, "Abandon your foreign perspective." They say, "You have to learn our company culture" and "That's not going to work here."

To benefit from a diverse workforce, organizations and teams must embrace varied perspectives from onboarding onward.

Fix Onboarding and Create a Welcoming Environment

Onboarding is the process of orienting and training new hires (or sometimes internal transfers). At some organizations, onboarding is limited to showing new employees to their cubicles and perhaps wishing them good luck—more like nonboarding. Failing to socialize new employees implicitly communicates that the employee (a) is not really valued and (b) is on their own.

Even when organizations have a more substantial process for socializing new employees, they tend to underestimate the magnitude of their internal jargon, norms, and assumptions. People often throw around obscure acronyms or terms that have different meanings to different people.

New hires need more extensive onboarding, including things like:

- an office tour;

- icebreakers, Q&A sessions, social events;

- documentation of team norms and practices;

- codebase walkthroughs;

- technical training related to the team's tooling;

- welcome emails, calls, kits (including, e.g., a glossary of buzzwords and jargon or lists of contacts), or meetings (with a representative from human resources or upper management);

- a buddy program and / or a mentor program;

- announcements of new hires; and

- a swag bag.

Some of these onboarding practices are simply intended to make new people feel welcome. However, as Cable et al. [161, p. 24] explain:

> *The traditional methods of onboarding ... assume that organizational values are something to be taught to and adopted by newcomers. This creates a tension: when newcomers are 'processed' to accept an organization's identity, they are expected to downplay their own identities, at least while they are at work. However, subordinating one's identity and unique perspectives may not be optimal in the long run for either the organization or the individual employee because suppressing one's identity is upsetting and psychologically depleting. Moreover, newcomers may not internalize the organizational values even if they appear to comply through external behaviors; over and above compliance, leaders need employee engagement if they want employees to contribute on their own and in ways that are not programmed. Socialization practices that get newcomers to behave inauthentically might not be sustainable because they do not fully engage the employee and they do not address broader issues concerning emotional exhaustion and work dissatisfaction.*

Instead of indoctrinating new hires, use the onboarding process to embrace the new hire's individuality and create an environment in which they can flourish by doing the following.

1. Encourage the new hire to "just be yourself" during onboarding events. Frame the workplace as a somewhere employees can be authentic. Accept myriad personal styles as long as people aren't hateful, toxic, or harmful to others.

2. Ask the new hire to identify their strengths and how their team can best take advantage of these strengths. Frame the job as endless opportunities to be your best self, to excel, and to grow as a person.

3. Ask the new hire to identify the conditions under which they flourish, and then manifest those conditions. For example, if the new hire does their best work at a standing desk, get them a standing desk.

4. During introduction sessions, specifically ask new hires to introduce themselves by talking about what they're good at, what they're like at their best, and their personal blockers (e.g., some people excel in hectic, high-pressure environments; others do their best work alone in quiet, low-stress environments). Try introducing someone from an often marginalized group "based on what they lead, and not what they do" (see Figure 12–1).

5. Provide a checklist for the new hire to chart their self-paced onboarding. The checklist is reviewed with their manager at expected intervals of day one, week one, month one, and month three. A written checklist (instead of verbal to-dos) facilitates self-assessment of onboarding progress.

6. Remind new hires that you expect them to be learning sponges for their first three months and not necessarily deliver work immediately. Acknowledge that they may still feel the need to deliver tons of value—that's normal—but you don't have that expectation.

This is not an exercise in lip service. If you tell people to be themselves and then expect everyone to dress / act / speak / be the same, or ask people their strengths and then assign them tasks unrelated to their strengths, or ask people what they need to succeed and then don't get them any of it, then they will rightly conclude that you're disingenuous. You have to follow through.

Embracing diversity doesn't mean abandoning all organizational norms. Teams can have coding standards. Organizations can have policies. Places can have ways of doing things. It just means respecting people as individuals and being open to new ideas.

aubrey blanche (she/her) ✔
@adblanche   ...

#Equity at work tip. Always introduce marginalized people by what they *lead* and not what they *do*.

Ex: I'd love to introduce my teammate NAME, who leads [organizing applications | ERG operations | new business development | etc.]. They can help you with THING.

9:52 AM · Jan 11, 2022 · Twitter Web App

Figure 12–1: Aubrey Blanche's Introductions Technique [162]

Practically speaking, whether your onboarding program includes icebreakers, a buddy program, technical training, etc., isn't as crucial as conveying that you value the new hire and their unique perspective.

Retain Diverse Talent

All this work recruiting and onboarding a diverse workforce will only pay off if organizations *retain* their workers. Significantly elevated turnover rates happen for people with underrepresented identities [163], [164], [165] because experienced or perceived discrimination reduces their organizational commitment, limits the ability to advance in their careers, and makes them want to seek other opportunities [166]. Employees from underrepresented groups have more negative experiences at work. From outright discrimination to lack of mentoring, these employees face more barriers and are therefore less included. Preliminary research in Paul's lab suggests that perceived organizational justice is one of the strongest predictors of employee retention. The most effective tactic for addressing this issue is sharing power.

Create an Inclusive Climate by Sharing Power

Creating an inclusive organization is about power. Who has the authority to make decisions? How are decisions made? Whose concerns are elevated, and whose are marginalized? Does everyone in the organization understand how decisions are made and who has what authority? How is the power wielded (justly or unjustly?), and for whose benefit?

To move beyond lip service, organizations must replace theatrics (creating the illusion of caring about inclusion rather than actually fostering an inclusive culture) with a focus on power-sharing and transparency. Write down who has what authority, discuss who *should* have what authority, and *include* everyone whose lives are affected by the outcome of a decision in the decision-making process. Consider the problems and fixes suggested by Okun and Jones [167] summarized in Table 12–1.

Be a Good Mentor

Employees at each stage of their career need mentoring to reach their full potential. Mentoring has the following three dimensions.

1. **Role-modeling**: exhibiting the attributes and actions you believe your mentees should exhibit; being an effective professional and a good person.

2. **Advising:** listening to the mentee's struggles, providing recommendations (especially around professional development and career progression), sharing insider knowledge about how to advance in the organization, helping the mentee strategize for advancement, and perhaps even teaching some new skills directly.

3. **Brokering:** taking an active role in driving the mentee's career forward by facilitating professional networking and actively creating opportunities for the mentee.

What differentiates mentoring from merely advising is a focus on career advancement (i.e., *brokering*). Brokering must be tailored to the mentee's goals. For example, when Paul has a graduate student who wants to be a professor, brokering means bringing the student

Table 12–1: Aspects of Organizational Culture That Prevent Inclusion (adapted from [167]*)

Problem	Symptoms	Fixes
Paternalism and Power Hoarding	Authority is centralized in people who believe they should make decisions for those without power.	Include in decision-making everyone affected by decisions; explain that effective leaders share power; demand economic democracy.
Opacity	Those with power don't explain why, how, or by whom decisions are made; authority is undocumented.	Demand transparency; document authority and decision rationale; reject organizational propaganda.
Defensiveness, Right to Comfort, and Fear of Open Conflict	The organization prioritizes protecting existing power structures, suppresses criticism, and maintains the status quo; making those with power feel uncomfortable is seen as deviant. Leaders suppress conflict, conflate raising difficult issues with rudeness and demand politeness.	Name defensiveness as a problem and explain how it sabotages the organization's mission; understand that discomfort is essential for growth and learning. Do not expect people facing serious problems to raise them in acceptable ways.
Only the Right Way	Our way is the only right way; anyone who can't see that is broken.	Accept that goals can be achieved in many ways, but once a group has chosen a way, honor it; call out people acting like their way is the only way.
Metrics Fixation	Only measurable outcomes matter; discomfort with emotion.	Find ways to measure important things that are being ignored; create your own scales; argue that qualitative accounts of the right things are better than quantitative measures of the wrong things.
Perfectionism	Focusing on what's wrong; failing to learn from mistakes because making mistakes is conflated with being a mistake.	Give balanced feedback; focus on learning from mistakes instead of assigning blame.
Sense of Urgency and Either-Or Thinking	Illusion of urgency leads to constant rushing; no time to be inclusive. Complex situations are reduced to false dichotomies: right vs. wrong; with us or against us.	Make realistic plans; include inclusivity goals and time to work on them. When stakes are high, reject pressure to make important decisions immediately, slow down, think more deeply, and *generate more than two alternatives*.
Objectivity	Believing that it is possible to be objective and that emotions are bad; mistaking one's own perspective for "facts" while other perspectives are "opinions."	Understand that all human phenomena, from music to financial accounting, is subjective; push yourself to understand and validate others' perspectives.
Inclusivity Theater	The organization prioritizes appearing to care about inclusion over actually being inclusive.	Focus on the problems listed in this table; dispute the usefulness of common inclusivity theater techniques (e.g., wellness committees, diversity-inclusion training); call out people paying lip service to inclusion while acting exclusionary.

*Adapted to apply more specifically to tech companies; *inclusivity theater* is our addition.

to conferences, introducing them to other influential professors, involving them in academic societies, getting them peer review work for scholarly publications, writing them reference letters, helping them apply for scholarships and awards, and most of all, involving them in many research projects and publications to expand their résumé.

Analogously, brokering for an ambitious young developer means actively driving their career forward by introducing them to influential people within the organization, getting them involved in the kinds of teams and projects that are likely to get noticed and lead to advancement, writing reference letters, publicly lauding their contributions, nominating them for internal awards, and putting them up for promotion. Brokering means taking an active role in advancing the mentee's career. A broker puts their own reputation at stake to advance the mentee.

Be a Good Ally

Brokering is related to allyship. An *ally* is like a broker for a person or group who faces some discrimination or oppression, for example, due to their gender, ethnicity, religion, sexual orientation, age, or disability. You don't have to be someone's mentor to be their ally. Allyship isn't usually a formal arrangement.

Juliet Bourke [168] recommends the following three simple allyship techniques.

1. **Helping each other out** by making introductions, sharing needed information, and amplifying others: "During my observations, I often saw peers subtly endorse and amplify each other (e.g., 'As Pedro said. . .'), thus helping to underscore a peer's point and increasing their potential influence over proceedings."

2. **Taking emotional care of others**, including showing honest interest in their personal lives, creating safe spaces for venting, or simply checking in on a peer.

3. **Making physical connections** with one's body and sharing space by "walking together to meetings, deliberately sitting next to each other, or if a meeting was virtual, sharing their personal backgrounds rather than using an impersonal corporate photo, and exaggerating positive non-verbal cues."

Try Reverse Mentoring

One effective technique for training upper management in inclusiveness is *reverse mentoring*. "Reverse mentoring is defined as the pairing of a younger, junior employee acting as a mentor to share expertise with an older, senior colleague as the mentee" [169]. While initially conceived as a means of sharing technical expertise, reverse mentoring facilitates the sharing of cultural perspectives and promotes diversity and inclusion. When a senior professional, manager, or executive from a dominant group takes on reverse mentors from frequently disadvantaged groups, the mentors can help the mentee get more in tune with the concerns of these groups. This isn't just about helping the mentee be more politically correct, it's about helping the mentee understand more diverse perspectives. Meanwhile, the mentors benefit from access to senior management, social capital, and leadership development [169].

Critical success factors for reverse mentoring include:

- "emphasize diversity;"

- "consult mentees before making the pairing formal;"

- address mentees' fear of revealing their lack of knowledge;

- "ensure strong commitment from mentees;" and

- train the mentors to structure their sessions with the mentees effectively [170].

In addition, reverse mentoring is *work* that must be *compensated*. Mentors must be released from regular duties to make time for mentoring, and mentoring must count for performance appraisal and promotion.

Avoid Fake Consultation

Many corporations, non-profits, and government agencies prepare for significant decisions through consultation (e.g., focus groups, town halls, questionnaires) to understand stakeholders' preferences and priorities. In our experience, consultations are often fake: they backfill justifications for already-made decisions, or gauge upcoming pushback and determine how to minimize it. Don't do fake consultations. Including people in decision-making means actually incorporating everyone's perspectives. Genuine consultation can be challenging. People have inconsistent—often incompatible—priorities. We can't make everyone happy, but people are much more accepting of decisions they disagree with when you're transparent about conflicting priorities and explain why you believe your solution is the best compromise.

Run Inclusive Meetings

Much of our advice in this chapter is directed to those in positions of authority, but one place where everyone can help foster a more inclusive culture is in meetings.

The most important inclusivity practice in meetings is to ensure that everyone who has a stake in the outcome of the meeting is invited to the meeting. This sounds obvious but is tricky in practice. Team members dynamically self-organize to solve problems. For example, an engineer facing a technical challenge might go directly to the team member they believe is most likely to be able to help and hash out the challenge one-on-one. For important engineering challenges, though, including the whole team is essential. This often takes longer, but if you ensure that the whole team understands the problem, the solution, and why this is the best solution, you'll have a more inclusive culture *and* the whole team will better understand the codebase.

The second most important inclusivity practice is good conversational turn-taking, meaning that:

1. only one person speaks at a time;

2. either no one interrupts, or there are specific rules about when and how someone is allowed to interrupt (e.g., a moderator is allowed to interrupt an off-topic discussion);

3. everyone in the meeting has a chance to speak; and

4. speakers are concise.

Good turn-taking does not mean putting people on the spot. If someone hasn't contributed to a discussion, you don't have to point at them and demand they add something. You can ask if anyone, especially anyone who hasn't already spoken, has anything to add.

Additional techniques to improve inclusivity in meetings include: speaking in reverse order of seniority (newest or least-experienced member first); repeating others' ideas to show that you're listening and confirm your understanding before offering your opinion; and amplifying ideas you agree with.

When amplifying an idea, explicitly credit its source (e.g., "I like Maryam's idea to refactor the service layer component..."). In our research, women often complained that their ideas were ignored until a man said the same thing and took credit.

Lastly, take care to avoid explaining things to people who already understand them and to avoid condescension.

Avoid Extra Work for Underrepresented Minorities

One pitfall to avoid is the tendency to volunteer team members from underrepresented minorities for extra work. Underrepresented minorities often take on additional work—not only mundane clerical work like note-taking but also education and advocacy work related to diversity and inclusion—which is often unrecognized, unrewarded, and unhelpful for career advancement.

When I (Todd) ran *Balancing Power Imbalances* workshops at Pivotal, I used to ask managers to recommend local co-facilitators. One recommended engineer explained that she'd prefer not to have been asked because she was tired of needing to say "no" to organizational justice efforts. Now I ask broader groups if anyone wants to volunteer so no one has to refuse explicitly.

Similarly, in Gusto's postmortem meeting template, the request for a volunteer note-taker is immediately followed by a reminder that underrepresented minorities disproportionately volunteer for the role, and maybe someone else could volunteer instead. Nudges like this can encourage better dynamics.

Confront Injustice in Real Time

> *Equality is a practice. It is how employees behave, leaders lead, and workplaces work.*
> – Michelle P. King

The old management adage "praise in public, criticize in private" is good advice unless a behavior causes significant, acute harm to others. Consider the following examples.

- Being late for meetings that require promptness (neither significant nor acute harm)— address in private. Sure, a consistently late teammate can be annoying and undermine a culture of punctuality over time, but that's not significant or acute enough to warrant calling someone out publicly.

- Misusing the travel budget (significant but not acute)—address in private. Despite being serious, nothing is gained by making a show about it in front of the whole team.

- Breaking the build (acute but not significant)—address in private, if at all. We've all broken the build. It's not a big deal. Publicly shaming someone for breaking the build will just make the team afraid to take risks.

- Calling someone a racist slur (acute and significant)—address immediately and publicly. In this example, calling out the offender publicly is not just about correcting the behavior, it's about ensuring everyone present sees that the behavior is unacceptable. Silence would imply that the behavior was OK.

Correcting behavior does not mean being a jerk. You don't have to yell, insult, or demean. In fact, calmly but firmly stating that some behavior will not be tolerated is often more powerful than losing your cool.

In practice, calling out misbehavior is intrinsically challenging because disturbing the interpersonal peace by "being rude" or "making a scene" is often seen as worse than the misbehavior itself. However, this attitude inhibits the organizational shift toward justice. Failing to confront injustice allows it to continue unimpeded and makes you complicit.

When you have to correct someone publicly, doing so calmly helps prevent others from protecting offenders by refocusing the situation on you "being rude." And yet, correcting people *too* kindly can also send the wrong message. If someone is abusing their co-workers, being too nice makes it look like you care more about the offender's feelings than the victim's. Calm but firm is usually best.

Confront Acute, Significant Injustice Immediately

When you must address injustice publicly, we suggest the following four-step process. Here, we are writing from the perspective of a concerned colleague who has no authority over the perpetrator or victim.

1. **Interject.** First, you must interrupt the situation by inserting yourself into it. You might say, "Wait a minute" or "Hold on" or "Hold up."

2. **Settle.** Take a deep breath. Give everyone in the situation a moment to settle down. If you are emotional, give yourself a moment. But don't wait long enough for the interruption to pass and the negative interaction to resume.

3. **Understand.** Ask the person(s) who engaged in the inappropriate behavior if you correctly perceived what just happened. You might say, "Did you just..." followed by whatever you think you saw or heard. Give them a chance to back down. Explain how the behavior could be harmful and specifically ask if that's what they meant. If they say, "Oh, that's not what I meant ..." (to say or do), play along.

4. **Educate.** If the perpetrator backs down, you might say, "In the future, let's try to..." and explain how the situation could be handled better. If the perpetrator doubles down, you might explain that the behavior makes you uncomfortable or isn't acceptable. Focus on how things should be done in the future. If the situation escalates,

suggest everybody take a break to cool down or include your manager or HR representative to mediate. Even if you can't de-escalate the situation, you still did your part. You voiced opposition to injustice. You showed the victim(s) of the injustice that you are on their side and that someone does care.

Here's an example of how this could go down. If you find intervening like this intimidating, really imagining specific co-workers in these roles and reading your lines aloud may help you feel more able to intervene.

```
Man [to woman]: You really should smile more.
You: Hold on, [deep breath] did you just tell her to smile more?
Man: Yeah. What's it to you?
You: There's this whole thing about not telling women to smile more.
It's like you're saying she's got to prioritize her appearance to you
over how she actually feels. Is that what you meant?
Man: Of course not. But everyone looks better when they smile. That's
not sexism, it's just human nature.
You: Sure, and you'd look better in a three-piece suit, but we aren't
the fashion police, so let's agree not to offer any unsolicited advice
about each other's appearances and get back to work.
```

In the fictional conversation, the "you" role used humor to take the edge off a difficult conversation. That's just one style, and other styles might work better for you. If you miss your opportunity to address an incident in real time, Michelle Mijung Kim [171] suggests the following prompts.

1. "Hey, can we check in about something that happened last week?"

2. "I'm sorry that I didn't address this earlier, but I've given it some thought and wanted to share this."

3. "I've not been able to get this off my mind. Can we have a quick chat?"

If you have more organizational power than the person, be more specific about the purpose of the meeting so that the person doesn't unnecessarily panic about a last-minute meeting with their boss.

Acknowledge Your Mistakes

Mistakes are inevitable, so we need to learn to acknowledge them, learn from them, and react gracefully when we are called out for making them. When you get called out, resist your natural impulse to be overly sensitive or defensive. You do not have to agree with what is being said to hear it, acknowledge that someone is upset, and consider their perspective. You don't need to decide whether you agree or not, or have a solution, immediately. You should probably take time to reflect on how to make it right. Calling someone out often takes significant emotional labor, and you can acknowledge their courage.

Finch [172] suggests the following phrases for acknowledging that you have room to grow:

- "I recognize that I have work to do."

- "I'm going to take some time to reflect on this."

- "I appreciate the labor you've put in."

- "I apologize; I'm going to do better."

- "I want to make this right."

- "What I'm gathering is [insert what you've learned]."

- "I'm doing some research now, but if anyone has a favorite resource on this topic that they'd like to share, I'm totally open to it!"

- "Thank you."

- "I believe you."

Re-envision the Tech Culture

We have to change our unconscious definition of what a software developer looks like, so we start recognizing talent that looks a little different than what we are used to.
– Ainsley Robertson [173]

Improving inclusion is all about culture change. One way to change an organizational or industry culture is through what Michelle P. King calls a "success prototype," the pattern or role model that others in an industry emulate to achieve success [174]. King argues that companies promote people who match their success prototypes.

Who are your engineering role models? Many tech professionals admire a brilliant engineer (who has spent years abusing colleagues who wrote code he didn't like) or an eccentric billionaire (who made some of that money through securities fraud). Is every role model you can think of a tall, attractive, wealthy, English-speaking, middle-aged, straight white man? Who does your organization put on stage? Who represents your team to outsiders? Who is in leadership?

You can help improve your organization's and industry's success prototypes by:

- identifying and praising people who don't fit existing success prototypes but have qualities you admire;

- getting your team to share opportunities for exposure (e.g., face time with upper management or clients, leading demos;

- choosing good role models for yourself and telling others about them;

- reflecting on and challenging who your organization and industry present as role models; and

- encouraging your organization to elevate more diverse success prototypes.

A good role model is someone who: you can relate to because they share some aspects of your background, challenges, or experiences; exemplifies the qualities you admire; and doesn't have a bunch of other qualities that are incompatible with your values. A role model can be a celebrity or someone you know personally.

At the start of my career, I (Todd) thought excellent engineering was a solo genius finding the best solution to a complex problem. In time, I realized that the best ideas usually emerge from collaboration. Being effective is not really about having the best idea; it's about collaborating with others to see ideas implemented. Unfortunately, many companies value engineers based solely on their technical skills, ignoring toxic behavior. They might reward individuals who "solve" complex problems over the weekend, despite negative impacts on the rest of the team who spend the next week fixing the "solution" so it actually works.

Many tech companies continue to devalue collaboration and communication. Consider Akila, a highly collaborative team lead who forged high-performing teams and routinely received excellent performance reviews. When her employer was acquired by a Fortune Future 50 and Fortune 100 Best Companies to Work For company, her new management devalued her collaboration skills and complained that she needed to be seen "doing more" by contributing to multiple projects simultaneously and reporting on the status of more work items—never mind that multitasking is inefficient [51]. She quickly moved to a new company that values agile principles and explicitly rewards and promotes engineers for improving team collaboration.

Another problematic trend is creating a two-tier system that disempowers young engineers by overemphasizing seniority. Does your organization make a big deal about who is a "senior" engineer and who is a "junior" engineer? Why? Years of experience is at best a weak predictor of developer job performance. Indeed, we routinely learn from our early-career colleagues despite our decades of experience. De-emphasizing hierarchy, especially within a team, usually produces better interpersonal dynamics. De-emphasizing hierarchy also helps organizations create more inclusive cultures because people from underrepresented groups are more likely to be perceived as "junior" and consequently disempowered.

Inclusive Software Process

Much has been written about optimizing software processes for efficiency, effectiveness, and agility, but what about inclusivity? Some argue that agile methods are more inclusive because they are more people-focused, which is true in principle but not always in practice. Agile was created by a relatively privileged, homogeneous group who were accustomed to having a lot of power within their organizations.

Consider the move from waterfall-like phased development to two-week sprints. A typical mid-career engineer in a medium-sized Silicon Valley company might find two-week sprints less stressful because they can manage their workload by controlling the sprint's scope. In contrast, a typical mid-career engineer in a large Indian tech firm might have no control over their bi-weekly deliverables. For them, two-week sprints create incessant crunch time. Agile proponents might despair that "you're not supposed to do it that way!" But that *is* how it's done in many companies [175].

Similarly, many members of underrepresented groups have had negative experiences in pair programming and code reviews (see Chapter 10). These negative experiences don't mean that sprints, pair programming, and code reviews are inherently exclusionary. An inclusive software process isn't really about selecting inclusive practices instead of exclusionary ones. *Inclusion is all about power: who selects the practices and determines how they're implemented.* Exclusion happens when practices are corrupted by power imbalances or imposed on people for whom those practices are problematic.

This is trickier than just letting a team determine its own software development process. The organization may have legitimate reasons for constraining the software development process in certain ways or standardizing the process across work groups. Even if teams set their own processes, the team as a whole could impose exclusionary practices on individual team members. And even if the team agrees on the practices, individual team members may still enact practices in an exclusionary way. So, how does one devise an inclusive software process?

Our advice is to apply the suggestions summarized in Table 12–1. To devise an inclusive software process, try the following.

- Include in designing the process everyone affected by the process.

- Transparently document both the process and its honest rationale. Consider co-authoring a norms document that makes the implicit, explicit.

- Leverage retrospective meetings to identify inclusivity problems.[7]

- Start from the assumption that there will always be inclusivity problems.

- Prioritize addressing inclusivity problems in the software process, *regardless of how those concerns are raised* (e.g., informally, impolitely).

- Be vigilant of people acting like there's only one right way to build software. You don't have to adopt a practice just because it's recommended by any particular book, community, or software engineering micro-celebrity. Finding practices that work for everyone on your team is more important than adhering to any particular guidelines.

Inclusive Product Design

Many tech companies seem pathologically unable to imagine any user who isn't like their employees. Too often, companies release software that doesn't work well for users who aren't tech-savvy, upper-class, young, English-speaking, disability-free, and dependent-free. Let's consider some examples.

Many software products (e.g., social media platforms) are used extensively by children and teenagers. Instead of providing an appropriate user experience, they simply state that minors aren't allowed to use the system and include some easily bypassed age verification questions in the account setup. Kids just lie about their age and carry on using the system. Meanwhile, the company sidesteps its responsibility to provide an appropriate experience for a potentially lucrative target market while sometimes harming its users.

---

[7]If the retro itself is identified as problematic for inclusion, adapt it as needed (e.g., conceal who proposed each retro topic, use a round-robin format where each person takes a turn speaking, in order, without interruption). For retros to surface inclusivity problems, the retro itself must be inclusive.

Every time a company changes the icon of a consumer-facing mobile application, many people *permanently* lose the ability to use that app. If Grandpa has moderate dementia, he might remember how to use a tablet to call his grandchildren. He might be able to figure out incremental interface changes. But if the *icon* changes significantly, it's game over. Grandpa can't find it, and there's a point at which many people with dementia just don't learn new things.

Meanwhile, much of the web is catastrophic for visually impaired users even though HTML that complies with the W3C Accessibility Guidelines[8] is among the best technologies for the visually impaired. Mobile apps frequently include infinitesimal fonts that screen readers cannot enlarge or read. Some products cannot be used without providing a home address, effectively excluding users who are unhoused, even when there is no reason to do so. And to this day, many products continue to feature binary "male or female" gender questions. It's not hard to include "other—please describe" with a free text response. Many of these apps don't really need to know the user's gender anyway.

Moreover, the hype around generative AI is palpable as we write this. Tech companies are scrambling to embrace the automated generation of text, audio, still images, and video in thousands of ways despite the demonstrable algorithmic bias.

While it may not be possible to design every product such that it works well for every possible user, greater awareness of user diversity and their involvement in product design is crucial for acting ethically and can provide a competitive advantage. If your product works well for the visually impaired and none of your competitors' products do, visually impaired users will be very loyal—they don't have a choice. Indeed, if you can foster a reputation of being friendly to any frequently victimized or disadvantaged group, you'll experience customer loyalty like never before.

Three keys to building more inclusive products are:

1. recruit a diverse team of professionals to build the product;

2. recruit a diverse group of users and other stakeholders for research; and

3. generate more diverse personas (see Chapter 7).

A more diverse team is more likely to recognize common falsehoods that programmers believe. For example, many programmers seem to believe that everyone has one first, one last, and maybe one or two middle names, all of which can be represented in ASCII and fit in, say, 30 characters. In contrast, the famous painter Picasso's full name was "Pablo Diego José Francisco de Paula Juan Nepomuceno María de los Remedios Cipriano de la Santísima Trinidad Ruiz y Picasso." Some people have names that mix character sets (e.g., including both Japanese kanji and Latin letters) that don't work in Unicode or include numbers or punctuation or words that are offensive in English. And that's just names. Programmers commonly hold similar incorrect beliefs about email addresses, dates and times, economics, geography, computer networks, measurement, and software engineering.[9]

More generally, designing more inclusive, accessible products is another area where your local university or nonprofit organization can be a fantastic resource. Want to know if your

---

[8]https://www.w3.org/WAI/standards-guidelines/wcag/

[9]For an extensive list, see https://github.com/kdeldycke/awesome-falsehood

system is hostile to minorities? Some scientists specialize in that. Is your system accessible to the local unhoused population? Go to a homeless shelter and pay people to try it. You'll get answers *and* feel like a good person.

Tailor Support

> *We can't tackle inequality if we are in denial it even exists.*
> *– Michelle P. King*

Equality refers to treating everyone the same regardless of individual differences. *Equity* refers to giving people what they need to succeed by considering their differences. For example, giving every employee the exact same chair aims for equality, while giving every employee a chair that fits their shape and needs aims for equity.

Equity means embracing individual differences and tailoring organizational support for each individual so that they can do their best work and be their best selves. For many developers, collaborating with people who act like they don't really belong is exhausting, demoralizing, and far harder than the technical challenges they face.

"Although all employees may behave more professionally at work compared to more casual settings ... conceal[ing] significant cultural aspects of themselves to minimize stereotyping ... is a necessary behavior for Black employees to be perceived as professionals" in many organizations [176]. Many women must routinely prove their technical abilities to their peers to be taken seriously. People transitioning between genders wonder how much of their authentic selves to bring to work for fear of discrimination. People hide disabilities to avoid being stigmatized.

We can create more equitable organizations by reducing these impediments in three key areas: organizational support, promotions, and feedback.

Support Diverse Employees

The more diverse your employees are, the more diverse their needs will be. The first step to supporting employees better is to *ask them what they need*.

To collect good data on employee needs, use *open-ended questions*. Simply choosing or ranking options generated by management produces junk data. Open-ended questions (e.g., "how can we best support you?") work much better.

You should also use *anonymous feedback mechanisms*. One-on-one meetings or focus groups may help in organizations that have high psychological safety. However, management tends to overestimate psychological safety, and the employees who need the most support are probably the ones who feel the least safe.

Some often-recommended ways of supporting employees include the following.

- Avoid hot-desking and open floor plans. Not having a space of their own makes already marginalized employees feel more marginalized and less like part of a team [177]. Encourage employees to personalize their spaces (e.g., with family pictures).

- Embrace flexible work locations. Having everyone in the office together is great, but some employees may sometimes need to work elsewhere for many reasons including caregiving responsibilities and personal safety.

- Embrace flexible hours. People from different cultural or religious backgrounds observe different holidays. People with complex family lives may need to work at unusual times. As discussed in Chapter 5, we recommend establishing core work hours and being flexible otherwise. Let each team set their own core work hours based on their unique constraints.

- Avoid overtime. Overtime, whether officially mandatory or an implied expectation, harms employees and usually backfires on organizations. The more hours people work, the *slower* they work, the more mistakes they make, and the less motivation they have.

- Allow employees to work part-time. For some employees, working part-time at a proportionately lower salary is a good trade. It's better to keep good people part-time than lose them entirely.

- Encourage breaks while pairing. While we are big believers in pair programming, it's OK to continue solo while your pair attends a medical appointment, picks up their kids, or shows a plumber the water heater that's just exploded in their basement.

- Consider paid time off, minimum vacation policies, and mandatory leave (i.e., employees are required to take all of their entitled vacation, parental leave, etc.).

We can look for ways to normalize different work hours. For example, Marchese et al. [178] suggest adding this phrase to communications for distributed teams: "My working hours may be different than yours. Please do not feel that you need to reply outside your normal working hours."

Fix Your Promotions Process

Creating a fair promotion process is exceptionally difficult. Promotion decisions tend to be intuitive and subjective or based on misleading indicators of performance (see the *Cognitive Biases Affect Promotion* sidebar on page 229).

Intuitive approaches to promotion suffer from significant biases because all sufficiently large organizations develop in-group / out-group dynamics. People naturally tend to divide the world into "us versus them." We divide ourselves based on nationality, race, gender, sexual orientation, religion, political ideology, etc. but don't always identify with others who are like us on any particular dimension.

We tend to perceive members of our in-group more favorably, pay more attention to them, and reward them. We are more likely to ascribe in-group members' successes to hard work and more likely to ascribe out-group members' successes to luck. Members of the in-group are, therefore, more likely to be promoted. This leads to the common pattern of organizations having homogeneous senior leadership despite efforts to hire more diverse employees.

The solution seems obvious: define a career ladder with clear performance standards for each step, and promote employees who exceed the performance expected at their step. Except *there aren't good, objective measures of job performance for software professionals.*

Hence a paradox: bias manifests due to subjective judgment, but it's not possible to remove the human from the equation. So how can promotion decisions be as equitable as possible? There's no simple answer, but here are some suggestions:

1. Promotion decisions should be made by a committee. The more diverse the committee, the more it resists in-group bias. In this case, "diverse" means including people at different career levels and roles (not just senior managers) as well as diverse demographics (gender, race, etc.). Structure the committee so that all members have equal say and feel safe giving their honest opinion. Failing that, vote by secret ballot.[10]

2. The committee should promote those who excel in the tasks *they are given*. Many organizations value some types of work (e.g., shipping new features; cross-team collaboration) more than others (e.g., crucial maintenance, unblocking team members) such that promotion is mostly determined by tasks assignment rather than performance. This leads employees to deprioritize their assigned tasks in favor of other work. More privileged employees and in-group members are more likely to engage in this kind of deviant behavior. If you're going to reward people for ignoring what you've asked them to do, you may as well forget promotions and just play musical chairs: when the music stops, everyone who has a seat gets a raise; everyone else, better luck next year!

3. The committee should review a list of common biases (as mentioned above) prior to the start of each promotion session.

4. The promotion process should be transparent. The promotion committee's deliberations should be observable, either live or recorded, to everyone in the company. Promotion statistics should be shared throughout the organization.

5. Promotion cases and reasons for decisions should be written down and provided to applicants *in writing*. Writing things down hinders murky, biased thinking.

6. Employee pay should be fully transparent. Ensuring everyone is being paid equitably for each career level is much easier when everyone can see what everyone else is getting paid.[11] Organizations should have an anomalies fund to enable imbalance corrections.

7. The organization should hold the promotions committee responsible for following its rules fairly. Employees should be able to appeal a promotion decision to someone outside their direct line of reporting, or (for small organizations) directly to the CEO. The appeals process must be genuine: if no appeal is ever upheld, the appeals process is fake. Promotion committees (or individuals) who display a pattern of unreasonable or biased decision-making should be replaced.

---

[10]Voting by secret ballot protects committee members, but those seeking promotion won't know who opposed their application.

[11]Management resistance to pay transparency has nothing to do with claims that it increases animosity within teams and everything to do with how it empowers workers to negotiate fairer pay.

Cognitive Biases Affect Promotion

Many biases that can affect promotions, including the following

1. Affinity bias—favoring people with similar backgrounds.

2. Recency bias—over-weighting recent accomplishments and experiences.

3. Halo and Horns bias—over-attending to first impressions, so an early stellar accomplishment can raise an overall mediocre performance, while a single dramatic failure may taint evaluations of an otherwise reliable performer.

4. Distance bias—over-weighting accomplishments from people who work near us compared to people who work in other offices or remotely.

5. Conformity bias—changing our beliefs to fit in with those around us.

As with other unconscious biases, redesigning the person-task system to prevent the bias is the most effective way of mitigating it. However, if you can't figure out how to redesign the system, reading the definitions of some common biases aloud at the beginning of a promotions committee meeting is better than nothing.

---

8. Promotion should be based on all of an employee's work at their current level, not just whatever they've done most recently. Employees should be encouraged to maintain an ongoing self-reflection document, including their accomplishments, professional development, and attempts at self-improvement. This shouldn't be onerous: a few minutes every few days should be sufficient. A good time would be immediately after the retrospective meeting. This self-reflection document will then be a strong resource for informing promotion decisions. Employees should be able to ask others for support compiling their promotion package.

9. Large organizations with multiple promotion committees should run an annual calibration process where each committee reads other committees' application packages and decisions and unifies job levels and pay organization-wide.

10. Promotion committees should not, under any circumstances, use AI for promotion decisions. AI systems simply conceal rather than prevent bias.

11. The promotion system should not assume everyone has a supportive manager (see next). In addition to the applicant's manager's appraisal, the promotions process should take into account feedback from applicant's peers and subordinates.

In many tech companies, employees are "put up for promotion" by their manager. The problem with this is that some employees and their managers just don't get along. Sometimes it's because the manager is a jerk or the employee is incompetent, but other times they're just incompatible. From the individual employee's perspective, if a manager's feedback seems unfairly negative, the employee should document their achievements and their objections to the manager's points in more detail.

In other organizations, the individual employee applies for promotion. The problem with this model is that in-group employees tend to be more aggressive in seeking promotions; out-group employees tend to wait longer.

The solution is threefold: (1) every year, all employees should submit a performance review and be considered for promotion; (2) promotion decisions should be based on the employees' self-appraisal as well as their manager(s) appraisal of them; (3) promotion committees should investigate significant discrepancies between manager appraisals and self-appraisals, and not automatically side with the manager. Promotion must not be based solely on the manager's evaluation.

If the manager is supportive, the manager and employee get along, and the manager has sufficient technical expertise in the employee's area, they can co-edit the employee's self-reflection document, and the performance appraisal can be based on this single, unified account.

Give Better Feedback

> *Every portrait that is painted with feeling is a portrait of the artist, not of the sitter.*
> *– Oscar Wilde*

Some feedback is *intentionally* destructive, such as when a supervisor encourages a subordinate to quit, a subordinate sabotages a manager's career, or a developer writes a nasty code review to get back at a rival. As explained earlier in this chapter, employees who continue to express conscious biases have no place in a just organization.

One extreme form of consciously biased feedback is gaslighting. The term *gaslighting* was popularized by *Gaslight*, the 1944 movie adaptation of the 1938 play *Gas Light*, in which the protagonist is manipulated into believing she is losing her sanity. Gaslighting thus refers to "psychological manipulation of a person, usually over an extended period of time, that causes the victim to question the validity of their own thoughts, perception of reality, or memories and typically leads to confusion, loss of confidence and self-esteem, uncertainty of one's emotional or mental stability, and a dependency on the perpetrator" [179].

For example, one woman we know was offended that her co-worker said "oh, just have your boyfriend help you" (thus assuming that she is heterosexual, in a dating relationship, and needs a man's help). When her managers minimized the experience—"oh, that's not so bad," "boys will be boys," etc.—that was gaslighting. Examples are easy to find on social media where people don't believe someone's experience, minimize it, or argue that their perception is compromised.

Gaslighting is closely related to *victim blaming*; that is, when the victim of wrongdoing, rather than the perpetrator, is held responsible. In a software development context, victim blaming could include blaming an individual software developer for failing to meet impossible goals or expecting a technical support rep to maintain perfect professionalism while being screamed at by an irate customer.

Well-intentioned feedback can also be biased and harmful as in the following examples.

- Urging a black person to soften their tone in meetings reinforces anger stereotypes.

- Discouraging a woman from ending statements with a question (as it makes her seem unconfident) ignores the fact that many women have found that seeming too assertive will hurt their careers.

- Telling an LGBTQ2S+ person, 'conceal your gender identity because it will help you advance' prioritizes the employers' bigotry over the employee's human rights.

- Encouraging a person to conceal a disability to appear more competent implies that their disability makes them incompetent.

- Suggesting that an indigenous employee stop wearing symbols of their indigenous identity (e.g., jewelry) to appear more professional reinforces the prejudice that indigenous people are somehow less professional or desirable in the workforce.

Dealing with unconsciously biased or hurtful feedback is difficult precisely because the giver doesn't perceive the harm and may be genuinely trying to help. When it's something specific, like a manager always telling their female subordinates to smile, the perpetrator can simply be informed of the problem. If they stop the behavior, the problem is solved. If not, it might be conscious bias after all and we're back to "isolate-educate-terminate." However, there are infinitely many ways of giving biased feedback, and no one can memorize all of the things that someone else finds hurtful. So we need more general advice such as the following.

- When receiving feedback that you feel is biased or otherwise problematic, have the courage to say why. If you don't correct problematic behavior, it may continue.

- Avoid tone-policing. Don't expect people who feel abused to be polite about it. Focus on the substance of complaints, not the way in which they're delivered. This is difficult because you need enough self-control to avoid defensiveness.

- When you witness people giving problematic feedback, speak up.

- When giving feedback, consider: (1) if your feedback could reinforce stereotypes; and (2) whether your feedback is phrased optimally to help the recipient. For example, sometimes people need to be told their work isn't good enough, but you don't have to be a jerk about it.

- Foster psychological safety within teams, especially with managers, so everyone feels secure enough to discuss problematic feedback (see sidebar on page 200).

- Encourage everyone in the organization to practice *reflexivity*; that is, reflecting on our own biases. Knowing oneself deeply helps us avoid problematic behaviors.

Share Power

Organizations blame injustice on individuals to avoid reforming their systems. To improve justice, dismantle the organizational structures that enable biased outcomes.

When a small group of people are permitted to hoard power, make decisions for others, act in secret, suppress dissent, and use junk data dressed up as "objective metrics" to obscure injustice, organizations cannot become just. When meaningful action is replaced with theatrics—mindfulness training, well-being apps, sensitivity workshops, wellness committees, adding a token minority on an advisory board, etc.—organizations will remain unjust [180].

"Inclusion" doesn't mean "included in the organization", it means "included in determining how things are done." The more power is decentralized and distributed to individual employees, the less individual prejudice can manifest as injustice.

Evolving your Organization toward Justice

To grow the organization toward justice, we must dismantle and reinvent the structures that enable injustice in the first place.

One woman we interviewed told us how she surfaced discriminatory comments to her manager. The manager intervened, and while the office culture initially improved, it quickly devolved back to old habits. She was frustrated. Her initial report was stressful and carried real risk to her career. Management thought they had "solved the problem." Injustice is not a singular problem that can be solved. Justice is an ongoing effort to improve our situations.

Resist any kind of one-and-done thinking. When you are the person receiving reports and intervening, set a reminder to follow up in a few weeks (or months) to see if initial improvements endure.

What Could Future Organizations Be Like?

If the reader will humor a little naked idealism, we'd like to explore what future organizations could be like if organizational justice was genuinely taken seriously.

Imagine working not for a publicly or privately owned company but for an organization that is effectively owned by its employees. Imagine if all your c-suite and director-level positions were elected by employees as well as investors, such that executives must balance employee and investor interests to maintain their positions. Imagine being absolved of the endless quest for unsustainable growth because the company is not driven by greed.

Imagine an organization where management and leadership were just different kinds of work, no more or less important than product design and development. Imagine if your pay was actually based on how well you do your job, not on which job you are assigned.

Imagine that you didn't have to worry about:

- getting laid off because the company wasn't allowed to lay off employees unless it was facing bankruptcy,

- being punished for taking parental leave because parental leave was *mandatory*,

- being punished for refusing overtime because overtime was *banned*, and

- being discriminated against because no one had the power to discriminate against you.

Imagine an organization structured around actively resisting prejudice instead of faking the appearance of social responsibility. Imagine selecting new hires based on their qualifications and experience without knowing anything about their demographics.

While this all may seem far-fetched, several organizations are making progress in this general direction—see Laloux and Appert [181] for further advice.

Many of these visions of a better future are based on economic democracy, a socioeconomic philosophy including the idea of broader participation in economic policy [182]. Economic democracy is not exactly capitalism, socialism, or communism. It is a roadmap for how economic activity could be organized to make the world better, and if you care about the Earth being a place where humans can still thrive in a century or two, economic democracy makes a lot more sense than how we're running things right now.

Summary

Most people think about organizational justice as a series of steps: first, you increase perspectives, then improve belonging, then eventually tailor support, then (one day maybe but probably never) share power. As usual, reality is less linear.

Increasing perspectives without tailored support is just public relations. Organizations can neither benefit from, nor retain, a diverse workforce without inclusion and tailored support. Furthermore, recruiting more diverse employees won't make an organization more just if that organization is saturated with structures (power hoarding, paternalism, opacity, inclusion theater, etc.) that reinforce and propagate injustice.

The main message of this chapter is that, while individuals can be problematic, focus on problematic structures. Focus on power: who has it, how do they use it, how do they abuse it, and how can it be better shared.

Changing the tech industry is a *generational* project. Maybe you think there's nothing you can do. Maybe you're not in a position of power. Maybe you are not a member of any particular minority group and don't see this as your fight.

But here's the thing: human history is not full of people in power having epiphanies and spontaneously giving away their power. Human history is full of people who are being abused, *and their allies*, demanding change. Human history is full of people forcing the changes they want to see in the world.

Expecting the most victimized people to peacefully and politely change the structures that are oppressing them, without any help, is totally unrealistic. Change depends on action from people who already have power. For most North American and European software companies, that's middle-aged white men. That's why the longest and most detailed chapter in this book—written by a couple of middle-aged white men—is about organizational justice.

Focus on what you *can* do. When opportunities arise, be supportive, call out injustice, and ask for change. Even if it doesn't seem to be working, just keep at it. Every time you bring up these issues, every time you voice support for a more just world, you shift perceptions of what is possible and necessary a teeny-tiny bit. If all you can do is tell someone who's having a bad day that you appreciate them and that, yes, they do belong here, you're still helping.

One of (the German philosopher) Hegel's central ideas is that we are all trapped in the zeitgeist of our time. Ideas around organizational justice are changing so fast that by the time you read this, some of our text may be cringey—we'll appear to have used the wrong words and failed to engage with key issues of our future / your present. But we have to try. So we did our best.

Remember: never mistake an imperfect ally for a deadly enemy.

Chapter 13

Conclusion

The most important characteristic of high-performing teams is that they are never satisfied: they always strive to get better. High performers make improvement part of everybody's daily work.
– Nicole Forsgren

 Key Takeaways

- An agile development culture helps teams build software faster.

- Blending user-centered design with agile helps teams design better software.

- Blending sustainable development with agile helps teams build more sustainable products in more sustainable ways.

- Every project is unique, so teams may have to adapt Sustainable Dual-Track Development to their specific circumstances.

- When adapting Sustainable Dual-Track Development, keep in mind the principles on which it is based: Humanity, Continuity, Balance, Share Knowledge, Rapid Feedback, Reduce Waste, and Embrace Change.

The Search for a Software Project Management Textbook

In 2010, I (Paul) was asked to teach a Master's course in software project management. I was excited to teach this topic because I wrote my dissertation on the scientific theories of the software development process, and felt well-informed and ready to share what I'd learned.

Teaching management isn't like teaching programming; you can't really practice it in a lab so students benefit from a good textbook or collection or readings. I therefore reviewed several popular textbooks on software management. They were all terrible.

Paul

A textbook should balance giving practical advice and explaining the science behind something. These textbooks had no science. They were loaded with unjustified opinions and concepts that had been thoroughly debunked by scientific research. Over the years, I moved on to standards like the International Standards Organization's *Guide to the Software Engineering Body of Knowledge* (SWEBOK) [183] and the Object Management Group's *Essence* [184]. They were even worse! They took the same unscientific, unjustified, opinion-based claptrap and dressed it up as universal truths. It turned out that SWEBOK was created not by reviewing data but by surveying professionals and summarizing their opinions. Essence just reformulated the old Unified Software Process as a "theory" that was never empirically tested, and, again, is replete with concepts that had been thoroughly debunked by scientific research.

I moved on to popular professional books about agile methods. These were better in the sense of containing less abject nonsense, but they didn't connect to the scientific literature and weren't based on any evidence beyond their authors' first-hand experience. They were doctrinaire: 'you should do it exactly this way because this worked for us'; never mind the differences between our situation and yours. The redefined 'agile' as the extent to which you use their practices without showing that their practices increase agility.

What I and my students needed was a book that combined first-hand experience, second-hand observation, and scientific theory to present practical, evidence-based recommendations without dogma. So Todd and I decided to write this book—the first-hand experience coming from Todd, the science coming from me, and second-hand observation coming from both of us. But this isn't a textbook—we wrote it for software professionals and students at every career stage.

Prior to its publication, I used excerpts and later complete drafts of the text in more than a dozen undergraduate and graduate courses, and I incorporated student feedback to improve its clarity and comprehensiveness. By the time it was done, many of my students liked the book more than their professor!

The Principles

Multitudes of practices have been proposed to improve software development, product design, product management, organizational justice and so on. Sustainable Dual-Track Development does not include every single promising practice. We decided which practices to highlight based on the amount and quality of scientific evidence supporting each practice, our personal experiences with each practice, and the following principles (Figure 13–1).

Humanity

When we spend most of our time configuring, updating, tweaking, and writing instructions for machines, we can forget that software is imagined, created, used, approved, and not infrequently condemned by human beings. For Sustainable Dual-Track Development to work—indeed, for any software project to succeed—it must focus on people. This means:

1. Understanding users and allowing the team's understanding of the user to drive not only the system's interface but also its features and architecture.

2. Understanding that you are responsible to all of your stakeholders, including the general public, not just customers.

3. Understanding team members as fallible, emotional humans, with diverse strengths, who need respect, support, and acceptance to do their best work.

4. Understanding that a team is more than the sum of its members and that team cohesion affects performance more than individual skill.

Humanity   Continuity   Balance   Share Knowledge

Rapid Feedback   Reduce Waste   Embrace Change

Figure 13–1: Principles of Sustainable Dual-Track Development

5. Understanding that everyone has had different professional journeys and that people with more privilege must support those with less.

6. Understanding the importance of welcoming people to the team; first impressions set the tone for a new team member.

Focusing on people means accepting team members, users, and other stakeholders with different strengths, weaknesses, motivations, worldviews, and emotional needs. It means identifying and making the most of people's strengths. It also means reflecting on our own behavior and listening deeply to each other. In Sustainable Dual-Track Development, people are not treated like widgets in some Taylorist horror film. Managers do not deploy a horde of key performance indicators to quantify every aspect of team or individual behavior. Teams need leadership more than management.

Some people seem oblivious to how their words and actions hurt others. The humanity principle means not only encouraging openness and honesty but also developing a thick skin. Honesty and mutual respect are impossible if everyone gets offended or indignant at every disagreement. This dual willingness not only to modify our behavior to protect others but also to give others a chance is essential for social sustainability.

The humanity principle is also about courage. Restarting a messed-up feature takes courage. Breaking the build for a large, important rewrite takes courage. Refusing overtime takes courage. Intervening to support a downtrodden colleague takes courage. Explaining that "we don't do fixed-price / -schedule contracts because they're too risky" takes courage. Refusing to create autonomous weapons systems, radicalizing recommender systems, or democracy-undermining advertising takes courage. Acting ethically in an unjust world takes courage.

Sometimes, you have to stand up for what you believe in, even if it costs you your job; sometimes, you have to do what's good for humanity, even if it's bad for you. That's why it's called the *humanity* principle.

Continuity

The most effective, efficient, and simple way to create good software is for a balanced team to own the entire software process and closely collaborate with stakeholders. Divisions or barriers between teams, temporal phases, or the team and its stakeholders must be avoided.

Organizing development into phases—especially, with different teams for each phase—is over-complicated, creates knowledge silos, inhibits communication, and engenders conflict. Designers trapped in such phase models often act paternalistic and downplay stakeholders' beliefs, values, and preferences.

In Sustainable Dual-Track Development, the balanced team imagines, creates, deploys, and maintains the product. The same team generates new feature concepts (Track One) and builds and maintains the software (Track Two). There is no tossing of projects from design to development, or from programmers to testers, or from development to operations. Meanwhile, the team tries to collaborate closely with its stakeholders to create products that delight or at least appease everyone involved.

In other words, *continuity* means that:

1. The team steadily delivers value. There are no iterations.

2. There is a single continuous development process (organized into two continuous, parallel but interconnected tracks). There are no phases.

3. A balanced team is responsible for the entire development process. There are no handovers from programming to testing, from development to operations.

4. The team works closely with stakeholders. There is no us vs. them thinking.

Continuity means preferring practices that remove barriers. It does not mean continuous delivery; delivery schedules should be based on stakeholders' needs. Continuity does not preclude different roles or third-party reviews (e.g., penetration testing and design reviews). Balanced teams, by definition, comprise diverse professionals with complementary skill sets. Getting feedback from a neutral third party is often beneficial. It's dividing development between separate teams with different identities (e.g., the programming team and the operations team) that causes problems.

Finally, the continuity principle implies that teams share core work hours and collaborate intensively. Remote, hybrid, and distributed teams can experience additional challenges in team maturation. These challenges can be mitigated by creating structures that encourage routine, intense interpersonal collaboration (see Chapter 2).

Continuity improve teams' resistance to disruption. Continuity improves economic sustainability by breaking down barriers between development, management, users, and customers.

Balance

The balance principle refers to the need to weigh the consequences of our actions across people and time.

Software development is full of what economists call *inter-temporal choices*: decisions that involve weighing impacts today against impacts in the future. Do we cut corners today for a short-term win, knowing it will give us a headache tomorrow, or do we go slower now and risk short-term failure to make our future selves more effective? Sometimes we should prioritize the present; other times we should prioritize the future. When software developers worry too much about the future, they over-engineer code for scenarios that may never arise, and endlessly fiddle with systems that are already good enough. When developers worry too much about the present, they skimp on tests, neglect security, compromise on code quality, and generally increase overall project risk.

In our experience, most software teams over-prioritize the present and neglect the future, not least because their companies create constant time pressure through artificial deadlines, unrealistic effort estimation, and misleading performance indicators. *However,* you can't *always* live for the future. *Balance* is needed. Sustainable Dual-Track Development includes practices like refactoring continuously (future-oriented) and designing code continuously (present-oriented), to encourage a more balanced approach to these inter-temporal choices. This kind of balance is essential to the technical and economic sustainability of our products, services, and organizations.

Similarly, designing great products involves what economists call *externalities*: often unanticipated, often negative impacts on third parties seemingly unrelated to the project at hand. For example, if social media foments polarization and radicalization in your community, leading to civil unrest, your window can get smashed in the riot regardless of whether you ever used social media. Avoiding and mitigating this kind of harm is perhaps the fundamental principle of ethical software design. Sustainable Dual-Track Development includes practices like stakeholder mapping, persona modeling, and interviewing to help anticipate negative externalities. This kind of balance impacts environmental and social sustainability, especially when one group reaps all the benefits from the product, while some other group endures the costs (or negative impacts).

Share Knowledge

The share knowledge principle means preferring practices that spread knowledge around rather than hoard it in silos. Engineers are always learning about the domain, the existing code, new versions of dependencies, and new technologies. But learning is not enough. The team must also share knowledge so it isn't lost when a team member leaves (temporarily or permanently) and so that anyone can work on any story in the backlog. The old way of writing everything down doesn't work because it creates documentation so voluminous that it's impossible to keep current or find anything. Keep the documentation minimal. Do write down how to build, run, and test your code and anything that's helpful to troubleshoot a production issue at 2 am. Sustainable Dual-Track Development encourages person-to-person knowledge sharing using numerous practices, including rotational pair programming, peer code review, story showcases, daily syncs, and retros. Documents and diagrams can support, but not replace, person-to-person sharing.

Effective communication does not always happen naturally. Engineers often want to focus on delivering features and don't want or can't handle the cognitive overhead of explaining what they are doing. Many engineers abhor meetings and interruptions. One reason pair programming is so useful is that it encourages engineers to share their reasoning in a way others can understand. Sharing knowledge is essential for social sustainability at the team and organizational levels.

Meanwhile, product designers must resist the temptation to simply ask stakeholders "what do you want?" and instead help stakeholders to construct and articulate their values, preferences, and ideas. Product managers, in turn, must learn to bridge the linguistic and cultural gap between business and development. And quite often, the whole team has to work on communicating clearly and amicably with people who think and act differently. This kind of knowledge sharing is essential for the economic sustainability of products and services.

Sharing knowledge is essential for work-life balance because it minimizes disruptions associated with people leaving or joining the team, taking vacations or sick days, work remotely, etc.

Rapid Feedback

A core tenet of agile software development is introducing and shortening feedback loops. Good feedback is constructive, polite, actionable, timely, and consistent. Short feedback loops help teams respond quickly to change, remove friction and waste, and evolve their practices. They are essential for learning. The faster we discover whether our actions are producing the desired effects, the better we learn. Sustainable Dual-Track Development has many feedback loops, including rapid build-test cycles, frequent releases with user validation, and regular retrospective meetings.

However, more feedback is not always better. Too much simultaneous feedback can be overwhelming. When training a person to do a task, it is usually best to focus on one area of improvement at a time. One of the best teachers Paul ever had would intently watch a student perform some action, then always say, "That's pretty good. Just one thing. . . " He saw lots of things, but addressed one problem at a time.

Moreover, a lot of feedback is noise. Feedback through anonymous comments and reviews can be abusive, inconsistent, and non-actionable. People give the best feedback in one-on-one conversations and the worst feedback in anonymous, faceless, online settings. That is why Sustainable Dual-Track Development emphasizes user interviews, not anonymous surveys. High quality, rapid feedback improves both the economic and social sustainability of software products by alerting developers to undesirable features or unintended consequences.

Reduce Waste

Ongoing, concerted effort to reduce waste is the backbone of any efficient organization. Waste is anything "that consumes resources without benefiting any project stakeholder" [185]; for example, over-complicating a product, working when you are so tired that you make loads of mistakes, or stressing out the team so much that they can't concentrate. Chapter 5 gives many more examples.

The Reduce Waste principle is about recognizing two things: (1) it's impossible to identify, in advance, the most efficient way to organize the development of any particular software system; and (2) no matter how efficient you are, waste seems to just pop up like weeds in Spring. It's just so easy for competent, well-meaning people to invent unnecessary bureaucracy, neglect stakeholder research, fall into multitasking, or forget to monitor how much power their software demands. Teams and organizations need to identify and eliminate waste *continuously* or they'll just naturally get less and less efficient.

Remember that eliminating waste is not about blame. Mistakes happen. Arguing about who is to blame just wastes time that could be used redesigning the product, test suite, build system, development process, etc., to make that mistake impossible. For example, if a developer accidentally leaks a private key in a commit to an open source repository, the team might install pre-commit hooks that examine each commit for secrets.

Seeing something as waste is half the battle. The Waste Workshop practice is specifically designed to help teams identify and prioritize waste. The other half is prioritizing waste reduction (which has long-term payoffs) over routine work (which has short-term payoffs). This second half is related to the Balance principle. More generally, reducing waste is essential for economic sustainability (because inefficiency wastes money) and environmental sustainability (because unnecessary power consumption is waste).

Embrace Change

The phrase "embrace change" comes from Kent Beck's classic work on extreme programming [46]. It is just as relevant now as it was in 1999.

The project environment will change because the world is a dynamic, often chaotic place. The stakeholders will change because humans grow, change positions, or have new problems. The team's understanding of the product, stakeholders, and environment will change because that's what learning means. The product changes with every commit.

Although we know, intellectually, that expecting everything to remain the same is naïve, many engineers find constant change frustrating. Here, we recommend taking a growth mindset and reframing the problem of change into the opportunity for change. For their own sanity, teams must accept—or better *embrace*—constant change.

Embracing change means many things. For instance, it means avoiding *silly planning*: generating detailed plans in which the details are made up, inaccurate, or very likely to change. Planning six months of iterations down to the story point in advance is silly planning. Silly plans do not survive first contact with stakeholders. We don't recommend Gantt charts, for example, because they encourage silly planning.

As another example, conventional wisdom recommends avoiding team disruption, but there is no sense fretting about team members leaving, arriving, or rotating between teams. Embracing change means embracing new team members. New team members create opportunities to improve our code and work practices. New team members often reveal understandability problems in the codebase and can detect problematic assumptions.

Embracing change also means committing to less work in advance. That's why we do not advocate organizing development into sprints or iterations. Commit to a story when you start it. The product manager can change a story (or its priority) up until the moment someone starts implementing it. An engineer should focus on the story at hand. Worry about tomorrow's story tomorrow.

Another way to embrace change is to carve out a little time every week, month, or quarter, for *method engineering*.

Method Engineering

> *Every time you say "we've always done it that way"*
> *my ghost will appear and haunt you for twenty-four hours.*
> *−Grace Hopper*

Your situation—your project, team, organization, and stakeholders—is unique. Sustainable Dual-Track Development may not work in your context exactly as we have described it. Indeed, we don't expect anyone to execute Sustainable Dual-Track Development *exactly* the way we have described it. As Irish scientist Brian Fitzgerald explained back in 1997: "There is a wide difference between the formalized sequence of steps and stages prescribed by a methodology and the methodology-in-action uniquely enacted for each development project" [186]. We hope you find this book a useful resource for constructing a "methodology-in-action" that works for you.

Even if you did apply our method exactly for a while, you, a clever person who reads books about software development, will probably think of ways to improve it. And that's great! Even better, you might systematically and iteratively modify your way of working and rigorously assess the effects of your modifications; that is, *method engineering*. Method engineering is an enormous and frequently overlooked source of competitive advantage in the software development industry. Yes, you need good people, a supportive environment, a viable business model, a quality product and all that, but a development process that makes sense will increase product quality, ensure the business model is viable, make the environment more supportive, and help you attract the best people.

The scientific literature on method engineering can be a little heavy, and you won't have as much control as a scientist in a lab when you're building a real product, but the general idea is as follows.

1. Write down the change you want to make. Writing clarifies thinking.

2. Determine, in advance, how you will decide whether the change worked or not.[1]

3. Get a baseline measurement from historical data, or carry on with your current process for long enough to establish a baseline.

4. Change something.

5. Monitor progress toward your goal. Wait long enough for the team to get used to the new way of working and notice its effects.

6. Write down your findings. Again, writing clarifies thinking.

7. Broadcast your findings across your company and, ideally, publicly. Many academic software engineering conferences have industry tracks specifically for this purpose.[2]

Our Core Message

Sustainable Dual-Track Development attempts to solve two problems:

1. Agile methods don't really explain how to design good software.

2. Software development products and processes are often unsustainable.

---

[1]Figuring out good ways of measuring the things we care about can be difficult [42]. The smartest software engineering researchers in the world can't agree on how we should measure *anything*.

[2]Maybe this doesn't seem like part of your job, but how cool would it be to have a popular practice or law named after you?

Blending User-Centered Design with Agile Methods

Agile methods, notably *Scrum*, just assume someone writes some stories. Sustainable Dual-Track Development explains how to use the principles and practices of user-centered design to generate *good* stories. Integrating user-centered design with incremental, agile processes gives rise to the dual-track structure. Track One generates a steady stream of *good* stories for Track Two to implement. The developers focus on the present while the product managers and designers envision the future, but it's not a strict division—they're always helping each other.

The team enters a rhythm where the product designer and product manager identify and refine upcoming features using mock-ups and information flows while supporting the engineers building the stories at the top of the backlog. Figure 1–1 on page 4 shows how the design from Track One flows into the development of Track Two. There are no iterations or sprints in the diagram; work flows between the tracks when it is needed.

The product designer might be drawing mock-ups for the next epic when developers interrupt the designer regarding the look of the user interface for their current story. The product manager might be writing user stories when developers interrupt regarding the acceptance criteria for their current story.

The dual-track structure helps teams stave off two competing types of failure: (1) going too fast, skipping user research and validation, and creating a product no one wants or that is difficult to use; (2) going too slow, over-engineering, or waiting to finish the entire product thus missing a product-market window.

The most common trajectory in failed software projects is building the wrong product. Having a *balanced team* (including a product manager and product designer as well as developers) and a whole track of work dedicated to understanding users and business opportunities helps the team build a product that users *want* to use, and someone is willing to pay for. Developers assuming they know best without ever talking to users has always been, and continues to be, a recipe for failure. Sometimes developers get lucky or work in an area where they have enough insight into users to squeak by, but most of the time, the dual-track structure is far less risky.

Sustainable Software Development

Similarly, most agile methods, including Scrum, ignore sustainability. Software developers routinely work in an unsustainable manner (e.g., constant overtime leading to burnout, individual code ownership leading to knowledge loss, poor coding habits leading to code without tests, management pressure leading to insurmountable technical debt) to produce unsustainable products (e.g., carbon-spewing cryptocurrencies, democracy-undermining social media applications, racist AI, unsellable consumer applications, incomprehensible and unmaintainable spaghetti code).

We organize sustainability considerations into distinct but interconnected pillars: environmental, economic, social, and technical. For example, many products become socially unsustainable *because* they are economically unsustainable: when the developers discover that users don't find the product useful enough to pay for it, they invent other, anti-social business models like selling users' personal data. Similarly, unsustainable environmental impacts can be driven by poor technical sustainability: how can developers optimize power consumption when the code is so laden with technical debt that no one understand how anything works?

Considering the interconnected nature of the sustainable development pillars, then, Sustainable Dual-Track Development includes many sustainability-enhancing practices.

Technical sustainability is enhanced by pairing continuously, refactoring continuously, test-driven development, team code ownership, and code review. These practices keep the code and test suite clean.

Economic sustainability is enhanced by user-centered design and ongoing user research (especially feature validation), which help teams avoid building products and features that users won't pay for. Furthermore, all of the practices that enhance technical sustainability reduce the cost of building and maintaining the project, which makes economic sustainability easier to achieve.

Social sustainability is enhanced by convening a diverse, balanced team and considering all project stakeholders, not just whoever is paying. Then, the same techniques that facilitate economic sustainability, with a little help from sustainability personas, help surface unintended negative effects on communities and society. Meanwhile, all the practices that facilitate knowledge sharing and prevent knowledge silos help support professionals' work-life balance because work depends less on specific individuals.

Finally, the same techniques that support technical sustainability help developers optimize efficiency, because the code is easier to understand. Meanwhile, the same techniques that support economic and social sustainability help prevent the enormous waste associated with building products and features that no one actually needs or wants. Including energy testing and sustainability personas further encourages attention to ecological sustainability.

Put another way, Sustainable Dual-Track Development helps professionals uncover the unintended consequences of their processes and products. Many software products have unintended negative consequences that are entirely predict*able*, but not predict*ed*. Just thinking about it is half the battle. If your product is wildly successful (i.e., widely adopted and used), what could go wrong? How could a malicious person abuse your product to do harm, and what can you do to stop that?

Merely limiting harm is a low bar. Ideally, we want products to be *pro-social* and *pro-environment*. While not every product can have meaningful positive effects on society or the natural environment, many can. Is there a way to counteract the product's carbon footprint? Are there specific choices that would encourage users to be more diplomatic, kind, and patient?

In the coming years, we hope to learn more about how software development can be more sustainable, but Sustainable Dual-Track Development is a good start to help your team build more sustainable products in more sustainable ways.

Final Thoughts

To conclude, we want to promote evidence-based practice[3] and what Hans Rosling calls a "fact-based worldview" [187]. Far too much software engineering practice is based on a microcelebrity's opinions, some parable about how "this worked for me," or evidence-free myths like the exponential cost of change curve. While we give opinions in places, we've tried to make recommendations based on facts, the findings of scientific studies, and the implications of widely-accepted scientific models.

For software engineering to mature as a profession, it needs to stop chasing fads, elevating gurus, and basing everything on opinions. It needs to move toward a fact-based worldview and evidence-based practice. Sustainable Dual-Track Development isn't just our opinion, it is based on our synthesis of facts, evidence, scientific findings, our first-hand experiences, and our observations of hundreds of software projects and professionals. We hope this book inspires more professionals to consider sustainability in their daily work, and inspires more scientists to study sustainable software engineering.

---

[3]Evidence-based practice is the main reason for modern medicine's effectiveness. It doesn't mean that scientists go around telling you what to do or that you should unquestioningly follow the results of the latest study. It just means professionals have guidelines based on research that inform their daily activities.

Bibliography

[1] S. Chamanara, S. A. Ghaffarizadeh, and K. Madani, "The environmental footprint of bitcoin mining across the globe: Call for urgent action," *Earth's Future*, vol. 11, no. 10, 2023.

[2] G. H. Brundtland, "Our common future—call for action," *Environmental Conservation*, vol. 14, no. 4, pp. 291–294, 1987.

[3] S. McGuire, E. Schultz, B. Ayoola, and P. Ralph, "Sustainability is stratified: Toward a better theory of sustainable software engineering," in *2023 IEEE/ACM 45th Intl. Conf. on Soft. Eng. (ICSE)*, pp. 1996–2008, 2023.

[4] T. Sedano, *Sustainable Software Development: Evolving Extreme Programming*. PhD thesis, Carnegie Mellon Univ., 2017.

[5] P. Devanbu, T. Zimmermann, and C. Bird, "Belief & evidence in empirical software engineering," in *Proc. of the 38th Intl. Conf. on Soft. Eng.*, ICSE '16, (New York, NY, USA), pp. 108–119, ACM, 2016.

[6] J. Highsmith, "The ghosts of project management's Iron Triangle still haunt agile teams." `https://www.linkedin.com/pulse/ghosts-project-managements-iron-triangle-still-haunt-highsmith-/`, 2023.

[7] J. Proctor, "Breaking the myth of the iron triangle." `https://www.inteqgroup.com/hubfs/file-437774667.pdf`, 2014.

[8] L. Bossavit, *The Leprechauns of Software Engineering*. Leanpub, 2013.

[9] K. Beck, M. Beedle, A. van Bennekum, A. Cockburn, W. Cunningham, M. Fowler, J. Grenning, J. Highsmith, A. Hunt, R. Jeffries, *et al.*, "The agile manifesto." `https://agilemanifesto.org/`, 2001.

[10] C. Doctorow, "Social quitting." `https://doctorow.medium.com/social-quitting-1ce85b67b456`, 2022.

[11] D. Norman, *The Design of Everyday Things: Revised and Expanded Edition*. Basic books, 2013.

[12] J. Bansler and K. Bødker, "A Reappraisal of structured analysis: Design in an organizational context," *ACM Trans. on Info. Sys.*, vol. 11, no. 2, pp. 165–193, 1993.

[13] V.-P. Eloranta, K. Koskimies, and T. Mikkonen, "Exploring scrumbut—an empirical study of Scrum anti-patterns," *Info. and Soft. Tech.*, vol. 74, pp. 194–203, 2016.

[14] L. Miller, "Case study of customer input for a successful product," in *Proc. of Agile 2005*, pp. 225–234, IEEE, 2005.

[15] S. A. Wheelan and J. M. Hochberger, "Validation studies of the group development questionnaire," *Small Group Research*, vol. 27, no. 1, pp. 143–170, 1996.

[16] J. Keyton, *Communicating in Groups: Building Relationships for Group Effectiveness.* Oxford Univ. Press, 2006.

[17] E. L. Deci and R. M. Ryan, "The "what"' and "why"' of goal pursuits: Human needs and the self-determination of behavior," *Psychological Inquiry*, vol. 11, no. 4, pp. 227–268, 2000.

[18] S. Sawyer, "Effects of intra-group conflict on packaged software development team performance," *Info. Sys. J.*, vol. 11, no. 2, pp. 155–178, Apr. 2001.

[19] J. Y. C. Liu, G. Klein, J. V. Chen, and J. J. Jiang, "The Negative Impact of Conflict on the Information System Development Process, Product, and Project," *J.of Computer Info. Sys.*, Dec. 2015.

[20] F. P. Brooks, *The Mythical Man-Month:.* USA: Addison-Wesley Longman Publishing Co., Inc., 1st ed., 1978.

[21] C. Alexander, *Notes on the Synthesis of Form.* Harvard Univ. Press, 1964.

[22] M. E. Conway, "How do committees invent?," *Datamation*, 1968.

[23] M. Simons and J. Leroy, "Contending with Creaky Platforms CIO," *Cutter IT J.*, 12 2010.

[24] E. O. Conchúir, P. J. Ågerfalk, H. H. Olsson, and B. Fitzgerald, "Global software development: where are the benefits?," *Commun. ACM*, vol. 52, no. 8, p. 127–131, Aug. 2009.

[25] R. Bareiss and T. Sedano, "Developing Software Engineering Leaders at Carnegie Mellon Silicon Valley," Tech. Rep., Carnegie Mellon Univ., Jan 2009.

[26] G. Paci, "Trucknumber. Portland Pattern Repository." `http://c2.com/cgi/wiki?TruckNumberFixed`.

[27] T. C. Lethbridge, J. Singer, and A. Forward, "How software engineers use documentation: The state of the practice," *IEEE Soft.*, 2003.

[28] E. Bolisani and C. Bratianu, "The emergence of knowledge management," in *Emergent Knowledge Strategies: Strategic Thinking in Knowledge Management*, pp. 23–47, Springer, 2018.

[29] R. Ruggles, "The state of the notion: Knowledge management in practice," *California Mgmt. Rev.*, vol. 40, no. 3, pp. 80–89, 1998.

[30] L. Argote and P. Ingram, "Knowledge transfer: A basis for competitive advantage in firms," *Organizational Behavior and Human Decision Processes*, vol. 82, no. 1, pp. 150–169, 2000.

[31] F. Zieris, *Qualitative Analysis of Knowledge Transfer in Pair Programming*. PhD thesis, Freie Universität Berlin, 2020.

[32] S. L. Star and J. R. Griesemer, "Institutional Ecology, 'Translations' and Boundary Objects: Amateurs and Professionals in Berkeley's Museum of Vertebrate Zoology, 1907-39," *Social Studies of Science*, vol. 19, no. 3, pp. 387–420, 1989.

[33] S. L. Star, "This is not a boundary object: Reflections on the origin of a concept," *Science, Tech., & Human Values*, vol. 35, no. 5, pp. 601–617, 2010.

[34] T. Ohno, *Toyota Production System: Beyond Large-Scale Production*. Productivity Press, 1988.

[35] S. Shingo and A. P. Dillon, *A Study of the Toyota Production System: From an Industrial Engineering Viewpoint*. CRC Press, 1989.

[36] M. Poppendieck and T. Poppendieck, *Lean Software Development: An Agile Toolkit*. Addison-Wesley Professional, 2003.

[37] D. J. Anderson, *Kanban: Successful Evolutionary Change for your Technology Business*. Blue Hole Press, 2010.

[38] M. L. Tushman, "Special boundary roles in the innovation process," *Administrative Science Quarterly*, pp. 587–605, 1977.

[39] M. Cohn, *Agile Estimating and Planning*. Pearson Education, 2005.

[40] J. Z. Muller, *The Tyranny of Metrics*. Princeton Univ. Press, 2019.

[41] K. Ball, "Workplace surveillance: An overview," *Labor History*, vol. 51, no. 1, pp. 87–106, 2010.

[42] C. Sadowski and T. Zimmermann, eds., *Rethinking Productivity in Software Engineering*. Berkeley, USA: Apress, 2019.

[43] K. Eichenwald, "Microsoft's lost decade," *Vanity Fair*, vol. 54, no. 8, 2012.

[44] L. D'Innocenzo, J. E. Mathieu, and M. R. Kukenberger, "A meta-analysis of different forms of shared leadership—team performance relations," *J. of Mgmt.*, vol. 42, no. 7, pp. 1964–1991, 2016.

[45] C. Larman, *Agile And Iterative Development: A Manager's Guide*. Agile software development series, Pearson Education, 2004.

[46] K. Beck, *Extreme Programming Explained: Embrace Change*. Addison-Wesley Professional, 1999.

[47] E. Derby and D. Larsen, *Agile Retrospectives: Making Good Teams Great*. Pragmatic Bookshelf, 2006.

[48] E. Bjarnason, A. Hess, J. Doerr, and B. Regnell, "Variations on the evidence-based timeline retrospective method: a comparison of two cases," in *2013 39th Euromicro Conf. on Soft. Eng. and Advanced Applications*, pp. 37–44, IEEE, 2013.

[49] T. Sedano, "Sedano waste workshop." `https://github.com/professor/waste-workshop`, 2019.

[50] T. Sedano, P. Ralph, and C. Péraire, "Software development waste," in *Proc. of the 2017 Intl. Conf. on Soft. Eng.*, ICSE '17, 2017.

[51] I. Koch, E. Poljac, H. Müller, and A. Kiesel, "Cognitive structure, flexibility, and plasticity in human multitasking—an integrative review of dual-task and task-switching research," *Psychological Bulletin*, vol. 144, no. 6, p. 557, 2018.

[52] M. Van der Hulst and S. Geurts, "Associations between overtime and psychological health in high and low reward jobs," *Work and Stress*, vol. 15, no. 3, pp. 227–240, 2001.

[53] H. R. Thomas and K. A. Raynar, "Scheduled overtime and labor productivity: quantitative analysis," *J. of Construction Eng. and Mgmt.*, vol. 123, no. 2, pp. 181–188, 1997.

[54] C. Mann and F. Maurer, "A case study on the impact of Scrum on overtime and customer satisfaction," in *Agile Development Conf. (ADC'05)*, pp. 70–79, IEEE, 2005.

[55] A. E. Dembe, J. B. Erickson, R. G. Delbos, and S. M. Banks, "The impact of overtime and long work hours on occupational injuries and illnesses: new evidence from the United States," *Occupational and Environmental Medicine*, vol. 62, no. 9, pp. 588–597, 2005.

[56] A. Cooper, *The Inmates Are Running the Asylum*. Indianapolis, IN, USA: Macmillan Publishing Co., Inc., 1999.

[57] D. Yeats, *Open-Source Software Development and User-Centered Design: A Study of Open-Source Practices and Participants*. PhD thesis, Texas Tech Univ., 2006.

[58] P. Ralph, "Improving coverage of design in information systems education," in *Proc. of the 33rd Intl. Conf. on Info. Sys.*, (Orlando, FL, USA), AIS, Dec. 2012.

[59] R. Mohanani, B. Turhan, and P. Ralph, "Requirements framing affects design creativity," *IEEE Trans. on Soft. Eng.*, 2019.

[60] F. P. Brooks Jr, *The Design of Design: Essays from a Computer Scientist*. Pearson Education, 2010.

[61] P. Ralph, "The Two Paradigms of Software Development Research," *Science of Computer Programming*, vol. 156, pp. 68–89, 2018.

[62] T. S. Kuhn, *The Structure of Scientific Revolutions*, vol. 111. Chicago Univ. of Chicago Press, 1970.

[63] P. Ralph and P. Kelly, "The Dimensions of Software Engineering Success," in *Proc. of the Intl. Conf. on Soft. Eng.*, (Hyderabad, India), pp. 24–35, ACM, June 2014.

[64] T. Donaldson and L. E. Preston, "The Stakeholder Theory of the Corporation: Concepts, Evidence, and Implications," *The Academy of Mgmt. Rev.*, vol. 20, no. 1, pp. 65–91, 1995.

[65] O. C. Robinson, "Probing in qualitative research interviews: Theory and practice," *Qualitative Research in Psych.*, vol. 20, no. 3, pp. 382–397, 2023.

[66] C. Liu, "Never ask what they want—3 better questions to ask in user interviews." https://medium.com/user-research/never-ask-what-they-want-3-better-questions-to-ask-in-user-interviews-aeddd2a2101e.

[67] S. Lichtenstein and P. Slovic, *The Construction of Preference*. Cambridge, UK: Cambridge Univ. Press, Aug. 2006.

[68] D. Martens and W. Maalej, "Towards understanding and detecting fake reviews in app stores," *Empirical Soft. Eng.*, vol. 24, no. 6, pp. 3316–3355, 2019.

[69] D. Graziotin, P. Lenberg, R. Feldt, and S. Wagner, "Psychometrics in behavioral software engineering: A methodological introduction with guidelines," *ACM Trans. on Soft. Eng. and Methodology (TOSEM)*, vol. 31, no. 1, pp. 1–36, 2021.

[70] P. Ralph and Y. Wand, "A proposal for a formal definition of the design concept," in *Design Requirements Engineering: A Ten-Year Perspective* (K. Lyytinen, P. Loucopoulos, J. Mylopoulos, and B. Robinson, eds.), pp. 103–136, Springer, 2009.

[71] P. Freeman and D. Hart, "A science of design for software-intensive systems," *Communications of the ACM*, vol. 47, no. 8, pp. 19–21, 2004.

[72] P. Ralph, "Software engineering process theory: A multi-method comparison of sensemaking–coevolution–implementation theory and function–behavior–structure theory," *Info. and Soft. Tech.*, vol. 70, pp. 232–250, 2016.

[73] L. Suchman, *Human-Machine Reconfigurations: Plans and Situated Actions*. Cambridge Univ. Press, 2nd ed., 2007.

[74] P. Ralph and E. Tempero, "Characteristics of decision-making during coding," in *Proc. of the 20th Intl. Conf. on Evaluation and Assessment in Soft. Eng.*, pp. 1–10, 2016.

[75] P. Graham, "Hackers and painters." https://www.paulgraham.com/hp.html, 2003.

[76] P. Ralph, "The sensemaking-coevolution-implementation theory of software design," *Science of Computer Programming*, vol. 101, pp. 21–41, 2015.

[77] N. Cross, *Design thinking: Understanding how Designers Think and Work*. Berg, 2011.

[78] D. Schön, *The Reflective Practitioner*, vol. 26. New York: Basic Books, 1983.

[79] G. Goldschmidt, "The dialectics of sketching," *Creativity Research J.*, vol. 4, no. 2, pp. 123–143, 1991.

[80] A. Clark and D. Chalmers, "The extended mind," *Analysis*, vol. 58, no. 1, pp. 7–19, 1998.

[81] R. A. Virzi, J. L. Sokolov, and D. Karis, "Usability problem identification using both low-and high-fidelity prototypes," in *Proc. of the SIGCHI Conf. on Human Factors in Computing Sys.*, pp. 236–243, 1996.

[82] R. Sefelin, M. Tscheligi, and V. Giller, "Paper prototyping—what is it good for? a comparison of paper- and computer-based low-fidelity prototyping," in *CHI '03 Extended Abstracts on Human Factors in Computing Sys.*, CHI EA '03, (New York, NY, USA), p. 778–779, ACM, 2003.

[83] D. G. Jansson and S. M. Smith, "Design fixation," *Design Studies*, vol. 12, no. 1, pp. 3–11, 1991.

[84] R. Mohanani, P. Ralph, B. Turhan, and V. Mandic, "How templated requirements specifications inhibit creativity in software engineering," *IEEE Trans. on Soft. Eng.*, 2021.

[85] N. Cross, "Design cognition: Results from protocol and other empirical studies of design activity," in *Design Knowing and Learning: Cognition in Design Education*, pp. 79–103, Elsevier, 2001.

[86] R. Mohanani, I. Salman, B. Turhan, P. Rodríguez, and P. Ralph, "Cognitive biases in software engineering: a systematic mapping study," *IEEE Trans. on Soft. Eng.*, vol. 46, no. 12, pp. 1318–1339, 2018.

[87] N. Dahlbäck, A. Jönsson, and L. Ahrenberg, "Wizard of Oz studies—why and how," *Knowledge-Based Sys.*, vol. 6, no. 4, pp. 258–266, 1993.

[88] C. Snyder, *Paper prototyping: The fast and easy way to design and refine user interfaces.* Morgan Kaufmann, 2003.

[89] D. North, "Behavior modification," *Better Software*, vol. 3, 2006.

[90] J. Faustino, D. Adriano, R. Amaro, R. Pereira, and M. M. da Silva, "Devops benefits: A systematic literature review," *Software: Practice and Experience*, vol. 52, no. 9, pp. 1905–1926, 2022.

[91] E. Petrovskaya and D. Zendle, "Predatory monetisation? A categorisation of unfair, misleading and aggressive monetisation techniques in digital games from the player perspective," *J.of Business Ethics*, pp. 1–17, 2021.

[92] W. Cunningham, "The WyCash Portfolio Management System." `http://c2.com/doc/oopsla92.html`, 1992.

[93] W. Cunningham, "Ward explains debt metaphor." `http://wiki.c2.com/?WardExplainsDebtMetaphor`, 2009.

[94] S. McConnell, "Managing technical debt," Tech. Rep., Construx Software Builders, Inc, 2008.

[95] M. Fowler, "Technical debt." `https://martinfowler.com/bliki/TechnicalDebt.html`, 2019.

[96] R. C. Martin, *Clean Code: A Handbook of Agile Software Craftsmanship*. Pearson Education, 2009.

[97] R. L. Oliver, "Effect of expectation and disconfirmation on postexposure product evaluations: An alternative interpretation.," *J.of Applied Psych.*, vol. 62, no. 4, p. 480, 1977.

[98] M. Fowler, *Refactoring: Improving the Design of Existing Code*. Addison-Wesley Professional, 2nd ed., 2018.

[99] B. Christel and T. Sedano, "Refactoring workshop." `https://github.com/benchristel/refactoring-workshop`, 2019.

[100] E. Tempero, T. Gorschek, and L. Angelis, "Barriers to refactoring," *Communications of the ACM*, vol. 60, no. 10, pp. 54–61, 2017.

[101] M. Fowler, "Design principles and design patterns." `http://www.objectmentor.com/resources/articles/Principles_and_Patterns.pdf`, 2000.

[102] B. Meyer, *Object-Oriented Software Construction*. Pearson College Division, 1998.

[103] B. Liskov, "Keynote address - data abstraction and hierarchy," in *Addendum to the Proc. on Object-Oriented Programming Systems, Languages and Applications (Addendum)*, OOPSLA '87, p. 17–34, ACM, 1987.

[104] E. Gamma, R. Helm, R. Johnson, and J. M. Vlissides, *Design Patterns: Elements of Reusable Object-Oriented Software*. Addison-Wesley Professional, 1994.

[105] J. Kerievsky, *Refactoring to Patterns*. Addison-Wesley Professional, 2004.

[106] K. Beck, *Implementation Patterns*. Addison-Wesley Professional, 2007.

[107] S. Freeman and N. Pryce, *Growing Object-Oriented Software, Guided by Tests*. Pearson Education, 2009.

[108] G. J. Myers, T. Badgett, T. M. Thomas, and C. Sandler, *The Art of Software Testing*, vol. 2. Wiley Online Library, 2004.

[109] P. C. Jorgensen, *Software Testing: A Craftsman's Approach*. CRC Press, 2018.

[110] J. Fields, *Working Effectively with Unit Tests*. Leanpub, 2014.

[111] M. Feathers, *Working Effectively with Legacy Code*. Upper Saddle River, NJ, USA: Prentice Hall PTR, 2004.

[112] Kubernetes Cluster API team, "Testing cluster API." `https://cluster-api.sigs.k8s.io/developer/testing.html`, 2021.

[113] J. Shore, "How do you get rid of the need for integration tests? email to extremeprogramming@groups.io." `https://groups.io/g/extremeprogramming/message/161233`, 2021.

[114] G. Calikli and A. Bener, "Empirical analyses of the factors affecting confirmation bias and the effects of confirmation bias on software developer/tester performance," in *Proc. of the 6th Intl. Conf. on Predictive Models in Soft. Eng.*, pp. 1–11, 2010.

[115] W. Wong, *Mutation Testing for the New Century*. Advances in Database Sys., Springer, 2013.

[116] W. Bissi, A. G. S. S. Neto, and M. C. F. P. Emer, "The effects of test driven development on internal quality, external quality and productivity: A systematic review," *Info. and Soft. Tech.*, vol. 74, pp. 45–54, 2016.

[117] F. Shull, G. Melnik, B. Turhan, L. Layman, M. Diep, and H. Erdogmus, "What do we know about test-driven development?," *IEEE Soft.*, vol. 27, no. 6, pp. 16–19, 2010.

[118] A. Causevic, D. Sundmark, and S. Punnekkat, "Factors limiting industrial adoption of test driven development: A systematic review," in *Fourth IEEE Intl. Conf. on Soft. Testing, Verification and Validation*, pp. 337–346, IEEE, 2011.

[119] J. A. Pereira, M. Acher, H. Martin, J.-M. Jézéquel, G. Botterweck, and A. Ventresque, "Learning software configuration spaces: A systematic literature review," *J.of Sys. and Soft.*, vol. 182, p. 111044, 2021.

[120] J. Hannay, T. Dybå, E. Arisholm, and D. Sjøberg, "The effectiveness of pair programming: A meta-analysis," *Info. and Soft. Tech.*, vol. 51, pp. 1110–1122, July 2009.

[121] A. Begel and N. Nagappan, "Pair programming: what's in it for me?," in *Proc. of the Second ACM-IEEE Intl. Symp. on Empirical Soft. Eng. and Measurement*, ESEM '08, (New York, NY, USA), p. 120–128, ACM, 2008.

[122] C. Schindler, "Agile software development methods and practices in Austrian IT-industry: Results of an empirical study," in *2008 Intl. Conf. on Computational Intelligence for Modelling Control & Automation*, pp. 321–326, 2008.

[123] F. Zieris and L. Prechelt, "On knowledge transfer skill in pair programming," in *Proc. of the 8th ACM/IEEE Intl. Symp. on Empirical Soft. Eng. and Measurement*, ESEM '14, (New York, NY, USA), pp. 11:1–11:10, ACM, 2014.

[124] T. Sedano, P. Ralph, and C. Péraire, "Sustainable software development through overlapping pair rotation," in *Proc. of the Intl. Symp. on Empirical Soft. Eng. and Measurement*, ESEM, 2016.

[125] S. Bryant, P. Romero, and B. Du Boulay, "Pair programming and the mysterious role of the navigator," *Int. J. Hum.-Comput. Stud.*, vol. 66, pp. 519–529, 07 2008.

[126] S. Salinger, F. Zieris, and L. Prechelt, "Liberating pair programming research from the oppressive driver/observer regime," in *2013 35th Intl. Conf. on Soft. Eng. (ICSE)*, pp. 1201–1204, IEEE, 2013.

[127] W. Zuill and K. Meadows, "Mob programming: A whole team approach," in *Agile 2014 Conf.*, (Orlando, Florida), 2014.

[128] K. Meadows and W. Zuill, *Software Teaming: A Mob Programming, Whole-Team Approach.* Amazon Digital Services LLC—KDP, 2022.

[129] T. Sedano, P. Ralph, and C. Péraire, "Practice and perception of team code ownership," in *Proc. of the 20th Intl. Conf. on Evaluation and Assessment in Soft. Eng.*, EASE, 2016.

[130] C. Bird, N. Nagappan, B. Murphy, H. Gall, and P. Devanbu, "Don't touch my code!: Examining the effects of ownership on software quality," in *Proc. of the 19th ACM SIGSOFT Symp. and the 13th European Conf. on Foundations of Soft. Eng.*, ACM, 2011.

[131] J. L. Pierce, T. Kostova, and K. T. Dirks, "Toward a theory of psychological ownership in organizations," *Academy of Mgmt. Rev.*, vol. 26, no. 2, pp. 298–310, 2001.

[132] S. Isaacs, "Social development in young children," *British J. of Educational Psych.*, vol. 3, no. 3, pp. 291–294, 1933.

[133] S. McIntosh, Y. Kamei, B. Adams, and A. E. Hassan, "An empirical study of the impact of modern code review practices on software quality," *Empirical Soft. Eng.*, vol. 21, pp. 2146–2189, 2016.

[134] J. Czerwonka, M. Greiler, and J. Tilford, "Code reviews do not find bugs. How the current code review best practice slows us down," in *2015 IEEE/ACM 37th IEEE Intl. Conf. on Soft. Eng.*, vol. 2, pp. 27–28, 2015.

[135] P. Thongtanunam, S. McIntosh, A. E. Hassan, and H. Iida, "Revisiting code ownership and its relationship with software quality in the scope of modern code review," in *Proc. of the 38th Intl. Conf. on Soft. Eng.*, ICSE '16, (New York, NY, USA), p. 1039–1050, ACM, 2016.

[136] A. Uchôa, C. Barbosa, W. Oizumi, P. Blenilio, R. Lima, A. Garcia, and C. Bezerra, "How does modern code review impact software design degradation? an in-depth empirical study," in *2020 IEEE Intl. Conf. on Soft. Maintenance and Evolution (ICSME)*, pp. 511–522, 2020.

[137] L. Braz and A. Bacchelli, "Software security during modern code review: the developer's perspective," in *Proc. of the 30th ACM Joint European Soft. Eng. Conf. and Symp. on the Foundations of Soft. Eng.*, ESEC/FSE 2022, (New York, NY, USA), p. 810–821, ACM, 2022.

[138] A. Bacchelli and C. Bird, "Expectations, outcomes, and challenges of modern code review," in *2013 35th Intl. Conf. on Soft. Eng. (ICSE)*, pp. 712–721, IEEE, 2013.

[139] S. D. Gunawardena, P. Devine, I. Beaumont, L. P. Garden, E. Murphy-Hill, and K. Blincoe, "Destructive criticism in software code review impacts inclusion," *Proc. of the ACM on Human-Computer Interaction*, vol. 6, no. CSCW2, pp. 1–29, 2022.

[140] R. Paul, A. Bosu, and K. Z. Sultana, "Expressions of sentiments during code reviews: Male vs. female," in *2019 IEEE 26th Intl. Conf. on Software Analysis, Evolution and Reengineering (SANER)*, pp. 26–37, 2019.

[141] P. Greenfield, "Revealed: more than 90% of rainforest carbon offsets by biggest certifier are worthless, analysis shows," *The Guardian*, vol. 18, 2023.

[142] Parametrix, "Crowdstrike's impact on the fortune 500." `https://www.parametrixinsurance.com/crowdstrike-outage-impact-on-the-fortune-500`, 2024.

[143] P. Ralph and E. Tempero, "Construct validity in software engineering research and software metrics," in *Proc. of the 22nd Intl. Conf. on Evaluation and Assessment in Soft. Eng. 2018*, EASE '18, (New York, NY, USA), p. 13–23, ACM, 2018.

[144] A. C. Edmondson and Z. Lei, "Psychological safety: The history, renaissance, and future of an interpersonal construct," *Annu. Rev. Organ. Psychol. Organ. Behav.*, vol. 1, no. 1, pp. 23–43, 2014.

[145] A. Edmondson, "Psychological safety and learning behavior in work teams," *Administrative Science Quarterly*, vol. 44, no. 2, pp. 350–383, 1999.

[146] S. Beyer, K. Rynes, J. Perrault, K. Hay, and S. Haller, "Gender differences in computer science students," in *Proc. of the 34th SIGCSE Technical Symp. on Computer Science Education*, SIGCSE '03, (New York, NY, USA), p. 49–53, ACM, 2003.

[147] S. Bradshaw, H. Bailey, and P. N. Howard, *Industrialized Disinformation: 2020 Global Inventory of Organized Ssocial Media Manipulation*. Computational Propaganda Project at the Oxford Internet Institute, 2021.

[148] E. Jelalian and A. G. Miller, "The perseverance of beliefs: Conceptual perspectives and research developments," *J. of Social and Clinical Psych.*, vol. 2, no. 1, pp. 25–56, 1984.

[149] J. Harvey, "White woman calls cops on black man over dog leash dispute in viral footage," *Huffington Post*, May 15, 2020.

[150] N. M. Daumeyer, I. N. Onyeador, X. Brown, and J. A. Richeson, "Consequences of attributing discrimination to implicit vs. explicit bias," *J. of Experimental Social Psych.*, vol. 84, p. 103812, 2019.

[151] B. Fischoff, "Debiasing," in *Judgment under Uncertainty: Heuristics and Biases* (D. Kahneman, P. Slovic, and A. Tversky, eds.), Cambridge, USA: Cambridge Univ. Press, 1982.

[152] D. Atewologun, T. Cornish, and F. Tresh, *Unconscious Bias Training: An Assessment of the Evidence for Effectiveness*. Equality and Human Rights Commission Research Report 113, 2018.

[153] R. d. S. Santos, G. Adisaputri, and P. Ralph, "Post-pandemic resilience of hybrid software teams," in *Proc. of the 16th Intl. Conf. on Cooperative and Human Aspects of Soft. Eng. (CHASE 2023)*, (Melbourne, Australia), May 2023.

[154] C. K. De Dreu and M. A. West, "Minority dissent and team innovation: the importance of participation in decision making.," *J. of Applied Psych.*, vol. 86, no. 6, p. 1191, 2001.

[155] M.-É. Roberge and R. Van Dick, "Recognizing the benefits of diversity: When and how does diversity increase group performance?," *Human Resource Mgmt. Rev.*, vol. 20, no. 4, pp. 295–308, 2010.

[156] N. Bassett-Jones, "The paradox of diversity management, creativity and innovation," *Creativity and Innovation Mgmt.*, vol. 14, no. 2, pp. 169–175, 2005.

[157] F. Beard and L. Morton, "Effects of internship predictors on successful field experience," *Journalism & Mass Communication Educator*, vol. 53, no. 4, pp. 42–53, 1998.

[158] S. Kuna and R. Nadiv, "The embodiment of otherness: Deconstructing power relations between staffing agencies, diverse jobseekers, and organizations in the israeli business sector," in *Diversity, Affect and Embodiment in Organizing* (M. Fotaki and A. Pullen, eds.), pp. 195–224, Cham: Springer, 2019.

[159] D. Gaucher, J. Friesen, and A. C. Kay, "Evidence that gendered wording in job advertisements exists and sustains gender inequality.," *J. of Personality and Social Psych.*, vol. 101, no. 1, p. 109, 2011.

[160] E. Derous and A. M. Ryan, "When your resume is (not) turning you down: Modelling ethnic bias in resume screening," *Human Resource Mgmt. J.*, vol. 29, no. 2, pp. 113–130, 2019.

[161] D. M. Cable, F. Gino, and B. R. Staats, "Reinventing employee onboarding," *MIT Sloan Mgmt. Rev.*, vol. 54, no. 3, 2013.

[162] A. Blanche. https://twitter.com/adblanche/status/1480960791310336005, 2022.

[163] C. Ashcraft and S. Blithe, "Women in it: The facts," *National Center for Women & Info. Tech.*, 2010.

[164] Bureau of Labor Statistics, "Employment and earnings, table 28—unemployment by reason for unemployment, race, and Hispanic or Latino ethnicity. Current population survey." https://www.bls.gov/cps/cpsa2005.pdf, 2006.

[165] R. Chordiya, "Organizational inclusion and turnover intentions of federal employees with disabilities," *Rev. of Public Personnel Administration*, vol. 42, no. 1, pp. 60–87, 2022.

[166] S. Jackson and L. T. Jackson, "Self-esteem: Its mediating effects on the relationship between discrimination at work and employee organisation commitment and turn-over intention," *J. of Psych. in Africa*, vol. 29, no. 1, pp. 13–21, 2019.

[167] T. Okun and K. Jones, "White supremacy culture," in *Dismantling Racism: A Workbook for Social Change Groups*, ChangeWork, 2000.

[168] J. Bourke, "3 small ways to be a more inclusive colleague." https://hbr.org/2021/12/3-small-ways-to-be-a-more-inclusive-colleague.

[169] W. Marcinkus Murphy, "Reverse mentoring at work: Fostering cross-generational learning and developing millennial leaders," *Human Resource Mgmt.*, vol. 51, no. 4, pp. 549–573, 2012.

[170] J. Jordan and M. Sorell, "Why reverse mentoring works and how to do it right," *Harvard Business Rev.*, vol. 3, 2019.

[171] M. M. Kim, *The Wake Up: Closing the Gap Between Good Intentions and Real Change*. Addison-Wesley Professional, 2021.

[172] S. D. Finch, "9 phrases allies can say when called out instead of getting defensive." https://everydayfeminism.com/2017/05/allies-say-this-instead-defensive/, 2017.

[173] A. Robertson, "How we doubled the representation of women in engineering at Clio." https://labs.clio.com/how-we-doubled-the-representation-of-women-in-engineering-at-clio-2d9a4a1a0282, 2019.

[174] M. P. King, *The Fix: Overcome the Invisible Barriers That Are Holding Women Back at Work*. Atria Books, 2020.

[175] P. Bjørn, "Dark agile: Perceiving people as assets, not humans," in *Rethinking Productivity in Software Engineering* (C. Sadowski and T. Zimmermann, eds.), pp. 125–134, Berkeley, CA: Apress, 2019.

[176] C. L. McCluney, M. I. Durkee, R. E. Smith, K. J. Robotham, and S. S.-L. Lee, "To be, or not to be...black: The effects of racial codeswitching on perceived professionalism in the workplace," *J. of Experimental Social Psych.*, vol. 97, p. 104199, 2021.

[177] A. Hirst, "Settlers, vagrants and mutual indifference: unintended consequences of hot-desking," *J. of Organizational Change Mgmt.*, vol. 24, no. 6, pp. 767–788, 2011.

[178] K. Catlin, "5 ally actions - oct 15, 2021." https://mailchi.mp/1ff8c383b7b2/5-ally-actions-oct-15-2021?e=69b9a3a391, 2021.

[179] Merriam-Webster, "Gaslighting," in *Merriam-Webster.com dictionary*, 2022. Definition.

[180] W. J. Fleming, "Employee well-being outcomes from individual-level mental health interventions: Cross-sectional evidence from the united kingdom," *Industrial Relations J.*, pp. 1–21, 2024.

[181] F. Laloux and E. Appert, *Reinventing Organizations: An Illustrated Invitation to Join the Conversation on Next-stage Organizations.* Nelson Parker, 2016.

[182] R. A. Dahl, *A Preface to Economic Democracy*, vol. 28. Univ. of California Press, 2023.

[183] P. Bourque, R. Dupuis, A. Abran, J. W. Moore, and L. Tripp, "The guide to the software engineering body of knowledge," *IEEE Soft.*, vol. 16, no. 6, pp. 35–44, 1999.

[184] I. Jacobson, P.-W. Ng, P. E. McMahon, I. Spence, and S. Lidman, *The Essence of Software Engineering: Applying the SEMAT Kernel.* Addison-Wesley Professional, 2013.

[185] T. Sedano, P. Ralph, and C. Péraire, "Removing software development waste to improve productivity," in *Rethinking Productivity in Software Engineering*, pp. 221–240, Springer, 2019.

[186] B. Fitzgerald, "The use of systems development methodologies in practice: a field study," *Info. Sys. J.*, vol. 7, no. 3, pp. 201–212, 1997.

[187] H. Rosling, O. Rosling, and A. Rönnlund, *Factfulness: Ten Reasons We're Wrong About The World—And Why Things Are Better Than You Think.* Hodder & Stoughton, 2018.

Index

Acknowledgments

This book would not have been possible without the love and support of our families. We'd also like to thank Cécile Péraire who was instrumental in the research that inspired this book, and everyone who gave us feedback on early drafts, especially Birgit Penzenstadler, Elisabeth Hendrickson, Mae Beale, and Therese Stowell. We wish to thank our editor Randi Slack who believed in this project and got us to the finish line.

Paul wishes to thank all of his students who read excerpts from and drafts of this book, both for their praise and for their patience, and all of the scientists and researchers who did the hard work of creating the knowledge we have attempted to distill.

Todd wishes to thank everyone he's pair programmed with at Pivotal, VMware, Enjoy, Gusto, and ID.me. Each of you made me a better programmer:

Ofri Afek	George Dean	Shane Hogan
Simeon Ajala	Garrett Denis	You-Sheng Huang
Christopher Amavisca	Kate Dontsova	Karen Huddleston
Andrea Angquist	Shelby Doolittle	Peter Huynh
Moh Anwer	Brian Duncan	Priyansh Jaiswal
Bridget Arthur	Yuliya Dzikovich	Sannidhi Jalukar
Jay Badenhope	Michael Edoror	Tim Jarratt
Mladen Bajić	Richard Enlow	Christopher Jobst
Oak Barrett	Hugo Estrada	Christine Jogerst
Oz Basarir	Alex Evanczuk	Nikhil Kak
Rachel Brindle	Ivy Evans	Michelle Kang
Andrew Brown	Inna Fedoseyeva	Daniel Keeney
Bryan Burr	Darcie Fitzpatrick	Wiley Kestner
Brian Butz	Davis Frank	Irina Khafizova
Max Calderoni	Nikhil Gajwani	Amil Khanzada
Kaiting Chen	Joëlle Gernez	Andrew Kitchen
Terry Chen	Phil Goodwin	Kalen Krempely
Eric Ti Yu Chiang	Chris Hajas	Tommy Kuntze
Heewon Choi	Ethan Hall	Maryam Labib
Benjamin Christel	Larry Hamel	Aaron Lawrence
Zac Clark	Jennifer Hamon	Kevin Lawver
Nicholas Coelius	Josh Harris	Christine Lee
José Miguel Colella	Perry Hertler	Kai Lee
Daniel Coo	Neil Hickey	Dominic Leung

Aaron Levine
Talal Mansoor
Nishad Mathur
Gregor MacDougall
Jamie McAtamney
Thomas Meyer
Caleb Miles
Sam Mirza
Sagar Muchhal
Maple Ong
Ngan Pham
Stuart Pollock
Nikhila Rao
Sudhindra Rao
Tom Robison
Richard Salloum
Amber Salome

Dany San
Aaron Severs
Parth Shah
Shoabe Shariff
Ramya Shenoy
Zach Shepherd
Daniel Shusta
Karina Sils
Bharath Sitaraman
Mike Stallard
Teal Stannard
Zornitza Stefanova
Vlad Stoian
Kelly Sutton
Tanel Suurhans
Eric Tsiliacos
Lenny Turetsky

Tyler Untisz
Rama Vempati
Joseph Villanueva
Nate Visconti
Aaron VonderHaar
Shimon Walner
Brandon Weaver
Alex Wilczewski
Ashley Willard
Luke Winikates
Stephen Wu
Victor Wung
Scott Yang
Zimeng Yang
Adrian Zankich
Lubron Zhan
Eda Zhou

Hopefully, our git commit messages captured all the fun.